# THE TEACHER
# AND COUNSELLING

# THE TEACHER
# AND COUNSELLING

## DOUGLAS HAMBLIN

BASIL BLACKWELL · OXFORD

ISBN 0 631 15230 X

Printed in Great Britain by
Burgess & Son (Abingdon) Ltd.
and bound by
The Kemp Hall Bindery, Oxford.

TO: URSULA AND ROSEMARIE
GEOFF AND PHIL

# CONTENTS

# PREFACE

The tradition of pastoral care which has always been a unique part of the British secondary school is growing more important as the length of education for each pupil increases. As the rate of social change accelerates, so does the work of the teacher and his contribution to the pupil's search for stable identity and purpose in life become vital.

This book is offered with great diffidence in the hope that it will be of use to my fellow teachers in secondary schools. This diffidence is accompanied by real belief in the creativity of teachers and the capacity of the schools to innovate. Any book of this type can only scratch the surface, and certainly this one is no exception. The main idea behind the discussion is that there are no final truths in counselling and no one "right way" of doing it. We all have to develop our own styles of counselling and our own methods. All that is offered is a starting point, although my intention has been that of presenting counselling in a way which gives pride of place to the concern and caring of teachers and which allows them to build on their teaching skills.

Throughout the book, illustrations from actual cases are used, but you will immediately realize that these describe only one point in a case. Complete case histories would occupy undue space in a book that is already long.

The most important thing in this preface is to pay my thanks to past and present students taking the Diploma in School Counselling at the

University College of Swansea. Certainly the teacher of mature teachers receives more than he gives, and I gladly acknowledge this. Many of them have read and commented upon the text, but I would like to mention Ursula Fanthorpe and Rosemarie Bailey who have checked my erratic typing and spelling without being too harsh in their comments. Mary Mott also selected the words for inclusion in the glossary. Despite one's firm intentions sometimes there is a need to be technical! George Buckton, Phil Davies, Walter Davies, Gwilym Lewis, Dudley Gray and Arthur Phillips looked at the original outline. I am indebted to Mr. A. H. Yates for his suggestions about the best method of presenting the critical incident analysis. Lastly, Gwynneth Edwards deserves commendation for her efficient typing of the manuscript.

It will be obvious that many writers have influenced my thinking. Certainly I would make no claim of originality for my work. I would like to acknowledge my debt to those who have taught me in the past and whose thinking has shaped some of my current work in counselling. Dr. A. N. Oppenheim stimulated my interest in the use of actual and ideal self scales. I have found his own scales very valuable in developing the ones presented in this book. The ideas underlying the discussion of the school as a socializing agency stem from a stimulating series of seminars at the London School of Economics conducted by Professor H. Himmelweit, Dr. A. P. Sealy and Miss B. Swift. I offer them my thanks, but fear they will consider me a poor pupil if they chance to see this result.

I would like also to thank the Open University for permission to use the three diagrams which appear on pp. 24, 26 and 28, and Faber & Faber Ltd. for permission to quote 12 lines from *Collected Poems 1909–1962* by T. S. Eliot.

Swansea.
*February* 1972.

# CHAPTER ONE

# COUNSELLING AND
# THE TEACHER

Each chapter will begin with a very brief outline of the main content of the chapter. Where possible the outline will consist of questions which we should try to answer.

## The content of Chapter One

This chapter consists of a breaking down of the counselling process into its basic elements. This provides a preparation for the model of secondary school counselling which follows in later chapters. It is the most difficult chapter in the book, but it will repay the reader for the effort expended on it. It would be very useful to re-read this chapter immediately after finishing the book.

## The questions asked in Chapter One

These are all concerned with the nature of counselling as it occurs within the school. We have to ask:

(i)  What is the connection, if any, between teaching and counselling? What are the similarities and differences between these activities?

(ii)  What is it that the counsellor is trying to do?

(iii)  Is there a "right" kind of person who is suited to be a counsellor?

(iv)  What do we mean when we talk about a counselling relationship?

### The final section of the chapter

Like all the other chapters, this one ends with a short summary of the main argument. It will be quite useful to read this summary before tackling the chapter as a whole.

### The link between counselling and teaching

"Counselling is a necessity, but counsellors are not." This statement, made by experienced teachers, indicates that as yet there is insufficient knowledge of the specialized role, functions and techniques of the trained school counsellor. Why do these teachers accept the activity, yet reject the role? It is possible to understand what happens through this simple illustration. As a teacher begins to read about counselling or explore it in some other way, he becomes aware of a feeling of familiarity. This crystallizes into the belief, "I've been here before!" They are then in the position of the man in Molière's play who suddenly discovered he had been speaking prose for years. The familiarity sprang from the fact that both counselling and teaching are deeply concerned with interpersonal relationships. Delight at the revelation that one has oneself already been counselling hides a vital point which seems to have escaped the man who spoke prose. Surely, once he had made the discovery, the sensible thing would have been to train himself to speak better prose. Discovering that we are, in some sense of the word, counsellors, seems to demand that we should take steps to improve that counselling. Not to do this, means that we have abdicated responsibilities and that we are not prepared to face up to the implications of our discovery. The first step is that of understanding more clearly the conditions for good interpersonal relationships, but this has to be followed by distinguishing between the counselling work of the classroom teacher and that of the specialized counsellor. Not only can words illuminate or obscure a problem, but the very discovery that teachers have counselling responsibilities can lead us astray. We may then falsely assume that "it's only a matter of commonsense". In our lives we know that commonsense advice is rarely sensible or applicable to us. If it is sense, then we usually find it is far from common.

Another link between counselling and teaching is found when we attempt to find out how counselling differs from a pleasant cosy chat enjoyed in a coffee-bar. We could confuse a caring process with good-natured niceness. Wrenn (1957) helps when he points out that counselling is different in emphasis from teaching because the subject of the learning experience is the learner himself. This is a key difference, yet it provides a link between teaching and counselling. Learning and learning processes are at the heart of counselling. It is therefore a particularly proper activity for a teacher, provided that he is able to allow pupils to learn and not simply instruct them in a rigid way.

The feeling of familiarity which follows acquaintance with ideas about counselling has a two-edged quality. At first, it produces a delightful glow and sense of well-being, but this is often succeeded by the experience of unease and sometimes real anxiety. Why should this be? British teachers usually feel they have a mandate to care for their pupils and to be concerned with wider issues than those of subject teaching and formal instruction. The term "pastoral care" draws our attention to the way in which the task of the teacher has something in common with that of the priest or parent. It is true that sometimes pastoral care in the school has been a myth behind which there was little reality. It has meant an operation similar to that of herding sheep in a predetermined direction. Yet for most teachers, the caring part of their job is not only important, but part of their very identity as teachers. Some teachers who try to find out about counselling end up believing that this part of their role will be taken away by a new specialist. Nothing is further from the truth, but it cannot be too strongly stated that the introduction of counsellors does not leave the class teacher without a caring responsibility. Unless this is understood, unnecessary conflict will develop between the counsellor and some of his colleagues.

This is the negative side of the picture. The really positive fact is that the effective school counsellor does not, indeed cannot, work in isolation. He depends on the help given by his fellow teachers. The subsequent discussion will stress this, coupling it with the need for the counsellor to be fully integrated into the daily life of the school and to be a full member of the school staff. Rather than eroding or competing with the pastoral care responsibilities of the teachers, the trained counsellor offers support and added strength in a spirit of humility. Tolerance and the avoidance of quick judgements about the other is demanded from both teacher and counsellor, but perhaps the most constructive thing that can happen is for the class teacher to begin to appreciate his own importance as a participant in the counselling process.

## The objectives of counselling

We have seen that both counselling and teaching are concerned with interpersonal relationships, but in a moment we shall see that counselling, like education, is a developmental process. If there is a wide discrepancy between the aims of the counsellor and those of the school, then conflict is likely, if not inevitable. If the goals of counselling are presented in such a way that they put the counsellor on the side of the pupil against the school, then the integration of counselling into the daily life of the school becomes unlikely. The school as a guidance community becomes a miserable mirage. In looking at this question of agreement between the goals of counselling and those of the school it seems useful to glance at a few definitions of counselling. (To examine them all would be impossible, whilst to do more than look at one or two is wearisome, but this means taking the risk of being highly selective.)

Carl Rogers (1942) said that "effective counselling consists of a definitely structured permissive relationship which allows the client to gain an understanding of himself to a degree which enables him to take new positive steps in the light of his new orientation". Nearly thirty years later, Lewis (1970) describes it as a "process by which a troubled person (the client) is helped to feel and behave in a more personally satisfying manner through interaction with an uninvolved person (the counsellor) who provides information and reactions which stimulate the client to develop behaviours which enable him to deal more effectively with himself and his environment". Note how this definition stresses interaction and to some degree a greater amount of activity on the part of the counsellor than Rogers. Krumboltz (1966) states that the counsellor should help to promote more adaptive behaviour. As a result of counselling the pupil "ought to be better able to solve future problems more independently and effectively".

There is no hint in these definitions that the object of counselling is that of changing personality. They stress self-knowledge and a change in behaviour, but never fundamental personality modification. The counsellor's job is to help a pupil find more effective ways of using what he has already got in terms of aptitudes, ability and personality in a truly satisfying way. "More of the good that exists" rather than the creation of a "different person" seems to be the theme lying behind these definitions.

It seems that a number of workers tie counselling with development. Tyler (1969) says that "the purpose of counselling is to facilitate wise choices of the sort on which a person's later development depends". This view is close to that of Blocher (1966) who says that the counselling task is that of ensuring that "Each individual has an opportunity to master the tasks that will equip him with the coping behaviours necessary for handling those roles and relationships that are involved in his next stage of development". Counselling is linked to developmental tasks, although we have not answered two associated questions. We must know what these tasks are. Then we must define when counselling is necessary for many pupils will master developmental tasks without difficulty.

It is useful to begin by taking Erikson's (1968) description of the developmental tasks of adolescence. The first key task is establishing a stable sense of identity. This is followed by the achievement of the capacity to make a truly intimate relationship. It is unnecessary to elaborate on these developmental tasks here, for they occupy the attention of every teacher of adolescents who is prepared to give more than lip service to his wider responsibilities. The identity crisis occurs during the earlier years of adolescence when the child is separating himself socially and emotionally from dependence upon his parents. He begins to build up a new social, vocational and sexual self, but this causes strain. Early adolescence is a period of storm and stress in some pupils because the boy or girl is uncertain. He adopts trial roles in a clumsy and exaggerated way. At the same time he is vulnerable to criticism and attack, not only from adults, but from friends of his own age. In early adolescence there is a push and pull into a wider range of relationships with both adults and peers, coupled with demands for greater responsibility. Growing uncertainty and self-doubt is countered by attitudes of bravado. Feelings of inadequacy about sex role behaviour can lead a boy to adopt a façade of toughness and a compulsive masculinity which hides inner confusion and a sense of despair. It is not unknown for a girl deliberately to court obesity to thrust off the risk of heterosexual contact. It is only too easy to pay attention to the aggression and the outer shell and fail to see the loneliness which lurks behind the bold front.

False solutions to these developmental crises are manifold. It is worth taking a brief imaginative journey into some of these aspects of adolescence. The basic need of the adolescent is for companionship, for the identity diffusion created by the physical and social changes of adolescence often means a great loneliness for some young people. This remains until the intimate relationship is achieved. Before this happens many young people, when truly known, reveal themselves as being like a lonely figure under a sullen bronze sky, trudging over a trackless moor, feeling the victim of blind forces and the pawn of coincidence.

In order to arrive there,
To arrive where you are, to get from where you are not,
You must go by a way wherein there is no ecstasy,
In order to arrive at what you do not know

You must go by a way which is the way of ignorance,
In order to possess what you do not possess
You must go by the way of dispossession.
In order to arrive at what you are not
You must go through the way in which you are not.
And what you do not know is the only thing you know
And what you own is what you do not own
And where you are is where you are not.

T. S. Eliot.

This then is the lot of that creature we so lightly label the adolescent. Under his superficial confidence and cheerfulness lurks the dilemma so clearly portrayed by Eliot. He has little clear identity, no sense of direction, so he is impelled to escape from loneliness and the facing of the empty shell self. Some of our pupils serve gang leaders faithfully, even court bullying and attempt to buy companionship and security. Sometimes we label as homosexuality an inchoate search for a relationship and an identity, which often ends in profound dissatisfaction.

Our greatest area of blindness lies in our failure to recognize destructive forms of competition. It is self-defeating for many young people. Life becomes flat and stale because they cannot enjoy what they are doing. Sometimes we have to face the fact that they are engaged in a process in which they can never win. The adulation they so earnestly seek from others will never serve as a substitute for the confidence in themselves they really require. Compulsive competition implies hostility to others, but more seriously, also to themselves. It is fundamentally destructive, for it occurs in a way which is self-punitive. A boy in such a situation will not speak in class or tutorial group because he feels unable to say the best and most perfect thing which has ever been said on that topic. His search is for the final and ultimate statement which will leave him the victor, for all other tongues will be silenced; but the very victory would create a desert. His triumphs are hollow and his dissatisfactions profound, for his triumphs feed his weaknesses. Such pupils come for developmental counselling, yet they cannot be reached easily. They reject the honest offer of help made by the counsellor, retreating into silence, rejecting or transforming what has been said. They may see counselling as foolish, the counsellor as weak and stupid and they may anxiously withdraw from the demands of the relationship. Yet we have a responsibility to offer acceptance, and must strive to provide this, for only then will the self-annihilating struggle cease. In one sense such an adolescent is a supreme conformist, for not only is he succumbing to cultural pressures in a total way, but to deeply internalized guilts and demands which scourge him. Such a person is not truly a person, merely a fragment. He will remain so until he achieves a real relationship with someone.

It is perhaps clearer that developmental counselling still means the facing of stark problems and involves great sensitivity mingled with not a little courage. Let us now try to get a guide to decide when developmental counselling is necessary. It will be needed when there is a discrepancy between the demands coming from the pupil's environment and his stage of development. This can be illustrated by what happens to *some* children when they transfer from the primary school to the secondary school. A number will immediately show signs of stress and anxiety which does not diminish with familiarity with the school. Their stage of development and stock of coping strategies is inadequate for the new demands. They cannot adapt to the widely varying demands made by the greater number of teachers who instruct them, the presence of older boys, the requirements of homework, the movement from classroom to classroom and the complexity of the new school. Some try to adjust, yet their adjustment is superficial and very costly. Parents report anxiety, night terrors, unwillingness to come to school, temper tantrums or a slight tic. Counselling, either individually or in groups, eases the stress and gradually provides the missing confidence and skills. Without it, the symptoms worsen, and some pupils begin to leave the school situation, either by truanting or by rejecting the school and its values. This cocking a snook at the school leads to the boy being labelled as a potential delinquent. Yet this label is simply the mid-point in a process which need never have occurred. The response to a gap between development and the need to make new peer relationships has already been described. If we realize that adjustment to work is closely linked with social competence, then the importance of efficient developmental counselling is obvious.

What is it that the developmental counsellor tries to do? He sets out to encourage:

(i) the *growth of self acceptance* in the pupil;
(ii) the *development of controls from inside* the pupil, rather than continuing his reliance upon external checks and pressures;
(iii) the *learning of relevant and competent coping strategies* and of problem-solving techniques which are both realistic and viable for that pupil.

This needs explanation. We can ask why self-acceptance is necessary in pupils who are destructive, inadequate and a nuisance to themselves and others. Surely self-acceptance should strengthen these tendencies? It is useful to retreat to an act of faith and ancient wisdom here. It has been pointed out that we should love others as we love ourselves, but it is equally true that we can only love others to the degree that we love ourselves. Matza (1969) illustrates the way in which a deviant person gets caught up in a process which steadily emphasizes his difference from others, until he finally accepts this definition of himself. As he is identified as being different, he begins to react to the signals of rejection and difference sent to him by his family, age-group and those in authority. In schools, just as in other settings, a process of labelling is at work which actually casts a pupil into a delinquent or deviant role. He is impelled to react to this labelling process, perhaps at first by distress or protest, but as pressures rise he takes it to be true. He acquires an identity as a thief, sissy or bully. This identity makes the activity more meaningful to him. It comes out in "All right, if that is what they say I am, then I'll really be like that". To be cast in the role of thief, girl of easy virtue or whatever, compounds and hastens the process of becoming that very thing. This labelling excludes the pupil from other identities and opportunities, so his chances of seeing himself in new or different terms becomes progressively smaller. We tend to treat a person, once we have seen him as delinquent or deviant in some specific way, as if he were deviant in every way. We seem to work very hard to create a self-fulfilling prophecy about such pupils. Acts of ban, exclusion, and punishment feed the negative identity until the individual is swallowed up in it. He has great difficulty in withdrawing from this or changing the definition of himself. He is held fast in the web of expectations which have built up. This connection between deviance and a poor self-picture exists even before the pupil has committed the overt acts. Reckless, Dinitz and Kay found that twelve-year-old boys named as potential delinquents by teachers were more likely to have negative self-concepts than those who were named as likely non-delinquents. Perhaps we detect here a picture of reaction to labelling. The first step for the counsellor who wishes to reverse or halt this process is to provide acceptance for the pupil. His concern is not with punishment, but with building up new self-respect in that boy or girl.

Controls which will continue after the pupil leaves counselling seem to be needed. Warmth and true concern are the first requirements for the counsellor. Usually children do not identify with the values and behaviour of harsh rejecting parents in a healthy way. Experience shows that they will not take over the values of a counsellor who is distant, cold and threatening. Without warmth we can perpetuate the situation which occurred when some young men were sent to Borstal and prison. External pressures existed to which they conformed, but as soon as these were removed on leaving the institution they reverted to their old behaviour. Nothing had happened to them: they were untouched by the experience. The school counsellor has to stimulate development, and this means understanding what the pupil thinks and feels. Then we work with him to change his feelings and thoughts so that he begins to view himself and life more positively.

We then try to develop problem-solving techniques in collaboration with our colleagues. This can only be done on the basis of fairly accurate knowledge about that pupil. We want to be able to provide him with success and this means our efforts must relate to what he is able to do, rather than to what he ought to be able to do. The school counsellor as a mature person must learn to adapt to each pupil and provide him with what will work for him. General recipes are useless. The mixture is indigestible, inappropriate or turns out to be a failure. Blanket advice, that is, the same advice handed out to each pupil, only works by chance. For some pupils it happens to be appropriate, but for others it may be grossly unsuitable if not downright destructive in its effect.

### The personality of the counsellor

It is at this point that we begin to see that not all teachers can be successful counsellors. The personality of the counsellor will influence the transactions which occur between him and the pupil, and not every teacher can create the conditions necessary for honest self-exploration and helpful communication. Particular personality qualities should exist in the counsellor if the counselling is to be successful. A great deal of discussion has taken place about such qualities, and interesting evidence exists in the research undertaken by Truax and Carkhuff (1967) in the U.S.A. Their research was concerned with investigation of the claim that *on the average* counselling and psychotherapy were no more effective than no counselling or psychotherapy.

This finding was confirmed in their examination of the evidence, but rather than let the matter rest there, they proceeded to isolate the conditions which make counselling an effective and creative process. They did this by comparing successful cases with failures. Their study was important because it brought home to us the fact that some counsellors do a great deal of good, whilst some do a great deal of harm. Pupils need to be protected from those counsellors who do harm.

Three conditions for success were found, all of which related to the counsellor's personality. The first of these qualities was the ability to empathize accurately with the person who was being counselled. Empathy is the capacity to "feel into" a person. It is a very special type of understanding. Certainly it is a complex ability, difficult to define in a few sentences. It is different from sympathy, for this suggests a difference between oneself and the person for whom one feels sympathy. Empathy is the ability to feel into the pupil, the capacity to take, for the purposes of counselling, his standpoint or perspective about affairs. From this we really grasp the implication of events for him, and for him alone. This description makes empathy appear an intellectual exercise, but it is far more than this: it is a type of momentary identification. Identification is an emotional merging with another person, and this is what empathy is. It can be illustrated quite simply by the phrase, "get into the other man's shoes, and if they pinch, then you feel the hurt". Once this kind of reaction occurs it is essential that the counsellor applies all his intellectual ability to discover the significance and import of his reaction. Empathy is a dangerous tool, although an essential one, for it can be misleading unless it is accurate. The counsellor is always in danger of pushing out on the pupil his own emotionally based attitudes and reactions. In other words, he ascribes to the pupil feelings and emotions which do not belong to the pupil. They belong to the counsellor. This can trap us into thinking that the pupil is bound to react in a certain way. We can try to impose on the pupil our idea of how we think people ought to feel in a particular situation, thereby sending the counselling process, off into a world which does not exist. The world is a creation of the counsellor and his needs and perceptions. A little thought shows us that what may be deprivation for a middle-class boy or girl is not necessarily deprivation for a child from a very poor home. The need for self-awareness in the counsellor becomes very clear when these points are mulled over. This is why self-knowledge is stressed in courses of counsellor training.

The second essential quality is one of spontaneity and genuineness. Difficulty arises, for spontaneity, like counselling, is a vague and fashionable term. In the counselling situation, spontaneity means the capacity to relate honestly to the pupil and reveal oneself as one human being to another. This means that there is no place for the false professional front, for this is detected and denounced by an adolescent immediately. Revelation of oneself is at variance with the usual constraints imposed by the formal teaching situation, and almost certainly evokes anxiety in some teachers who manage their classes by keeping social and emotional distance between themselves and the pupils. It may be that this is what lies behind arguments about the conflict of teaching and counselling roles. We certainly have to come down from any protective pedestal and be prepared to talk honestly and openly to pupils, allowing them to criticize us for our stupidities and pretences when necessary. This does not mean a loss of standards or the disappearance of the counsellor into a morass of loose liberalism. It does mean that he cannot take up a remote or omnipotent role, and must honestly confess when he does not know the answer. When questioned about his beliefs and values he must answer frankly, phrasing his reply in a style near to, "Well, this is the way I see it", indicating that other viewpoints exist. It means the counsellor must be open to new evidence, change his course if necessary, admit his errors and generally function in a way which provides the pupil with a model of purpose and maturity. He should be able to reveal himself as a human being and not indulge in defensive manoeuvres to maintain a position of false authority and security. Counselling often is anxiety provoking, and it is all too easy to run away from the anxiety. There is real authority in counselling, but defensive and destructive types of authority have to be avoided. Constructive authority springs from the concern, skill and knowledge of the counsellor, from the fact that it is his responsibility to set the limits to the relationship and from his refusal to get emotionally involved. In this he is like the nurse or doctor who have to remain detached from the pain of the patient in order to deal with it efficiently. The counsellor who becomes swamped with sympathy or whose emotions blind his judgement is one who can do a great deal of harm to the adolescent. There is a kind of equality in the interaction between pupil and counsellor because the pupil is the focus of concern, and it is a process in which the counsellor receives the pupil's statements with respect whilst both are participants in a problem-solving situation. The authority in counselling is constructive and containing and not coercive. This may well be what Carl Rogers meant when he spoke of a "structured permissive relationship".

The third essential quality is the counsellor's capacity to show a non-threatening, safe and non-possessive warmth towards the pupil. This means that one has to know what a pupil can accept. To ladle out praise to someone who has a very negative picture of himself is to awaken grave suspicion. If they have bad experiences with adults in authority, then not only will there be suspicion, but contempt and exploitation. To demonstrate warmth blindly and too quickly is to invite rejection from some pupils. This underlines the fact that a counsellor has to learn to assess and adapt to a pupil. He must not indulge in an undifferentiated approach to all pupils, however well intentioned this may be. Even in areas connected with crucial personality qualities, there is still the need for conscious and accurate adaptation to each pupil.

Counsellor trainers accept the importance of these personality characteristics. They try to devise courses of training which bring out these qualities more fully and place them under the control of the counsellor. You can see that the personality of the counsellor forms the sub-structure upon which a super-structure of more technical skills has to rest. There is undoubtedly a complex interaction between the counsellor's personality and the effective use of these skills. Although we have insufficient precise empirical knowledge about this at the moment, Carkhuff (1969) produces very useful suggestions. Certainly the most important tool the counsellor possesses is his own personality. Without the qualities just described, his efforts would be abortive, if not actually destructive.

### The counselling relationship

The previous section has brought us to a discussion of the counselling relationship, for the personality of the counsellor has meaning in the relationship between him and the pupil. The counselling relationship is a giving and a forgiving relationship. It is true that it is more blessed to give than receive, but sometimes we have to maintain our giving in the face of hostility and rejection by those to whom we are giving. This means that sometimes we shall feel that what we have to give is useless, whilst we are worthless. Self-doubts crowd in, and we then begin to ask whether we have anything to give, or even if we have the right to give. Sometimes we can feel so drained and empty that we want to retreat from this exhausting work. This is the lot of every counsellor. He has to learn to live with this, and all the training in the world does not stop it happening. I have shared this experience with many colleagues. At these moments it is tempting to make noises about "unhealthy involvement", but this usually turns out to be a preliminary for an attempt to evade responsibility.

Counselling is both exhausting and rewarding. It is a strange paradox that although one gives more, there is always more left to give. We are not diminished by our counselling, but enriched. We demand effort and honesty from the pupil, but we are required to invest energy and involve ourselves. The really unhealthy relationship is the sterile one which is devoid of wamrth and life. It is the psychological equivalent of the diluted gruel which Victorian matrons offered to the undeserving poor. Today we are uneasily aware that relationships in our secondary schools sometimes seem to have reached the level of futility represented by those ladies.

The relationship which is the core of school counselling is centred upon acceptance of the pupil as he is, not as we would wish him to be. Above all it should not be overtly judgemental in character. This statement instantly arouses concern, for many pupils who come for counselling possess attributes that are regarded as undesirable by most people. Such attributes may harm their possessor and his associates. It is sometimes thought that the counsellor's acceptance strengthens these tendencies in the pupil, but from the earlier discussion you can see that this is not the case. The counsellor is neither overtly judgemental nor is he collusive. The latter term will be discussed in detail later.

Sometimes we think that the counselling relationship is always pleasant and positive. A mature relationship is never solely positive, but involves elements of like and dislike, love and hate. The counselling relationship is no exception. It is dangerous and delusory to expect purely positive responses from the pupil to one's actions and concern. Such expectations may be due to the counsellor's need to be liked and his fear of aggression. It may be vital for the pupil to express dislike, hate and aggression and still experience acceptance and understanding. This does not mean one stimulates negative feelings, but we cannot avoid or gloss over them when they appear. A teacher background is a liability here, for such expressions of feeling may be seen as a challenge and thus something to be extinguished or avoided by the teacher in a counselling role. A relationship which denies tensions, anxieties, dislikes and the expression of hostility is not a counselling relationship, for it is based in phantasy and does not help an adolescent to come to terms with his difficulties.

The counselling relationship which is built up in developmental counselling is simultaneously a means and an end. It is the end in the sense that when established it can satisfy important needs in the pupil, such as the need for affiliation or reinforcement of his concept of himself as a person of worth. Developmentally it is more important as a means, for the relationship is the basis upon which the counsellor supports the pupil in his sometimes painful, and certainly demanding, problem-solving efforts. There is nothing mysterious about the counselling relationship, for it develops as a result of the co-operation of the pupil and counsellor as they work towards defined goals. It is based upon the concern and competence of the counsellor as he interacts with the pupil. Developmental counselling can be seen as a process in which the pupil learns to modify his behaviour so that it yields more satisfying outcomes for him. The relationship between counsellor and pupil provides motivation for this process, but is also strengthened as the process develops. It should be clear that the relationship is brought into being when developmental counselling is necessary, and also when long-standing problems, not necessarily anti-social, exist. Counselling is not the prerogative of the disadvantaged or delinquent: it should be available to any pupil with developmental or environmental problems, including that of under-functioning in academic work. There are certain levels of counselling where this relationship is not necessary, indeed it would be wasteful to create it. Some problems of subject choice, or career problems of an informational type provide examples where the relationship is superfluous. We should note that this provides us with a means of discriminating between counselling and guidance. The latter is a largely informational process without the therapeutic relationship.

The counselling relationship is aimed at the eventual production of autonomy, but this does not mean that dependency is to be excluded from counselling. We tend to shy away from dependency, particularly in the adolescent, because it conflicts with the general tenor of demands upon them. This is to ignore the fact that often independence cannot be achieved without experience of dependence. It is akin to the situation of a small child who cannot explore with confidence unless he has a safe base to which he can return if hurt or alarmed. Sometimes our own immaturity prevents us from seeing that dependency will only be temporary. Certainly dependence in the counselling relationship really means that the counsellor is dependable. He must show continuity of concern and he must be reliable in the sense of doing what he has promised to do. Dependency is one of those responsibilities in coun-selling which we would evade if we could, but to do so would be to be avoiding reality.

One of the most mis-used terms in discussion of counselling relation-ships is that of reassurance. It has a place, and certainly we are not setting out to disturb the pupil. Yet it is merely a palliative technique used to reduce anxiety as a temporary expedient. Anxiety which rises beyond a certain level distorts perceptions and destroys viable coping techniques, therefore we have to reduce it at times. Sometimes we cannot. Reassurance contains certain hazards which, although obvious, are ignored at times by those who rely on it as an important technique. It is given, and then it is found that it does not match reality. So the pupil then begins to suspect the competence of the counsellor, if not his integrity and the reality of his concern. A recent example met in the supervision of a student counsellor illustrates this. The boy com-plained that he was a poor writer, although his handwriting was legible and certainly no worse than many boys of his age. The student wanted to give immediate reassurance that he was not different. This was avoided, and it was found out that "bad writing" was linked with vocational aspirations, pressures from parents and, above all, a sense of being different from other boys. The complaint, which seemed unreal, encapsulated a number of conflicts and stresses which can be dealt with during counselling. Not only can easy reassurances stifle the emergence of the real meaning of the situation, but if given in excess, they become something needed by the pupil. This goes against the declared aims of counselling, which are those of increasing com-petence and decision-making ability. Even less obvious, but more important, is the fact that constant reassurance is likely to make a pupil feel he is different. The counsellor and his behaviour make a looking glass in which a boy or girl can see themselves. When we are ill it is disturbing to be given constant reassurances that we look well, will be better soon and that everything will be all right. We might well begin to suspect that we are marked out for an early end, possibly a painful one, and we almost certainly feel suspicious. The counsellor intends his reassurances to be helpful, yet the pupil may interpret them as evidence that he is both inadequate and grossly different from other pupils. Reassurances can be evasions by the counsellor. They avoid exploration of the situation and confrontation of difficulty. Yet without this tension, change is unlikely.

The relationship built up in counselling is a disciplined one. This is a favourite word in educational discussion, therefore we need to be careful in using it. When we apply the word *discipline* in the school situation, we normally focus our attention on the pupil. In counselling, the onus falls on the counsellor, for he must exercise self-discipline and constantly question the motives lying behind his actions. We may see our own weaknesses and personal problems in the pupil, rather than what is there. We may unwittingly repeat the reactions we met from others during our own adolescence. It is easy to mis-understand the meaning of the pupil's problem and his situation. It is hard to accept that the behaviour of rational people can be tied closely to their pasts. Yet when I looked at my teaching methods and relation-ships with pupils I used to get an unpleasant shock. I accepted the findings of research and tried to innovate, yet all too often I recreated a classroom situation similar to that experienced in my own school-days. If we learn to listen to ourselves, then we may well hear our own teachers and parents talking through us. Something like this may lie behind the findings of Oliver and Butcher (1968) that the attitude changes induced by an expensive course of teacher training are largely reversed and eroded in the first year of teaching. It is not just this, but it seems to be one factor in the business of adjustment to the classroom situation. If we do recreate the past in our major professional task, then it is even more likely to happen in the more emotionally threatening area of counselling.

### Summary discussion

There is a clear link between counselling and teaching because inter-personal relationships are at the heart of both activities. This produces a sense of familiarity which obscures the real difficulties and the need for special skills in counselling. The counsellor works closely with colleagues and is dependent upon their good-will and support. The teacher has a real place in the counselling process, and his pastoral care role is strengthened by the presence of a counsellor in the school.

Counselling is concerned with developmental tasks. It is not restricted to the deprived and disadvantaged pupils, but it should be available where there is a gap between the stage of development reached by the pupil and the demands made on him by the environment. Counselling is usually concerned with the inability to meet demands, but it can also be necessary when a very able pupil is also far ahead of others in his social, emotional and intellectual development. Counselling is concerned with finding creative and efficient solutions to developmental crises. It is concerned to understand the situation as it appears to the pupil; once this is achieved the counsellor begins to build up missing skills and to develop adequate coping strategies in the pupil. The counsellor is concerned with healthy and realistic development of the social, sexual, vocational and philosophical selves in the pupils who come to him.

Certain personality qualities are essential for counsellors. In themselves, these qualities are insufficient, but training will refine them and bring them under the disciplined control of the counsellor. Without these qualities, the counsellor is almost useless, because the lack of them prevents him from making the interpersonal relationships essential to counselling. These qualities distinguish counsellors who are ineffective, if not actually harmful, from those who do really help someone. The first quality is that of accurate empathy, i.e. the ability to feel into a person and really know what he is feeling without imposing our own feelings on him. Next come spontaneity and genuineness. If the counsellor puts on a phoney professional front or simulates concern which he does not feel, then he will not make a relationship which facilitates development of the pupil. Last we have the capacity for non-possessive warmth. This is not merely heartiness and a cheerful manner, but the ability to show real concern and acceptance and be human in interaction.

The relationship central to counselling is one based on acceptance of the pupil as he is rather than as we would like him to be. It is not overtly judgemental, and it is based on the belief of the counsellor that every individual is fundamentally good and worthwhile. It does not mean that the counsellor gets on the side of the pupil against adults, neither is it merely pleasant warmth. The counsellor uses the relationship to help a boy or girl become the best that he or she can be in every aspect of life where the need for counselling exists.

## REFERENCES

Blocher, D H (1966) *Developmental Counseling,* New York: Ronald Press.

Carkhuff, R.R. (1969) *Helping and Human Relations,* Vols. 1 and 2. New York: Holt, Rinehart & Winston.

Eliot, T.S. (1944) *The Four Quartets,* London: Faber & Faber.

Erikson, E. (1968) *Identity,* London: Faber & Faber.

Krumboltz, J.D. (Ed.) (1966) *Revolution in Counseling,* Boston: Houghton Mifflin.

Krumboltz, J.D. and Thoresen, C.E. (Eds.) (1969) *Behavioural Counseling,* New York: Holt, Rinehart & Winston.

Lewis, E.C. (1970) *The Psychology of Counseling,* New York: Holt, Rinehart & Winston.

Matza, D. (1969) *Becoming Deviant,* Englewood Cliffs: Prentice-Hall.

Oliver, R. and Butcher, H. (1968) 'Teachers' Attitudes to Education', *Br. J. Educ. Psychol,* Vol. 38. 38–44.

Rogers, C.R. (1942) *Counseling and Psychotherapy,* Boston: Houghton Mifflin.

Rogers, C.R. (1951) *Client Centred Therapy,* Boston: Houghton Mifflin

Truax, C.B. and Carkhuff R.R. (1967) *Toward Effective Counseling and Psychotherapy: Training & Practice,* Chicago: Aldine.

Tyler, L (1969) *The Work of the Counselor.* 3rd. Edn.: New York: Appleton-Century-Crofts.

Wrenn, G. (1957) Status and Role of the School Counselor. *Personnel & Guid. J.* 36. 175–183.

# CHAPTER TWO

# A MODEL OF COUNSELLING
# FOR THE SECONDARY SCHOOL

### *The purpose of this chapter*

This chapter looks at counselling in the setting of the school, showing by means of a simple systems analysis the forces and influences to which the counsellor has to adapt. It then looks at some of the basic dimensions which shape the way the counsellor sees his job. After this, the discussion moves on to the important step of creating a model of counselling which seems to meet the needs of the British secondary school.

### *The questions asked*

(i) How do the activities and procedures of the counsellor link with what is happening in the classroom and school?

(ii) What basic ways of looking at his task can be used by the counsellor? Do these have any consequences for his role and behaviour in the school?

(iii) What are the major functions of the school counsellor?

(iv) In what ways can the counsellor and class teacher collaborate with profit for the pupil? Are there stages in counselling where the contribution of the form teacher may be at least as important as that of a specialist counsellor?

*The summary discussion*

This underlines the fact that no rigid prescriptions can be given for the counsellor's task without denying the complexity of the real life situation. It also draws attention to the importance of the team approach to counselling.

*The need to relate counselling to the school*

Counselling does not occur in a vacuum. Yet we tend to discuss it as if it were a situation completely insulated from the rest of the pupil's life. There are intimate and strong connections between counselling and what happens in the classroom and in the rest of the school. This is not a trite statement, but one which has far-reaching implications. The situation of complex relationships between the needs of the pupil, the personality and training of the counsellor, the regime of the classroom and the expectations of the school has important consequences. What will work with one pupil will not work with another; what one counsellor can do, cannot be done in the same way by another; what is an effective strategy of counselling in one case or in one school will be useless, if not destructive or self-defeating, in another school or with a different pupil. There may be a few schools in which counselling is impossible and where only the foolhardy would attempt it. There are some schools where counselling could be misused, because it is seen as a more subtle form of discipline—a form of discipline applied to condition pupils painlessly to unthinking conformity. Such schools are rare, but it is not uncommon for weaker teachers to see the counsellor as an efficient disciplinary agent. We must always ask *who* is the counselling for. Is it for the school or for the pupil? We must guard against misuses of the concept of counselling which creep in very easily. Labels given by a counsellor, such as immature or inadequate, lead to the delusion that something has been solved and something real has been done. But these labels may be simply stating expectations about a pupil, which he then begins to meet, conveniently confirming our "diagnosis". Sometimes these labels take blame away from teachers and the school (where it properly belongs) and put it on the pupil. We then evade situations which should have been energetically tackled. Awareness of the links between counselling and the school do not allow this to happen.

The first step in our model is that of a very simple "systems" description of the counselling process. This is presented in three steps:

   (i) A basic process model.
  (ii) A Chinese Box concept of counselling.
 (iii) The situational constraints on the counselling process.

## The basic process

When we undertake counselling in a school, we counsel within a social system. If we are to understand the meaning of this, then we have to put ourselves into the position of a social anthropologist who tries to see the relationship of each part to the whole society. Introducing counselling into a school is like throwing a stone into a pond. Ripples are set up: they move plants in the pond. But once it is there the stone itself is influenced by the life of the pond. Perhaps it gathers various bits of plant life; perhaps it becomes a shelter for some forms of animal life; perhaps it merely is lost in the mud. What we do as counsellors has an impact on the rest of the school, whilst the school situation in its turn, shapes and limits what we can do.

The first step is to look at the counselling interview as a three-part process composed of input, process and output. This is shown on p. 24.

This little model shows us a number of important things. If we change either the counsellor or the pupil then we alter the input drastically. Counselling will vary with change of counsellor and we must see that the goal of counselling can be reached in a number of different ways. Perhaps the most crucial thing is that this diagram calls our attention to the need to look at the consequences of our counselling. The output is change of attitude, new goals, new motives and new behaviour in the pupil; but we have a moral responsibility to look at the consequences of this output. It may lead a pupil into a further sense

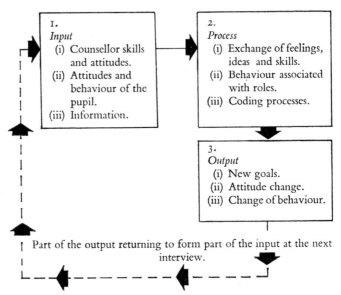

Part of the output returning to form part of the input at the next interview.

of inadequacy. He may try to gain his goals without fully realizing the difficulties, or before sufficient supports have been arranged for him. We end by increasing his sense of being different. It is possible to send a pupil away from the session in a mood of elation, failing to understand that this alone may lead him into trouble with the teacher who has to receive him. We may have allowed something to emerge towards the end of the interview, which we did not have time to deal with adequately, so that he returns to the classroom in a state of tension. Some boys in this state are then liable to blow up when the teacher signals disapproval to them. The counsellor must look carefully at the output and anticipate how this will fit into the classroom situation otherwise he will be unnecessarily at odds with his colleagues. Naturally they only see the pupil's overt behaviour and not the reasons for it. In any case, the counsellor is working economically when he assesses the impact of the output on others. Part of that output, with the reactions of the boy's teachers and age mates to it, is brought back to the next interview. A good counsellor acquires sensitivity to this feedback for it tells him whether or not he is "on course" and whether he needs to modify the output for the benefit of the pupil. Sensitivity to this feedback process is necessary because it is possible to reinforce views and opinions against counselling very easily. This can be avoided by the careful "reading" of feedback.

The middle box is concerned with the basic process which will be discussed more fully in Chapters Three and Four. Here we must simply see that the interview or group session is an exchange process. Pupils trade feelings, information and attitudes for the concern, acceptance and skills the counsellor has to offer. This idea of exchange draws our attention to the fact that there are costs involved in counselling. If these are too high for the pupil, or if he can get what the counsellor has to offer more cheaply outside the counselling situation, then it is sensible to expect him to opt out or be resistant to counselling. The costs of counselling for the pupil may include the knowledge that friends see him as going to someone who deals with "nutters". If he accepts the counselling situation, he may be put into conflict with important peer groups, especially if these are anti-school or delinquent.

Even more important than the costs, is the fact that counselling is a two-way process. We tend to talk as if a boy or girl made responses and behaved in isolation. In fact, he or she is responding to the comments and activities of the counsellor. The counsellor shapes responses, initiates new ideas and activities and the pupil responds to this. We are concerned with a set of reactions, not the pupil's verbal behaviour alone. The process will be shaped by a number of things. If the boy feels "picked on" because he has been sent for counselling, and the counsellor does not recognize this, many distortions of meaning and threats enter the counselling. If the counsellor fails to see that a boy or girl holds expectations about the counsellor's job which are not true, then there is grave danger of the creation of a spiral of misunderstanding in which both partners feel confused. All this underlines the need for skill and sensitivity, but above all for clear recognition of the fact that counselling involves costs for a pupil which we may ignore until he refuses to be counselled and rejects the good intentions of the counsellor. We then often try to find some explanation which puts the blame on the pupil, instead of recognizing that our own insensitivity has led to this state of affairs.

### The Chinese Box concept of counselling

Counselling is similar to the old toy composed of boxes nesting inside one another. To understand it, we also have to use Talcott Parsons' (1957) idea of transactions taking place across the boundaries of systems. The diagram makes this clear:

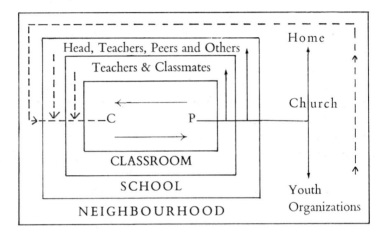

The heart of the "nesting box system" is the one containing the pupil interacting with a counsellor. The output from this box feeds into all the boxes enclosing it. How far what is produced in the inner box matches the styles of communication, controls and interaction usually found in these larger systems is crucial. A counsellor may have determined, perhaps obstinate, ideas of the "right" way to counsel and may refuse to modify them. As a result he may be pushing a pupil into behaviour which brings him into conflict in the classroom with his teachers or with other pupils. I remember a student who was determinedly liberal in his approaches to pupils, whether or not this was appropriate or in the boy's best interest. In one case, where the boy needed firm containment and his background led him to interpret the counsellor's behaviour as both weak and as approving of his mis-behaviour, this resulted in an increase of clowning behaviour in the classroom, increased punishment from the teachers and a reinforcement of the tendency of classmates to use this boy to bait teachers. If the role of the "good pupil" is defined rigidly by the school, to induce attitudes and behaviour which go against this in an extreme way, is to push a pupil into trouble. If the counsellor objects to such rigid ideas in the school, he may have to bring them out into the open in a constructive way or decide not to counsel in that school. He must not behave in a way which harms the pupil. There may be conflict between the values of church or home and the output from the counselling situation. The counsellor has to face the consequences of such conflict squarely, rather than deny its existence. This might well occur where middle-class parents have vocational aspirations for their child which are conventional, academic and safe. The counsellor might produce a situation in which the boy is clear that he will have none of this and comes to a firm decision to do something quite different. Whilst respecting the autonomy of the pupil, the counsellor also has a duty to anticipate the reactions of parents and understand their feelings, even when he may disapprove of their attitudes.

The larger systems of school, home etc., produce values, ideas and standards of behaviour which feed into the counselling interview. To ignore them is to float off into cloud cuckoo land. It is important that the counsellor learns to understand the impact of these pressures on what he is doing. It is always useful to sit down and try to assess what is happening in cases where no improvement is occurring. On a number of occasions, I have found that I was attempting something without asking if the steps were appropriate in the situation. The outer boxes set limits on what the counsellor can do; they also show him which lines of attack on a problem will work and which will not.

*Situational constraints on counselling*

The next step brings out the need for the counsellor to adjust to the situation. This does not, however, mean a passive conformity. It means that the counsellor has to assess each situation and see what is likely to be effective. He must develop flexibility in his style and techniques of counselling. There is always the same underlying deep concern for the pupil and belief in the value of individuals but to attempt to apply the same approaches to different situations is unintelligent. The situational constraints on the counsellor are represented in the diagram:

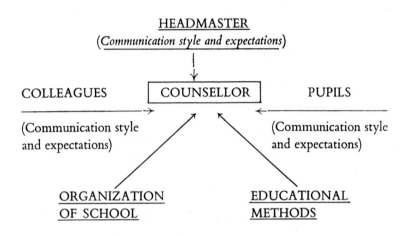

In every school a specific style of communication and of relationships develops, carrying with it expectations. Pupils have expectations about the staff which are not always flattering, whilst staff hold definite expectations about the pupils. Each group, staff and pupils, also hold expectations about the ways in which their peers will behave. The expectations and styles of communication acquire an almost coercive character in the sense of "rightness" that develops around them. They gain a quality of legitimacy which can only be violated to a certain degree, unless the violator is prepared to face severe repercussions. This fact sets limits to what the counsellor can do in a particular school, and it also constrains the form of his interventions. There is a certain elasticity in these styles and expectations, but to go outside them is to invite rejection. Students training for teaching sometimes make this mistake: they introduce methods or strike postures which violate the expectations of pupils, and the pupils then reject them ruthlessly. Perhaps we need to allow for the fact that adolescents are often more rigid in their expectations than adults. They bring into the counselling interview certain expectations which have been well learned, and which act as anchors in their relationships with adults: to breach these expectations too quickly or without due cause creates anxiety and hostility.

Colleagues too have very clear expectations of the counsellor. Sometimes these have to be quietly but firmly refuted, for instance, when they turn him into a disciplinary agent, or when they foist on him unrealistic and almost messianic expectations. The trained counsellor quietly refuses such claims, pointing out that he needs to work with his colleagues and that there is no quick answer or easy solution to many problems. He will meet the expectations of colleagues in a positive way, by observing meticulous professional courtesy and adapting to their requirements within the limits of integrity. One of the ways in which he can do this is by carefully adhering to the normal period when calling a pupil for interview and by ensuring that pupils are not sent back late for the next lesson. Other points will be discussed in subsequent sections of this chapter. The enthusiastic counsellor sometimes feels that the need to keep to the timetable distorts his work. This is false: every professional helper, social worker, psychotherapist or probation officer has to keep to a timetable. Far from being a hindrance, it provides a basic structure. The expectations of colleagues underline the need for the school counsellor to be a good organizer, setting out his aims and objectives clearly, and learning to work economically.

### An analysis of the counsellor's task

We need some method of describing more exactly the activities of the counsellor. To say that effective school counselling means the adoption of methods which are appropriate to a specific situation may give the impression of vagueness. Though each situation is different from the last, and no two problems are dealt with in an identical way, we should still be able to analyse the process. Certain dimensions exist in counselling, and these give us a means of comparing one counsellor's activities with those of another. They could be used by a counsellor to define his own work and relate it to the needs of the school.

The first of these dimensions is that of *field*. It has been traditional to divide counselling up into three fields: personal problem counselling, vocational counselling and educational counselling. These distinctions are very useful in exposition, but in practice the boundaries are very indistinct. A personal problem often leads into a vocational choice problem, and a vocational problem may be produced as a respectable admission ticket to counselling which ultimately serves several purposes. To seek the help of the counsellor over a vocational problem defends the pupil against the queries of others, and it also gives him a chance to assess the counsellor before committing himself in perhaps a more intimate way. Some counsellors find themselves to be at their best in one specific field; although others may well be undertaking activities in one field, but labelling it as something else. One counsellor I know works best when he is able to give a personal problem a label which places it in either the vocational or educational field. He then feels secure and that he has a legitimate right to tackle the problem. Field is not a rigid concept, however, for counselling is concerned with adolescent development, and development is not easily confined in watertight compartments.

The type of field preferred by the counsellor does have an effect on his technique. This will be discussed in later sections. If he works mainly in the vocational field, this may highlight the need for the efficient storage and retrieval of information. The educational field would demand a greater knowledge of subject options and of topics such as retardation and underfunctioning. Field becomes important when a school provides a well-developed counselling service with a team. A team means division of labour, and this in turn means some specialization in a particular field. But even in these conditions there would be considerable overlap.

Before we discuss these dimensions further, it is useful to draw attention to the way in which the counsellor's idea of personality influences his approach to counselling. It is possible to detect three basic trends in the theoretical and research work in the field of personality. First, there is the concept of *man as a reactive being*. This is the behavourist approach, emphasizing stimuli and responses. In this type of personality theory the discussion is phrased largely in terms of conditioning, reinforcements, i.e. rewards and punishment. It seems that if counselling were to be based solely upon this theory of personality, it would be a highly technical process of behaviour modification. Second, we have the concept of *man as a reactive being in depth*. This stresses the ideas, familiar to the psychotherapist, of repression, resistance and defences. The basic point is that this view of personality tends to assume that the cause of current behaviour lies in the past, and that early experiences are of central importance. Adult and adolescent achievements and interests are seen as almost entirely the product of these early experiences, mainly because they have set the directions which later development has followed. It also draws our attention to the function of repressed or unconscious factors in shaping behaviour in the here and now. If this view of personality were to become the basis for school counselling, it would require skills and abilities beyond most school counsellors. This approach should not be neglected. Certainly the counsellor must be aware that irrational factors will intrude into the counselling process. But where such factors are strong, this is an indication that clinical referral is necessary. Thirdly, we have conceptions of personality such as those of Maslow (1954) and Allport (1955) which look at *man as in a state of continuous development,* or in the "process of becoming". This model implies that all of us are in a continuous state of development and have potentials and capacities which only gradually emerge, this emergence being helped or hindered by environmental factors. It suggests that each one of us has a future which we face with mingled hope and anxiety. According to this model, the counselling process should be one which aids the pupil achieve his or her idiosyncratic goals.

I am guilty of distortion and over-simplification in emphasising these three approaches out of the bewildering amount of research and difficult theory concerned with personality. I have done it because it seems to me that the counsellor's implicit, often almost totally unrecognized ideas about personality undoubtedly influence his position on the dimensions of counselling under discussion. To subscribe to the "man as a reactive being" model might well mean that one's major concern would be with reinforcements or rewards and the deliberate shaping of behaviour. This is important, indeed the counsellor and teacher need to ask what reward power they possess which is meaningful to pupils, and is also thought-provoking, for the work of Hargreaves (1967) has shown the way in which the rewards of the school can be found meaningless to certain groups of pupils. The second approach, "man as a reactive being in depth", alerts us to the importance of irrational factors, and certainly sets limits to the school counsellor's job. There is always a temptation to become fascinated by the abnormal and pathological nature of counselling when this model is central in the counsellor's thinking. "Man in the process of becoming" is a view of personality which fits the creative skills of the teacher and allows the counsellor to work within the school, seeing the school experience in positive terms as a means for development. It leads us eventually to what will be called the *active model* of counselling.

Views of personality as well as the personality of the counsellor lie behind this attitude and approach to his job. If he is tied to the "man as a reactive being in depth" view of people this will be shown in the *level* at which he works. He tends to see himself as a specialist whose skills are totally different from the rest of the staff, consequently sharply demarcating his role from that of the teacher. He will not see the constructive possibilities of the fact that counselling takes place on many levels of sophistication and specialism. Certainly he is in danger of alienating himself from his colleagues, and he also loses the supports and strengths given to pupils when other teachers are involved as real participants in the counselling process. There is a danger in this approach, for a teacher can feel that he is being used or is being pushed into a subordinate position. Such feelings are understandable and the counsellor respects them, although they mean that the situation has been misinterpreted. Counselling is a team effort, which means that a division of labour exists. We can distinguish the trained counsellor from the classroom teacher or form master without allocating people to inferior or superior positions. They do *different* things in the interests of efficiency. The teacher is present in a number of situations where a pupil shows stress or strain. This allows him to *deal with things in context*. He can supply supports, modify conditions and give the pupil important rewards, working very closely with the counsellor to achieve this. The counsellor uses the techniques described in this book to prepare the pupil to work with the teacher in this way.

The next dimension is that of the *normal versus the pathological*. This is a doubtful distinction anyway, because we are never sure whether we mean by normal the statistical idea of the most frequently found type of behaviour or our own moralistic ideas of what people ought to do. If the counsellor loses sight of the creative and developmental view of counselling and personality, he is also in danger of separating himself from the objectives of the secondary school. He may then tend to concentrate on a small proportion of pupils, seeing himself as an outpost of the child guidance service. Like many of those who man outposts, he may feel under threat, and this colours his relationships with the school staff. He is in danger of missing the fact that developmental crises hold the seeds of positive movement towards maturity and that his job is to stimulate growth. This is illustrated by the case of a boy whom we will call John who was aged thirteen and in difficulties. His student counsellor, who was conscientious and sensitive, began by concentrating on John's feelings about his father and unsatisfactory home background. His mother was divorced and the father lived many miles away. John was attached to his father, whilst his mother found great difficulty in adjusting to the increased family responsibilities. Nothing seemed to happen, despite the sympathy and concern shown to John. It was then decided to look at John in developmental terms and assess what he needed in social skills and to gain competence in classroom situations. John was then taught to make better relationships with other pupils on the basis of a systematic analysis of the situations in which he was involved. He was shown how to avoid arousing the resentment of other boys when he was successful in English and metalwork. In addition, the P.E. master took special trouble to improve the boy's performance in the gym, where he was a figure of fun. Many of the situations began with this. Lastly, he was encouraged to take a pride in his appearance and taught to care for his clothes. He had wanted to look nice, but seemed unable to keep his clothes in a clean condition. As progress occurred, John showed all-round improvement. His mother then came to the school counsellor, having noticed the great improvement, and was able to work constructively with him. Not every case works out like this, but it is possible to find creative solutions to such combinations of developmental and environmental problems. The normal and developmental features of the situation were the focus of attention, and the teachers were involved in the counselling programme.

The next dimension is that of *event versus process*. We have tended to discriminate between crisis and developmental counselling in our discussions, but here a slightly different line will be taken. Crisis counselling can be seen as a form of emotional first aid, which can be massive and time consuming. If these crisis situations occur too frequently and too severely, then something is wrong somewhere. The most likely thing is that preventative and developmental work is not done early enough in the school. Crisis counselling is uneconomical, because it allows a pupil to continue under stress before the crisis is given manifest shape. Process versus event also allows us to share out the functions of form teacher and trained counsellor to advantage. Quite a lot of counselling requires only a single interview, and this is likely to be the case where the school is conceived as a guidance community. The form teacher is, if given some in-service training, able to undertake such counselling, using his counselling session as a filter or screen. Some pupils are then passed on to the trained counsellor for developmental counselling, while form teacher and counsellor continue to work closely together. Sometimes, of course, the counsellor refers the pupil to the appropriate outside agency. The trained counsellor is not only necessary for the developmental and long-term counselling, but as a source of support and training for the form teacher. The skills of the counsellor need to be diffused throughout the school, but this has to be done with integrity and the realization that there is no substitute for real training.

The next dimension is the one around which most argument centres and which is also at the heart of models of counselling. It is that of *non-directiveness versus directiveness*. Misunderstanding of the ideas behind non-directive models of counselling lead to fears that the counsellor's action could lead to the subversion of legitimate authority in the school. Stated coldly, this looks ridiculous, for it is unlikely that the discipline structure of the school is so shaky and the power of the counsellor so great that this could happen. Such a reaction reflects the concern given in teaching to problems of control, although it may also include irrational guilt which leads to the added fear that the counsellor will encourage pupils to talk about their teachers in a destructive way. This, of course, would be a gross act of collusion in which no trained counsellor would engage.

The non-directive model springs from the seminal work of Carl Rogers (1942, 1951) and contains the central assumption that the pupil should lead the process, the counsellor taking care neither to direct the pupil nor to give him instructions and advice. The functions of the counsellor seem to be those of providing an atmosphere of unconditional acceptance for the pupil, thereby making it possible for him to undertake self-exploration, without any undue sense of threat. He also acts in such a way that he reflects back to the pupil the thoughts, feelings and attitudes which he holds, thereby facilitating self-discovery. The counsellor is a kind of looking glass in which the pupil can discover for himself his own strengths and weaknesses, his aspirations and fears. This means that counselling is seen as a fairly free process, the form of which cannot be predicted, because each pupil has different aims in life and probably needs to take a unique path to gain his goal. There is, nevertheless, a sense of purpose, because attention is focused on the development of a positive self-picture in that pupil. Coupled with growing recognition of himself as a person of worth is the extension of his personal autonomy. Both of these are vital aspects of healthy adolescent development. But does non-direction always achieve this?

The non-directive approach appears to take two things for granted; that the desire to discuss such abstractions as *the self* will be present in pupils, and (more crucially) that the language capacity to do this exists. We are only too aware of the impact of language development upon educational attainment, but there is also a relationship between this and the establishment of inner controls and attitudes towards the social world. Despite some criticisms and unresolved doubts about the valuable work of Bernstein (1961, 1962, 1965), it does seem that disadvantaged pupils function with restricted language which is not solely a matter of deficient vocabulary, but also of the structure and organization of their language. They possess a closed and circular code or structure which handicaps them in appreciating the relationships between events, and prevents them from perceiving crucial associations. Even more important is the fact that they cannot easily integrate new events and associations into an accurate and coherent schema. The relevant point for the counsellor is that these pupils may be action-orientated. They are, as Lawton (1968) suggests, concerned with events, rather than with reflection about those events.

It has been held that one of the virtues of the non-directive model is that it is value free. In fact, it seems to encapsulate middle-class values which stress that self-exploration is a desirable activity. But some sections of the public would regard self-exploration as meaningless and undesirable. More than this, is the non-directive emphasis upon the self-concept, although a necessary one for developmental counselling, sufficient *by itself*? It certainly is pertinent, for many pupils who seek or are recommended for counselling will have negative or distorted self-images which will need modification. This approach also stresses the acquisition of insight, but we know that the acquisition of insight alone is insufficient to change behaviour. Just as many pupils show shame and guilt when they fail to resist temptation, so do many boys and girls continue to do things although they have gained insight into why they do it. Caseworkers and probation officers would probably nod weary agreement to this. Perhaps enough has been said to suggest that although this non-directive approach to counselling contains many features that are essential to school counselling, it cannot be applied without considerable thought, for it may be ineffective, if not actually harmful, with some pupils in the school.

The idea that different methods are necessary for the lower and higher streams is in tune with general teaching method. It is realistic, but we have to be careful because distasteful associations are attached to the idea. Plato in *The Republic* (BK. III) produces the myth of the four metals. Into the compositions of those fit to rule the gods mixed gold. Their assistants were given silver, but the farmers and craftsmen were restricted to brass and iron. It was recognized that children of gold could be born to parents who had the nature of iron and brass, and that these should be trained as rulers. Yet the emphasis is on the different natures of children. It would be shameful if counselling were to underline differences between children, or were misused to reintroduce the idea of different types of ability and lead to some pupils being regarded as drawers of water and hewers of wood. We need to adapt our methods to fit the needs of the pupils without falling into this trap. Many special programmes for statutory age leavers seem to fail because they separate these pupils from others, a strategy which seems to emphasize that not only are they leaving school, but that they are failures as well.

One way of solving this problem lies in the sophisticated version of the directive approach presented by Krumboltz (1966) and which has been developed by writers in the volume edited by Krumboltz and Thoresen (1969). His view of counselling is quite simple and offers possibilities. The aim of counselling is that of promoting adaptive behaviour. This definition, although somewhat alarming in relation to the Platonic myth, is helpful, because the end product is seen as the development of efficient problem-solving skills. The job of the counsellor is that of learning to break problems down into simple components which show both the pupil and the counsellor the steps needed to solve them. This gives counselling a more immediate and visible purpose. The task of the counsellor is that of arranging conditions in counselling which allow the pupil to discover more adaptive ways of coping with his difficulties. This approach is attractive, for it means that the skills of the teacher can play a real part in counselling.

It is always useful to see what an approach is protesting against. Krumboltz is arguing against the traditional mental health view that has permeated discussions of counselling from Beers (1939) onwards. He is saying that one can be deluded into believing that the pupil's mental health can be blamed for what is actually a deficiency in experience of success and of positive learning experiences. Many teachers will know how valid this is, for many of their pupils come from backgrounds marked by deprivation and negative learning. The world is a jungle for these pupils, and they have spent most of their energies in maintaining an uneasy containment of hostile forces. Krumboltz is arguing that we should get away from what he calls an "implicit disease paradigm" concealed in the non-directive approach to counselling. It is this aspect which makes teachers suspicious, I suspect. There is an idea that counselling releases bottled-up constructive behaviour, but like many teachers I suspect that this is not entirely realistic. Many pupils will be suffering from a deficiency of good experiences in learning situations; they will lack adequate decision-making and problem-solving skills; and they will have very limited experience of success. Perhaps it is sensible to question whether there is anything to be released through non-directive counselling, and what this is likely to be. If a strictly non-directive approach were to be used with such pupils they might well see the whole thing as meaningless or as an intolerable threat. Certainly nothing would be done to remedy the above deficiencies. Krumboltz says that the behavioural goals should be set through the mutual agreement of both counsellor and pupil, the behavioural changes being worked out as a co-operative effort. This makes a situation which can be carefully tailored to suit each pupil, although some will present greater challenges to the ingenuity of the counsellor than others.

This approach seems to be relevant because it utilizes the skills of the teacher. We need, however, what will be called the active model of counselling to deal with the old problem of transfer of training. The danger with this technique is that very often the problem with which a pupil comes is not the real one. If this is the case and the counsellor goes ahead with planning, then real harm could be done to the pupil. This is poor counselling, and certainly trained counsellors are aware of the need for flexibility and change of aim. Care is needed to ensure that a pupil is not pushed too rapidly into accepting a goal, or that he is not forced into a passive and over-dependent position where everything is spelt out for him. The real mistake lies in the way in which an enthusiastic counsellor can create for himself a role of benevolent paternalism which is against the aims of developmental counselling.

To create new father figures at a time when independence of them is at the centre of developmental tasks is a strange way to induce development. The counsellor can assume too easily that he knows the problem and hence the answer. But this is not always as straightforward as one likes to imagine. A serious danger is that the counsellor can begin to manipulate the pupil, producing superficial and conforming responses which are not in tune with what is happening inside the boy or girl. Such responses will not lead to constructive development and the whole procedure becomes abortive.

If we look at the non-directive and the directive approaches we can see that they have more in common than is evident at first sight. The extreme non-directive approach is a protest against the fact that it is very easy to put the pupil into a passive and vulnerable position, instructing him as to what he ought to do. The importance of this reaction can be gauged by the fact that an ex-student of mine said in the last day or two of his training that for the first time in his life he had not been told what to do. Before his training it had seemed to him that the world was full of people who were prepared to direct him and give advice, but none who would listen and accept his needs. A very serious question is whether non-directiveness is actually non-directive. This was in my mind when the man just mentioned was talking. If we bring an adolescent into an ambiguous situation when he is having some difficulty, we bring him into a situation which lacks the clear signals of the classroom. One can argue quite plausibly that ambiguous situations cause anxiety, and this, together with the fact that the pupil has a problem, leads to a search for cues which indicate to the pupil that he is doing the right thing—the right thing being then what the counsellor wants and expects. Blocher's (1965) thesis is that a very subtle and probably unrecognized process of conditioning, based upon non-verbal cues such as gestures, tones of voice and the facial expression of the counsellor, is operating in many ostensibly non-directive counselling situations. This might well be true of many pupils who work in a restricted language code, for it seems that they are more responsive to *how* a thing is said, than to *what* is said. In non-directive situations many unintended and unrecognized reinforcements are given, which eventually result, if the process is continued long enough, in a convergence of the viewpoints of counsellor and client. Researchers in the evaluation of psychotherapy have pointed out that this convergence of viewpoints is sometimes the implicit criterion for describing an outcome as successful. If we subscribe to the developmental approach to counselling this is a questionable yard-stick, unless it represents a satisfying adjustment to the school situation, needless to say, satisfying from the pupil's point of view.

It is essential to integrate the two approaches into a model which meets the needs of secondary school pupils, or we may be caught in a trap hidden in both the "man in the process of becoming" model of personality and in the non-directive view of counselling. This is what Gellner (1964) has called the "hidden prince" theory of personality. It is illustrated by the fairy tale of the enchanted prince who has been given the shape of a frog, i.e. the idea that inside an antisocial pupil or a boy with negative attitudes to school is a social and positive pupil struggling to get out. This is not completely false, but we usually do not know the magic formula. Certainly studies of the ideal self of such pupils confirm that they want to be different and they would like to be successful in school. This is not the whole story, for it ignores the facts that the concept of self is partially derived from experiences with important people in our environment, and that a complex link exists between behaviour and the self image.

The weakness of the non-directive model is that it seems to take it for granted that a new positive self can emerge without any change in the environment or in the behaviour of the individual and those around him. The active model of counselling will suggest that we may need consciously to integrate what is happening inside the person with what is happening in his environment, especially in school and at home. We can take the position of the fairytale princess quoted by Gellner, who says to the frog, "How do I know that you will turn into a prince if I kiss you?" How indeed? We can ask whether the kiss of non-direction and unconditional acceptance may lead to no change or even to negative change in the frog-pupil. Counsellors can do harm. Some of this harm comes from the fact that it is not too difficult to find a counsellor taking a non-directive approach to his work, whilst simultaneously holding some cloudy version of Freudian theory, which says that deep dark urges of an instinctual type are at work within the pupil. Sometimes we then stress the fact that such forces need to be controlled and modified whilst the other part of our theory says that we must let the hidden prince out of his darkness into the light of day. The muddles in our models are many, and we need to go on thinking about this.

Some time has been spent on the directive versus non-directive dimension and the associated controversies, but this was essential to provide understanding of the need for an eclectic model of counselling.

The way in which these dimensions of the counsellor's role influence his style of work can be seen more clearly if we look at two extreme types of counsellor. One we will call the "integrated" and the other, the "separated". These names indicate the tendency to work as part of the school team or to separate themselves from colleagues. The diagram shows what happens in these extreme positions:

## COMPARISON OF THE ISOLATED AND INTEGRATED COUNSELLING ROLES

| Dimension | Isolated counsellor | Integrated counsellor |
|---|---|---|
| 1. Field. | Stresses personal counselling. | Works in all three fields as determined by the needs of the individual pupil and the expectations and resources of the school. |
| 2. Specialist activities. | Sees counselling as a very specialist skill. Overtly stresses the therapeutic nature of his skills. | Builds his counselling on teaching skills. Carefully relates what he does to the normal activities of the school. Emphasizes the "normality" of counselling. |
| 3. Directiveness. | Claims to be non-directive. | Is prepared to advise or be directive if this seems to be in the best interests of the pupil. |
| 4. Separation from the teacher role. | Emphasizes his differences from the teacher. | Tries to link the counselling and teaching roles. Looks for points of similarity. |
| 5. Counselling seen as a long-term process. | Emphasizes this. | Looks at the situation and makes decisions after looking at the evidence. Is prepared for short-term counselling. |

These types are caricatures, yet school counsellors do tend to move towards one or the other. There is no right way of counselling, and although this book stresses the integrated approach, there are some schools where the "separated" counsellor may be most useful. Such counsellors may be necessary when the outside agencies are unable to deal with the large numbers of difficult adolescents who appear when the school does not meet the needs created by social deprivation and disorganization through modification of its educational methods and the development of therapeutic teacher-pupil relationships. What seems important, is the need for an individual counsellor to work out the costs and the consequences of the position he takes up on these basic dimensions, and then proceed to justify this, both to himself and to those to whom he is responsible. Failure to do this can lead to unnecessary inefficiency.

### The active model of counselling

The active model of counselling tries to be eclectic in using the contributions of both the non-directive and the directive school. It should be made clear that no attempt is being made to state in precise terms what the counsellor should do. We would be engaging in a self-defeating strategy if we tried this, for the essence of the active model is adaptation by the counsellor to both the pupil and the school. The systems analysis has already shown that the school itself imposes many constraints upon the counsellor, yet the counsellor is also engaged in a delicate process of role-making and role-taking which calls for maximal sensitivity to feedback from colleagues and pupils. He does not go to occupy a clearly defined position which remains the same for each incumbent. The best way of looking at this model is to begin by looking at the broad functions the counsellor performs. You are again warned that these are only analytical outlines, for each counsellor will give a different weighting to each function, just as some counsellors may prefer the vocational field as their major area of operation, whilst others favour the personal or educational.

### I. THE COUNSELLOR AS A RESOURCE PERSON

The biggest use of the counsellor as a resource person in the active model lies in his capacity to provide his fellow teachers with information about pupils which allows them to be more effective teachers. The results of tests of interests, of aptitudes and attainment can provide teachers with a new understanding of a pupil. The very fact of having an explanation about apparently inexplicable behaviour puts the teacher back into control of a situation in a constructive way. An instance of the way this works is given by the case of Stephen, a fourteen-year-old who was considered to be unpredictable by those who taught him. He would suddenly provoke an incident in the class causing complete disruption. He had been referred to the local hospital clinic who found little the matter with him. Counselling revealed that Stephen had learned a pattern of behaviour which made sense of what he did. If a teacher annoyed him or he disliked the lesson, he grew resentful, yet he always contained his feeling until the next lesson. Then some minor irritation or opportunity was sufficient to provoke violent discharge. To the observer there seemed no pattern or sense in this. The way in which the boy had learned a pattern of coping with his feelings of aggression does not concern us here; the relevant point is that once the teachers understood this, then they could take steps to cope with it constructively, and they could also feel better about the boy as they made sense of his behaviour. Behaviour which is apparently meaningless is very threatening to a teacher coping with a class. The counsellor operated as a resource person in transmitting this kind of information to the teacher. Some teachers were very co-operative, taking the strategy further, informing the others when Stephen appeared tense so that the teacher receiving him could take the necessary tension-reducing steps. New feelings of concern on the part of the teachers and positive expectations were aroused, and these communicated themselves to the boy. He then began to change certain attitudes, despite strong counter pressures from peer groups in which he was involved.

The fact that the counsellor talks to teachers about pupils he is counselling should not be taken to mean that he is indifferent to the need for confidentiality. A boy or girl is always consulted before such action is taken. Indeed, such consultation is often an essential requirement for success. The counsellor is a resource person when he allows himself to be available to discuss pupils who are under stress. Teachers are concerned about pupils, yet it is a surprising fact that there has been very little conscious provision of supports or opportunity for professional discussion of pupils in schools. This is especially true of young and probationary teachers, who often tend to avoid discussion of difficult pupils because they feel they ought to be able to cope. They fear being exposed as inadequate, although it is highly unlikely that with some pupils anyone else could be more successful. Young teachers are sometimes shattered to find how different full-time teaching is from teaching practice. As one such probationary teacher said, "I've just realized that my teaching practice was a dream—it was so protected and sheltered. Now I don't know what is going on". The counsellor can apply his skills here, not only in understanding the complex feelings concealed in such statements, but also to help young teachers with simple things that seem so obvious that they are missed: how to mark a register in two minutes, avoiding the chaos which often begins during this operation when the teacher is slow; how to scan a situation in the classroom to detect the source of trouble; how to speak to a pupil with fairness, yet in a way which quietens the others, rather than bleating ineffectually for silence at the whole class. Simple practical situations of this type structure a process which is concerned with a young colleague's professional self-image. The trained counsellor can allow this to happen at the teacher's own pace and in his own way, doing it with humility and without having to impose constricting stereotypes which hamper innovation and creativity in his colleague. My tepid phrases do little to convey the real vigour and excitement of this aspect of the counsellor's role.

### 2. THE COUNSELLOR AS A MOBILIZER OF RESOURCES

One of the central features of the counsellor's role in the active model is that of a mobilizer of resources on behalf of the pupil. Counselling can be seen as composed of two parts:

(a) Attention is given to the needs, feelings and emotions of that boy or girl. In this phase the counsellor is concerned with the main things emphasized by the non-directive school. These are acceptance of the pupil as he is rather than as we think he should be, the fact that he is central in the counselling process, and above all belief in his worth as a person.

(b) A phase concerned with adaptation and careful use of environmental resources to help the pupil attain his or her goals. In this phase, the counsellor works very actively with his colleagues to give the pupil the maximal chances of achieving his aims and using the resources of the school constructively.

This two-phase approach to counselling which lies behind the active model can be understood through the diagram on p. 46, which is based on a modification of the valuable work of Carkhuff (1969, 1971). This writer brings out the idea of *emergent direction* as the basis of counselling.

Providing that one does not follow this model slavishly or interpret it rigidly, the two-phase diagram explains the need for the school counsellor to operate as a mobilizer of resources. It shows that the first phase is not an unnecessary luxury, but an essential for creating a sense of purpose and direction in counselling. The first stage is one where the counsellor builds up a highly personalized communication system between himself and the pupil. A boy or girl can be seen in the position of the man in Stevie Smith's poem who drowned because the onlookers thought he was waving. He was drowning and yelling for help, yet some people on the shore probably waved back cheerfully. As teachers we may prefer to wave back rather than recognize a shout for help which is concealed in defensive behaviour and indirect statements. The very difficulties in communicating lead us to think that the first phase is a cosy chat period, when in fact it is concerned with facing realities, becoming bitter and sour at times as unpalatable truths emerge for the pupil. All the skills are needed to support and move towards action which is sound and constructive.

The fact that a child is in a good school is no guarantee that he sees it as good or that we can assume confidently that he will be able to

## THE TWO PHASES OF THE COUNSELLING PROCESS

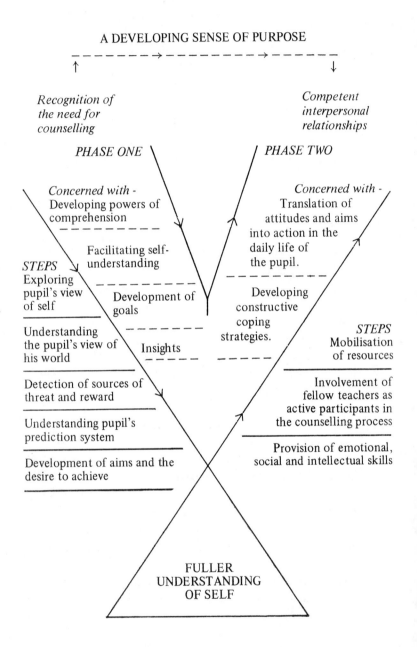

A DEVELOPING SENSE OF PURPOSE

*Recognition of
the need for
counselling*

*Competent
interpersonal
relationships*

*PHASE ONE*

*PHASE TWO*

*Concerned with -*
Developing powers of
comprehension

*Concerned with -*
Translation of
attitudes and aims
into action in the
daily life of
the pupil.

Facilitating self-
understanding

*STEPS*
Exploring
pupil's view
of self

Development of
goals

Developing
constructive
coping
strategies.

Understanding
the pupil's view of
his world

Insights

*STEPS*
Mobilisation
of resources

Detection of sources of
threat and reward

Involvement of
fellow teachers as
active participants in
the counselling process

Understanding pupil's
prediction system

Provision of emotional,
social and intellectual skills

Development of aims and the
desire to achieve

FULLER
UNDERSTANDING
OF SELF

use what the school offers, or indeed that he wishes to use it. Sometimes it is necessary to help a pupil change false views of the school. These are not necessarily negative views, for the non-academic sixth former or the one taking C.S.E. or O Levels may have unrealistic ideas of the benefits of staying at school and of the value of minimal educational qualifications. Bright working-class boys may reach the sixth form and then find themselves unable to use the experience. The demands for independent study and thought overwhelm them, whilst many factors prevent them from continuing their self-investment in study. Such pupils sometimes are fighting parents who see school as unnecessary and who deny the legitimacy of the boy's educational aspirations. The first phase of counselling operates to create the conditions in which a boy rediscovers himself as a person of worth, able to achieve the things he desires.

Once direction has been achieved, the counsellor needs to work very closely with his colleagues, trying to solve the major problem of transfer of training. If the pupil's new attitudes and skills remain within the counselling sessions, then the exercise is scarcely worthwhile. The conditions must be created in which a pupil can translate his new self-image into action, exercise his problem-solving skills and have a realistic opportunity for the experience of success. The active model is an adaptation to the implications revealed in the systems analysis, namely that effectiveness in counselling depends upon the constraining and shaping forces of classroom and school organization. The counselling interview cannot be insulated from the rest of the school, because the pupil goes back into it after the session and feedback is then brought back into the next interview. The counsellor becomes a figure almost totally dependent upon the co-operation of his colleagues in the second phase of counselling, and he reinforces the pastoral care functions of his colleagues through this dependency upon their co-operation.

The precise form taken by the counsellor's work will depend upon his position in the hierachy of authority within the school. If he is head of a department of guidance and counselling, then he will be more absorbed in administration and the making of situations of contact with other departments. If he works at a lower level in the authority and power structure of the school, then he will use different methods of gaining co-operation and involving colleagues, but in every case it seems desirable that he should be a fully integrated member of the school team, working together with colleagues for the welfare of pupils. He will learn to use educational situations creatively to aid the personal development of pupils and to provide them with coping strategies which are viable. Some indication of the way this can be done will be given in the accounts of group guidance and group counselling. The educational techniques of role playing and simulation offer many possibilities, but the last chapter will emphasize the need to call on the specialist skills of colleagues.

This reference to different levels of complexity in counselling is a reminder that we must not forget that the trained counsellor has a special place in the school. As a specialist he will have to deal with the most difficult and demanding developmental and crises cases himself. He knows that he is not equipped to deal with all the problems of the school, referring some of them outside, and he steadfastly refuses to become absorbed in a small percentage of hopeless cases who have been rejected by the skilled specialist agencies. He knows he is neither a social worker nor a therapist, although he draws techniques from these professions, using them in a modified way. In describing counselling in the secondary school it is useful to see the counsellor as a variety of specialist teacher concerned with creativity and the development of flexible and relevant coping strategies in pupils at the crucial period before they take up more committed roles in society. The danger lies in seeing the familiar and not recognizing the differences. Counsellors do not "just speak the prose of counselling". They do speak prose, but they are trained to speak it better, and sometimes they have to speak it in a language which is unfamiliar to the school, although necessary for the pupil. They have skills going far beyond those of the ordinary teacher. The active model is looking forward to new developments in secondary education, which are themselves the product of a more fundamental move towards new ideas of the nature of the school. In the not-so-distant future many secondary schools will become places where pupils are given carefully designed opportunities of learning the skills of social interaction, methods of problem solving and the development of effective styles of thought, rather than being the recipients of traditional subject teaching. Schools seem to be moving towards a state in which they will become centres containing resources for learning, which means that the current role of the teacher will be modified drastically. Simultaneously there will be a greater need for developmental counselling as the school career of each pupil will be designed for the development of decision making and personal responsibility. The teacher will be released from the constraining tie to a classroom and a form group, whilst educational technology will have produced machines which perform many functions now carried by teachers. We are foolish if we ignore these things.

A curious paradox permeates this discussion about the need for the trained counsellor to be active in the school setting whilst giving other teachers a participant and helping role in counselling. We have seen that school counselling is one of many special skills within the teaching profession, yet this seems to be a contradiction of the fact that every teacher sometimes has to be a counsellor. The confusion arises because of two things. First as a special skill it is centred upon interpersonal relationships. We know that the major cause of difficulty in many deviant and neurotic people is the lack of capacity to make relationships. The Underwood Report (1955) defines a maladjusted pupil as one who has an impaired capacity to make a normally satisfying relationship. Yet by the very nature of the learning situation every teacher should be concerned with relationships. The answer to this paradox which seems to take away the need for a trained counsellor is that there are many aspects of interpersonal relationships, and many different levels of involvement. The position of the counsellor is somewhat like that of an English specialist. Every teacher can claim to be a teacher of English with justification, but there is still a need for an English specialist with well-defined duties within the school. The school counsellor is in a similar position, although he is even more directly dependent upon the efforts of his colleagues than is the English specialist.

Later chapters will show very clearly the need to understand the pupil's view of his life situation. Again this is not confined to the counsellor, for every teacher who struggles to and succeeds in making his material meaningful has to take this into account. We have to make an attempt to understand the difficulties in building a communication system. In primary school children the language of the space age is part of their basic vocabulary, whilst those who have been taught mathematics in a modern way are familiar with multibase number systems and understand the binary number system lying behind computer work. Those of us who are well into middle age find this difficult and often artificial. We must see that information now flows to pupils from many sources that are far more significant than parents and teachers. We may lack credibility as sources of information. The horizontal flow of communication from peers, the mass media and other sources outside the school render it essential that a counsellor should make a real effort to understand and comprehend the world view held by a pupil. This does not apply only to those pupils who are younger and disadvantaged but to sixth formers. One of the most helpless positions the counsellor can occupy is that of attempting to counsel a group of sixth formers who have committed themselves to a religion of world rejection. Faced by a morally based rejection of the system, its pressure and rewards, what does one do? There is so much real morality in the attitudes and beliefs that one wonders whether it is right to intervene. We may, of course, show them the consequences of certain behaviours without appearing to threaten or indirectly blackmail, and sometimes we may help an individual who has opted out psychologically, to find his way back in. We know that once we see the standpoint of the pupil, behaviour that appeared obstinate and anti-authority becomes very reasonable. In most cases it seems proper to try to aid a pupil to see the school in a constructive way, and also see himself as having the potentiality for achievement if it is there. It could be objected that this presupposes that meaningful courses and activities can be found in the school, but even in the most sterile and unimaginative school it is possible to help a pupil identify resources which he can use. Once this point is reached we can enter the second phase of the counselling process, becoming a mobilizer of resources. We need to ensure that the changes in self-image are translated into successful activity in school and that the sense of direction which has emerged is given concrete behavioural form. We must see that the skills used in the session are brought into use outside it, for this further step cannot be left to chance. The counsellor would approach those having responsibility for pastoral care, explain the pupil's problems and needs as they emerged in the counselling process, and ask for help in providing the necessary experiences and reinforcements. The pupil is consulted, mainly because the counsellor cannot take credit for what others do, but also because the positive attitudes developed toward the counsellor should be spread to the staff. The counsellor has a responsibility to ensure that the change in attitude and the positive relationship does not remain tied to him. It is important that the pupil should realize that a number of people are actively prepared to help him, the counsellor on his part seeing that his efforts are of little use in isolation. He does not conceive of counselling as a rigidly insulated situation: instead he views the counselling interviews, whether individual or group, as a focal point within a process which involves the pupil's total school life. Specialized skills are used within the interview, but only an unintelligent counsellor would consider these skills sufficient to attain the goals by themselves. The counselling interview can be quite usefully seen as a central point in a team effort at real pastoral care. A counsellor failing to appreciate this runs grave danger of arousing unrealistic expectations in others about what he can achieve, and is implicitly assuming a messianic role. History seems to suggest that those claiming such attributes usually get the treatment they deserve, and one hopes that school counsellors will not be exceptions.

The counsellor's skill in communication is one which has to be continuously practised and assessed, for despite undoubted goodwill one's fellow teachers can acquire stereotypes and expectations of pupils which ensure that they continue their undesirable behaviour and keep negative attitudes operating. This is a self-defeating strategy by the teachers: if re-socialization is to occur, then these stereotypes must be modified, and the labels, which are probably inaccurate and certainly unhelpful, must be removed from the pupil. This is achieved by skill in presenting information, reducing implicit threat and showing the teachers why the boy or girl behaves in a particular way. This realizes the latent goodwill of the many teachers who, once they understand the "why" of the situation, are prepared to be extremely helpful.

Two devices exist to aid the counsellor become a mobilizer of resources, and they are of equal importance: informal contacts and individual discussion, and the more structured device of the counselling conference. A counselling conference is useful because it provides the participating teachers with structured and immediately usable information, although the counsellor gains at least as much as he gives. Teachers often possess information without realizing its significance, sometimes because they lack the other piece of information to which it is related.

The counselling conference is called at points in the counselling process when there are clearly articulated problems to be solved in which the help of colleagues is essential to the counsellor. This means counselling conferences have different functions in the two phases. If they are called early in the first they will be concerned with information, either from the teachers to the counsellor or the reverse. The counselling conference is more essential and more productive during the second phase where it is task-orientated and aimed at the solution of some problem which inhibits progress to a goal which is desired by the pupil. The objective is usually that of thrashing out a common policy for the treatment of the individual and finding a mode of action that gives him a real chance of success. It is more positive than this, for it aims at finding means and routes of helping a pupil achieve the goals he developed in the first phase of counselling. It strengthens pupils' autonomy because it is based on the idea of "emergent direction" rather than directiveness, and certainly contains no benevolent paternalism which tells that pupil what "is best for him". It is an effective tool for the mobilization of resources, for the participants are encouraged to indicate what they feel they can do, making the process of support consistent and clear. It is a team effort, aimed at fulfilling the responsibilities of the school for the full education of a pupil. The counsellor provides information, and acts as a co-ordinator. The conference also provides a means of assessing the changes occurring in a pupil, and it gives the team a chance to detect the means by which they can modify stress situations. It is a flexible instrument, for counselling conferences are called when they are necessary, which means that the strategies and supports can be changed to fit in with changes in the pupils. Because it is an internal affair in most cases, it can be arranged during the lunch period or immediately after school.

The counselling conference serves to help colleagues to understand the pupil's view of the world, thereby making sense of his behaviour. The situation and stimuli to which he sharply reacts can be exposed and discussed but, more important, the participants gain some knowledge of the functions the behaviour serves for him. It is a fundamental point in counselling that behaviour is purposive. If crisis counselling is necessary, then it seems very likely that the counsellor will need to call an emergency conference. The purpose then is different, for the counsellor's role may well be that of gathering and collating information. He will probably have little to communicate, but may have to gather as much information as possible for the purpose of reaching some decision about action. The discovery of drug taking on the school premises or a dramatic breakdown of an unusual type might be the situation necessitating a crisis counselling conference. More important than the gathering of evidence is the fact that such a conference allows one to mobilize internal supports for a pupil, even if outside referral is necessary. It cannot be emphasized too strongly that, just as the presence of a trained counsellor does not relieve teachers of pastoral and counselling responsibilities, so the school cannot shed its responsibilities through the act of referral.

A realistic approach is essential in organizing a counselling conference. There is a limit to the amount of adaptation that can be properly accepted by teachers, and a ceiling to the level of demands they can meet. The more counselling is developmental in nature, the less likely one is to demand too much of the teacher. This danger of excess and unrealistic demands is one reason why the counsellor should be a teacher who fully understands the stresses and strains of the classroom and the degree of elasticity in the school structure. Some schools can adapt more readily than others, but perhaps it is very useful to keep Tyler's (1960) theory of minimal change in mind. This would mean that the counsellor should learn to ask for the minimal amount of support and adaptation necessary to achieve positive change in a pupil. To ask for more is to run the risk of negative feedback upon the others in the class, and sometimes to cause difficulties in other areas. I remember the case of David, a rather sensitive delinquent fourteen-year-old. He had been shocked by his experience of a remand home and was able to talk about this to his student counsellor who had an excellent relationship with him. The counsellor did sterling work in mobilizing resources, but suddenly things began to go sour. Investigation showed two things which represented a misuse of the principle of mobilization of resources and of the counselling conference. First, the boy felt that things were being taken out of his hands; his remark was "I want to stand on my own feet . . . I'm not different". The last phrase led to the discovery that the woodwork master who was very supportive had begun to act unwisely. He had done good work, but then he took it too far. The boy came from a deprived and fatherless home where the mother was under a suspended prison sentence. He wanted to make his mother a Christmas present and the master was letting him do this when the others in his group were confined to making rather dull joints. David therefore began to feel disassociated from the rest of his group. In fact, further investigation showed that his mother was giving him a pound a week pocket money out of a family income which was officially below £10. He was found a part-time job and given greater responsibility for himself, whilst the woodwork situation was unobtrusively changed.

The nagging doubt in every counsellor's mind is the fear of being unable to preserve confidentiality. The following procedures will aid this by providing a real structure to the counselling conference. The counsellor prepares a clear statement of the pupil's general problem leading to his need for counselling, followed by the specific problem which has led to the counselling conference. This is followed by a statement of the counsellor's view of the pupil and his reactions to counselling. The pupil's position should be presented with sympathy, thereby inviting co-operation, but without sentimentality. The counsellor in drawing up his draft for the conference will probably hold in mind the general principles:

(i)   that human behaviour is caused,

(ii)  that it is modifiable,

(iii) that the objective is to provide the participants with insights into the pupil and his behaviour,

(iv)  that a pupil is worthy of respect and assistance.

This will lead to a working hypothesis about the reasons for the behaviour of the boy or girl, and this in turn is succeeded by a brief statement of the objectives of the counselling conference. In this way, the counsellor avoids plunging into the trap of giving precise methods and routes for achieving the objectives, for not only would this be stupidly arrogant, but other teachers almost certainly will produce better strategies and modes of action than those thought of by the counsellor.

The constructive part of the conference lies in the interchange of views and the gradual movement towards a united plan for action. This requires all the skills of the counsellor as he notes the trends, and in highlighting potentially useful statements made by members. He will need to develop good techniques of chairmanship, summarizing the discussion and clearly stating what is to be done. If the counsellor is working in a school where the principles of counselling and pastoral care are fully built into the organization, then it is safe to duplicate the information before the conference and also do a summary of the decisions which were reached once the conference is over. Teachers who are involved in pastoral work are capable of treating such documents in a professional way, although the trained counsellor will always look around for a forgotten sheet or one which is on the floor. He is aware that cleaners can read, and that they usually know a number of pupils in the school.

As with most educational activities, the case conference is productive to the degree to which preparation has been invested in it and the amount of efficient follow-up which is established. The number of counselling conferences which can be undertaken by the trained counsellor is limited, but there is no reason why they should not be initiated by other members of the pastoral care team. The principle is that the conference is determined by the needs of the pupil and the utility of it for him in the energence of realistic supports. To undertake the counselling conference too soon, and before the participants can be given real information, is not only ineffective, but it may be damaging to the pupil. Timing of the conference is important, and although the counsellor will know when to hold a conference for one of his own cases, he will have to train the pastoral care team to deal with less severe problems. Timing is critical and only the counsellor's real integration into the staff team will allow him to assess this with accuracy. To foist a premature counselling conference on unwilling participants adds nothing helpful, yet if one waits a month it is often possible to hold a conference with profit. Knowledge and changed perceptions of the pupil account for this. This counselling conference helps to put pastoral care into a professional, yet truly educational, framework, making the skills of the trained counsellor more widely available. As varied systems of pastoral care develop in the comprehensive school, so will various versions of the school welfare team emerge, to which the counsellor, careers advisory officer, careers teacher, the educational welfare officer and the representatives of other outside agencies can make relevant contributions. The counselling conference is just one way of giving the participation of other people a helpful form, allowing the counsellor to be a real mobilizer of resources for a pupil.

### 3. THE COUNSELLOR AS A LINK BETWEEN THE SCHOOL AND OTHER AGENCIES

One British trainer of counsellors has remarked that from inside the school the counsellor appears to be a specialist, but from the viewpoint of the specialist agencies he is seen as the equivalent of the general practitioner. This means he should know when, where and how to refer pupils for specialist help. This referral function, and his knowledge of emotional and other signs indicating a problem requiring the help of an outside agency, is undoubtedly an important part of the counsellor's role, although his relationship with outside agencies is not limited to this. One of the difficulties hindering collaboration between the schools and other agencies springs from the fact that teachers and social workers used to have very different training and markedly different attitudes to their clientele. This has made for a lack of understanding on both sides, although there are more similarities in present-day training than we think. It is true, however, that teachers often fail to appreciate the objectives of social workers and are suspicious of the relationships they establish with their clients. Social workers fail to understand the nature of modern educational practices: the rate at which change is occurring in the schools; the demands of teaching; and the relaxed atmosphere found in the good secondary school. Rigid stereotypes are at work, and these are not confined to one side. In this situation, the counsellor who has been given a training which incorporates some of the elements found in the training of social workers can perform a valuable function. He is able, as the need arises, to interpret the position of one party to the other. He can act as a filter for communication, facilitating meaningful co-operation. The position has its dangers, for he may alienate himself from both sides if he is clumsy and can precipitate a breakdown in relationships. If this were all the counsellor did in relation to the outside agencies, then it would be scarcely worthwhile. The relationship between the counsellor and the pastoral care team and the outside agencies is deeper than this, for children often attend school while they are clients of the outside agency. The counsellor can offer special support to these pupils, either providing this himself, or, more profitably, gaining the co-operation of his pastoral care colleagues. This can take the form of general support, or the counsellor may operate the equivalent of an early warning system by keeping an unobtrusive eye on certain pupils. He then alerts the social services or probation officer to signs of stress and tension noticeable in school, but which are unlikely to be reported by the pupil or his family. This type of surveillance requires skill and diplomacy for it is a not unreasonable fear among social workers that teachers will treat a child differently if it becomes known that he comes from a children's home or is on probation. This does not mean that the social agencies are saying that such children are discriminated against, simply that he or she will be perceived as different, and that this perception will become noticeable to the pupil, even although it is well meant and sympathetic. I remember seeing Paul, a boy of just fifteen, who was in the top stream of a comprehensive school and about to take his O Levels. The school was extremely worried about him, describing him as deep, odd and different. They were extremely worried because he was on probation. With the permission of the probation officer the boy was interviewed. It was found that he had ambitious parents who worked hard for everything and who did not understand his aspirations to be a social worker. It was then discovered that Paul's parents were having a new house built and that they had to live with the paternal grandparents. Paul was fond of his grandparents, but the whole burden of entertaining them fell on him. This intelligent and active boy was left to play dominoes with them evening after evening. One night it was too much, so he and his friends went into a nearby town, and into an off-licence taking a bottle of wine. They did not drink it; they put it into a waste bin where it was found by the policeman. There was no sign of oddity, just strong feelings of stress, which were given sudden expression in a rather silly way from the outsider's viewpoint. No more than this was found, yet Paul was being bombarded with signals from teachers that he was seen as odd and different. He was beginning to respond by opting out of the school situation, dropping his standards and beginning to absent himself. Considerable time had to be invested in reversing these signals and the associated expectations of the teachers. This illustration makes it easier to understand the doubts of social workers, although the possibility of very constructive strategies of co-operation between school and agencies is strong. It does demand an imaginative Head and willing caseworkers. One successful strategy is for the counsellor to see the child in school, whilst the caseworker deals with the home. The two co-operate very closely, and in some situations joint visits of caseworker and counsellor to the home have been extremely helpful.

It seems almost inevitable that very close contact will develop between the counsellor and the child guidance team, the educational psychologist being the central figure in this. It is essential that this contact spreads to the whole pastoral care team and to other teachers as the occasion demands. It has been strongly stated that counselling is not primarily intended for the delinquent and deviant population of the school, but should be available to all. Buckton (1971) in a survey of sixth-form pupils found that they clearly recognize that they have developmental problems, and feel that their performance in school would be facilitated if a counsellor were available with whom they could discuss individual worries. It is noteworthy that they saw their major area of problem and anxiety as lying in school. They felt that difficulties with home had come several years earlier and that the vast majority of them had achieved equilibrium between themselves and parents. Despite this, it is a hard fact that secondary schools have to contain pupils who need residential placements, but for whom no facilities exist. Many pupils receiving child guidance treatment are to be found in schools. Sometimes it is useful for the counsellor to work with these boys and girls under the direction of the educational psychologist or psychiatrist, providing support and trying to ensure that recommendations are implemented. The counsellor has to assess this matter carefully, or he may find himself become a "Department of Lost Causes". How much work he does in this area depends on his feelings about the basic dimensions, especially those of the *normal versus the pathological* and *separation versus integration* into the school. Only the individual concerned can make up his mind, but it is an area of work where confusion begins. It is tempting for a counsellor interested in maladjustment and abnormality to begin thinking of himself as a representative of the clinic within the school or as an outpost of progressive thought set in barbarian darkness. It should be stressed that clinic staffs do not think of schools in this way. Most school counsellors work closely with clinics and educational psychologists without doing this. They do not duplicate the function of the psychologist, for they do not have sufficient background in psychology, but they do use their training in the service of the pupil whilst remaining full members of the school. Psychologist and counsellor co-operate to feed into the school greater understanding of the contribution of family relationships and regime, social class membership and differences in developmental progress to the particular pupil's difficulties.

One very important function of the counsellor in linkage with agencies is that of ensuring that information gets to the people who need it and can use it. Information is very much linked with the power struggles which sometimes occur in the secondary school. Those in the category of "those in the know" are at a distinct advantage to "those not in the know". Information essential to wise and creative handling of pupils often does not reach those concerned. It is often filed away without any action being taken. The counsellor will take pains to see that teachers receive information which is helpful to them.

The information function is two-way in nature. The presence of the counsellor in a school helps the social agencies to make more effective contributions to the development of pupils, and in turn the school can become more helpful to them. A school does hold a great deal of critical information about a child, but this rarely reaches an outside agency in any coherent form, mainly because the collection of it is not the responsibility of any one person who also knows what is needed in individual cases and what is helpful to a specific agency. Many pupils may, for example, appear before a court deprived of the benefit of information which the school could have given and which would make their actions more comprehensible. This may be more important as the new approach to child care develops. Even the best probation or child care worker cannot acquire these facts in every case, and it is here that the school counsellor has a valuable part to play in communicating information at a professional level.

Social agencies are very willing to assist the school, but quite reasonably want some assurance that the information they provide will not be misused. Above all, they need to know to whom they can go with it. Headmasters are often fully committed to the educational leadership aspect of their role, and certainly often over-worked, whilst the social worker feels frustrated because of his growing awareness that he is imposing on a busy person and that the visit is not being appreciated. He is also aware that his contact with the Head is probably a fleeting one. It has been an essential principle of all therapeutic work that continuity of concern should be maintained, and although the system of pastoral work is designed to allow this, whilst the active model of counselling reinforces this, the social worker may find it difficult to make this a reality for his client without fairly constant contact with the same person. The school counsellor has an essential role to play by being the person to whom the social worker can relate. None of this denies what has been implicit throughout the discussion so far, namely the fact that the Head is ultimately responsible for all the pupils in his charge, the school counsellor and others working with delegated authority.

### 4. THE COUNSELLOR AS A LINK BETWEEN SCHOOL AND HOME

The school counsellor functions as a link between school and home, although the difficulties are great. The major discussion of the home and school link will occur in the chapter on problems of counselling. Sir Alec Clegg (1968) commenting on the Seebohm proposals remarked that it would be regrettable if the control of the link between home and school passed to a new agency with no experience of educational needs and problems. I agree with this. It now seems unlikely to happen, but it is my belief that effective developmental counselling can only be done when the resources of the school are mobilized in some variant of the active model. Although the Seebohm Report remarks (1968) that "Social work in schools should be the responsibility of the social service department" this does not mean the schools can be content with what they have done, for what happens in a school is the responsibility of teachers, and not as Seebohm suggests of an outside agency.

The counsellor is amongst the first to realize that he is not necessarily the right person to visit a home, seeing that the Educational Welfare Officer may be more suited for this task. A counsellor who visits a home without checking may disrupt relationships established by other caseworkers, providing parents with the opportunity to manipulate the agency against the school, rather in the way some children play one parent off against the other. This simple example suggests the need to evaluate carefully before undertaking home visiting and to recognize the possibility of producing unintended reactions which complicate and distort the counsellor's work with the pupil in school. The counsellor has almost to work out a balance sheet of costs and benefits connected with home visiting, looking at the impact on his work in school as well as on the pupil whose home is to be visited. He will see if his objectives can be obtained more economically by tactics other than home visiting.

Close co-operation with the educational welfare officer is necessary. Although there is a great deal of variation and difference in training and background of these officers, it is very likely that they can be an important source of help for the school counsellor and pastoral care team. In recent years their role of "child chasers" has diminished, although the public image of them is still that of the "school board man". Their training is improving, and the best now function in a way scarcely distinguishable from other social workers. Considerable anxiety has been expressed by them about the nature of the counsellor's work, and fears have been expressed that counsellors will take over their work or make it unduly difficult. Such fears are largely groundless, for in practice school counsellor and educational welfare officer work closely together as colleagues. Both gain from this. Recently I was visiting a school when the educational welfare officer brought in a boy who was a school refuser, mainly because of poor home conditions. He remarked as he came into the room, "Here's Robert . . . and it's nice to have somebody to hand him over to who will carry on with my work". This shows the kind of relationship which can develop between the E.W.O. and the counsellor. This healthy co-operation is increased by inviting the E.W.O. to case conferences where home conditions are important. Certainly cases of truancy (itself an ambiguous term) cannot be discussed fully without the presence of this officer.

### Summary discussion

The idea behind this active model of counselling is that the secondary school is a community essentially concerned with guidance and preparation for life. Next to the family the school is the great institution of socialization-developing values and standards, and also personality. In this process, the trained school counsellor is only one facet, although an essential one. Jeffreys (1957) says "It is the teacher's obligation to combat everything that disintegrates human personality, undermines the value set upon persons such as, or reduces human life to abstractions". What is true for the counsellor is also true for the teacher. This view lies behind the active model of counselling. Although there is a real place for the trained counsellor, he is dependent upon his colleagues He rejects the view that if a specialist exists, paid to do the job, the form teacher need not bother. The abdication and rejection of responsibility by the classroom teacher would be disastrous, both for school and the individual pupil. What is needed is continuity of concern, which can only be achieved by the integration of a counselling approach within the daily life of the school.

We have seen that there are key dimensions which influence the counsellor's work. The position taken on these dimensions will decide how much the counsellor co-operates with the pastoral care system and the degree to which he works within it as a member of the team. It is impossible to offer specific and rigid role prescriptions for a counsellor, because this denies the fact that he has to make realistic adaptations to the school. This reminds us that there are sometimes conditions in which counselling is impossible and in which no self-respecting counsellor would work.

The two-phase description of counselling provides a way of discriminating between the work of the teacher who has some counselling responsibilities and the trained counsellor. When the downward and inward phase is likely to be prolonged because self-confusion is high or immaturity is marked, the trained counsellor's skills are necessary. In the stage of task achievement the form teacher and the counsellor work together as equal participants in the counselling process. The counsellor has more to contribute in the first phase, whilst it is possible that his colleagues will be contributing more than he does in the second phase. There is no loss of standards in counselling, because once it becomes clear what a pupil wants and can do, the counsellor works to achieve this. Counsellors may begin by accepting, but they are always trying to reach the position where they do not have to accept a pupil at anything less than he can be.

The team approach becomes crucial, otherwise the change of attitudes and behaviour is not taken out into the everyday school life of the pupil. The counselling conference is an essential technique for achieving team co-operation and co-ordinated action. This team approach is extended to the outside agencies with whom the counsellor works closely.

Above all, the trained counsellor is aware that he can do a great deal of harm as well as a great deal of good. This leads him to see that he is dependent upon his colleagues and cannot work in isolation. His dependency springs from the fact that he is working within a social system. What he does has an impact on the school, whilst the expectations, style of relationships and the organization of the school determine what he can do which is effective. What can be done in one school, cannot be done in the same way in another.

## REFERENCES

Allport, G. (1955) *Becoming*, New Haven: Yale University Press.

Beers, C.D. (1939) *The Mind Which Found Itself*, New York: Doubleday Page.

Bernstein, B. (1961) "Social structure, language and learning", *Educational Research*, 3, June, 163–176.

Bernstein, B. (1962) "Linguistic codes, hesitation phenomena and intelligence", *Language and Speech, 5*.

Bernstein, B. (1965) "A socio-linguistic approach to social learning", *Penguin Survey of the Social Sciences*, Gould, J. (Ed.), London: Penguin.

Buckton, G. (1971) *Problems of Sixth Formers and the Implications for the Counsellor*, D.S.C. Dissertation, Swansea: University College.

Carkhuff, R.R. (1969) Helping and Human Relations, Vols. 1 and 2, New York: Houghton Mifflin.

Carkhuff, R.R. (1971) *The Development of Human Resources*, New York: Holt, Rinehart and Winston.

Clegg, A. (1968) "Seebohm: A sorry tale", *Education*, Vol. 132, No. 41. 395.

Gellner, E. (1964) *Thought and Change*, London: Weidenfeld and Nicolson.

Hargreaves, D.H. (1967) *Social Relations in a Seconday School*, London: Routledge and Kegan Paul.

Jeffreys, M.V. (1957) "Existentialism", Judges, A. V. (Ed.), *Education and the Philosophic Mind*, London: Harrap.

Krumboltz (1966) *Revolution in Counseling*, Boston: Houghton Mifflin.

Krumboltz and Thoresen (Eds.) (1969) *Behavioural Counseling*, New York: Holt, Rinehart and Winston.

Lawton, D. (1968) *Social Class, Language and Education,* Routledge and Kegan Paul. London.

Maslow, A. (1954) *Motivation and Personality,* New York: Harper.

Parsons, T. (1957) *Economy and Society,* Glencoe, Illinois: Free Press.

Rogers, C. (1942) *Counseling and Psychotherapy,* Boston: Houghton Mifflin.

Rogers, C. (1951) *Client Centred Therapy,* Boston: Houghton Mifflin.

Seebohm Report (1968) *Report of Committee on Local Authority and Allied Personal Social Services,* London: H.M.S.O.

Tyler, L. (1960) "Minimum Change Therapy", *Personnel Guid. J.,* 1960. 38. 475–479.

*Report of the Committee on Maladjusted Children* (1955) London: H.M.S.O.

# CHAPTER THREE

# THE ROLE OF
# THE COUNSELLOR AND THE
# COUNSELLING INTERVIEW

### *The purpose of this chapter*

This chapter describes the basic processes and dynamics of the counselling interview. It demonstrates the need to consider our own contribution to what goes on within the interview and the output from it. It looks at the underlying processes of negotiation and bargaining between the counsellor and the pupil.

Some description is given of the basic role requirements which are necessary if the counsellor is to be effective within the context of interaction which makes up a therapeutic interview. I discuss one way of building up a structure for the interview where feelings and emotions, often of a strong type, are to be expressed. Sometimes the interview becomes distorted because the pupil feels he is not being understood or is being manoeuvred into saying what he does not really feel.

### *The questions which are asked*

#### (a) THE ROLE OF THE COUNSELLOR

(i) What basic behaviours are essential if the counsellor is to help a pupil?

(ii) What role stresses exist for him when he tries to counsel in the school situation?

### (b) THE INTERVIEW

(i) Is the interview anything more than an attempt to discover facts?

(ii) If it is more than this, what exactly are we doing?

(iii) What can the counsellor do to ensure he builds up a structure which makes the interview a safe place in which a pupil can express feelings and changes begin to occur?

(iv) What aids or destroys efficient communication between the counsellor and a boy or girl?

(v) What factors distort the interview, making it almost worthless and the counselling a waste of time?

*Two simple ideas*

This chapter deals with the role of the counsellor and the general structure of the interview. The ideas put before you are taken from complex theoretical work, but they are basically simple. Your attention should focus on two themes which underlie the discussion. These can be illustrated diagrammatically:

(a) *Basic Interaction Diagram*

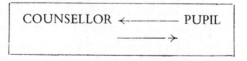

(b) *The Chain of Responsiveness*

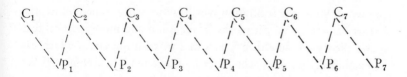

These two diagrams draw our attention to fundamental features of the interview which are easily lost sight of. We often begin to talk about counselling and interviews as if they consisted of only one person, the client or pupil. The first diagram draws our attention to the fact that the counsellor and the pupil are constantly in interaction. What one says influences the other; therefore if a pupil makes a statement and the counsellor makes a friendly response, the pupil follows this up with a more revealing remark. If the counsellor had responded with coldness or criticism, then the boy or girl would have said something quite different—a concealed expression of "Do I have to come and see you?" We seem to have the idea that it is possible to talk about the pupil's responses $P_1$, $P_2$ . . . etc. as if they made sense in isolation or were complete by themselves. It is easy to laugh at this now, yet this is what happens in the situation. The chain of responsiveness diagram draws our attention to the fact that a pupil's responses only make complete sense when the counsellor's contributions are also considered. It is true that it takes two to make a quarrel, and it is equally true that it takes at least two to make a counselling situation. A counsellor with a severe headache produces different responses from the pupil, from those he would get on a day when he felt the world was his.

## The role of the counsellor

This book is concerned with the act of counselling, rather than with the counsellor as a person who occupies a set position and performs certain fixed duties. It describes counsellor behaviour, showing the reader what must be done. Any worthwhile book on counselling must contain some theory, and it is important that it is given, otherwise the reader would be reduced to blind trial and error techniques. Even worse, he might begin to use the book as a kind of recipe book for instant counselling. Certainly he must know why he is doing something, and we all know the frustration which comes when something works, but we cannot say why it works. There is nothing more practical than sound theory, because theory provides us with objectives which can be examined, and ideas which can be translated into techniques. We have already become aware of the variation within schools which makes it pointless to discuss counsellor role in terms of the division into personal, vocational and educational. These divisions are mainly of use in exposition. The sensible approach is to follow up the work on the qualities of personality discussed above, by asking, "What kinds of behaviour are crucial for counsellor success?". Little empirical work has been done in Britain on this, but the topic has been the subject of research in the U.S.A., the work of Allen and Whiteley (1968) and Carkhuff (1969) providing examples, whilst experience of training and supervision of trainee counsellors provides relevant ideas. The key behaviours needed are:

1. The ability to adapt realistically to both the pupil and the situation which led to the counselling.

2. The possession of intellectual ability, especially sufficient imagination and flexibility of thinking to look for new solutions to problems.

3. The ability to communicate effectively and consistently.

4. The possession of sufficient sensitivity and skill to note very low level signals coming from the pupil.

### I. THE POWER OF REALISTIC ADAPTATION

In a recent morning's supervision, I saw four boys aged from twelve to sixteen. I had to behave very differently with each one, yet remain honest and spontaneous. The first boy, Mark, needed a slow pace of interview, and the emphasis was on Mark's feelings about certain delinquent episodes. The next boy, John, was like quick-silver and was full of phantasy. The rate of the exchanges was rapid, with a great deal of symbolic communication. The school had thought the boy was odd, but could say no more. I found that the basic problem was that the parents were divorced, the mother living in England and the father in Wales. The boy loved both parents dearly and he was in a state of acute conflict. A number of delinquencies emerged which were linked with his desire to be masculine. The third boy could only be reached through the technique of drawing. He produced a great deal of material in this way, whereas he would not do much in the field of verbal communication. His material was deeply meaningful, for it was concerned with the tragic death of his brother, but he needed to express his feelings indirectly. This indirect technique took much of the threat out of the situation and allowed him to express only as much as he could tolerate. The fourth boy was concerned with a surf-riding culture. He was highly articulate and used sociological concepts quite accurately. This interview was intellectually stimulating and resulted in the boy setting himself some real objectives for future sessions. The morning's work was composed of constant adaptations, none of which could have been avoided, because it is the counsellor's duty as a mature person to make the necessary adaptations. This is difficult for teachers, because we are still liable to think that we should treat every pupil alike. This is educational nonsense, but we still do it because we feel that we are being unfair if we give one pupil more attention than another, unless the attention is unpleasant and we then tell ourselves it is good for him!

The active model of counselling is based on the idea that the school counsellor has many roles in the counselling interview. These different roles are taken up by the counsellor according to his assessment of the needs of the pupil. The idea of one ideal type of behaviour is a myth, because it denies differences between pupils. The basic skill the counsellor has to acquire is that of observing closely and accurately, so that he can shift roles as the occasion demands. Not only does one take up different roles with different pupils, but it is necessary to modify one's role with the same pupil as counselling moves from the first into the second phase. Initially, there may be more toleration of dependency, more acceptance and support than is given in the task-orientated phase, where the pupil is trying to achieve his goals. Some pupils, like the third boy in the situation described above, need more concrete aids such as drawing, and this changes the quality of the interaction. The argument is for flexibility, but many people could confuse this with inconsistency and the production of insecurity in the pupil. This is not so, for flexibility does not mean that the counsellor makes sharp or erratic swings in his behaviour, rather that he continuously and sensitively adjusts his contributions and demands to the pupil's current state. Consistency and security come from the relationship, and also through the counsellor's continuity of concern, even when he feels "let down", as well as through his willingness to explain to the pupil what he is doing. There is no one universally correct type of counsellor behaviour: simply specific behaviour from a particular counsellor suitable for an individual at that point in his counselling.

Many types of behaviour have a place in the counsellor's repertoire. The criterion for inclusion is that the behaviour should meet the needs of the pupil. We tend to under-rate advice, probably because we have experienced it ourselves as something freely offered by the well-meaning, yet rarely relevant to our needs. We can think of advice as something we offer which is not often taken, and if it is taken, is taken only to prove us wrong. In this sense it is obviously a fruitless activity. Yet there are situations of gravity and extreme urgency where we have a moral duty to give implicit and direct advice to prevent grave damage to a pupil. Normally, it can take more indirect forms, but we can fool ourselves about our advice giving. If we work to establish a good relationship with a pupil, then we make ourselves important to him. Suggestions we make have the power of commands, just as the young child tries to please his mother by doing what she wants because he loves her. This is the basis of socialization, and the process is not so very different in counselling. It is a self-defeating strategy to deny our influence on pupils: indeed we should be suspicious of our motives when we do this. Sometimes a situation exists where there is only one course of action, e.g. in a pregnancy which is fast reaching the stage where abortion would be ill-advised or impossible, when medical advice has to be sought and the girl may have to be persuaded to talk to her parents.

We encourage a boy to try out alternatives, but we may need to give him practice in the behaviour. This means that our techniques will include role playing in which we play a part. Many other behaviours are part of counselling. We need to listen without interrupting or distorting by undue comment. We confront the pupil very carefully with discrepancies in what he says, and we give information to pupils. All this means that we behave quite differently with different pupils.

We know that some pupils will need greater support or rely more heavily on reassurances, and that without these they tend to go to pieces. We supply them for such pupils, whilst working to create development which will do away with their great need for such reassurances.

We are strangely reluctant to accept that teaching plays a real part in counsellor role. Yet this is very important. It includes the explanation of test results, ways of problem solving, engagement in explicit role-playing situations and providing models through tape recordings. This catalogue of counsellor behaviours only touches on some of the rich variety of behaviour which has to be brought into counselling, but it does serve to point out that adaptation to the pupil calls for real flexibility. We have to see what is right for that situation and pupil, rather than take a haphazard approach, for a haphazard approach is just as bad as maintaining the same kind of behaviour whether or not it is suited to the pupil. The interview is a chain of responses, which means that serious mismatch of counsellor behaviour to pupil needs could send the interaction right off the rails.

### 2. THE POSSESSION OF INTELLECTUAL FLEXIBILITY

It is possible to overstress the personality qualities and undervalue the intellectual demands made by counselling. This is demonstrated by the Head who once said with complete confidence, "Well, he's the right sort of chap, you know, but not too bright, so I thought he'd be happy counselling". Even worse is the situation where a counselling post is used as a reward for long and undistinguished service when it has become clear that all other chances of promotion have passed the teacher by. Such individuals find themselves floundering, or say wonderingly, "Nobody ever comes to me with any personal problem". The truth is that the counsellor has to respond in diverse and creative ways, which means he *must* possess intellectual ability. A prime requirement is the possession of sufficient psychological knowledge to build up a series of tentative hypotheses about the individual and his behaviour, which after a process of testing and checking finally coheres to give a meaningful psychological picture. This then leads into appropriate action. A counsellor needs to develop the ability to combine intuition with clear thinking, seeing the significance of apparently isolated scraps of information, and using a wide range of personality and behaviour theory in his work. Unless this real background knowledge exists, the counsellor could begin to resort to pseudo-Freudian explanations of behaviour. It need hardly be said that Freudians would be the first to reject this type of explanation.

### 3. THE MAINTENANCE OF EFFECTIVE AND CONSISTENT COMMUNICATION

As honest counsellors we try to keep what is going on inside us in line with what we do and say. Like most other human beings, we dislike having to play a part which does not fit our ideas of ourselves. We feel fraudulent when we catch ourselves out in this. Yet there is a way in which we can be ineffective and inconsistent in communication with a pupil. Communication occurs both verbally and non-verbally, and what Carl Rogers has called congruency is of major importance in successful counselling. Boys and girls with limited language ability or those who are very anxious appear to pay great attention to non-verbal signals. It is very easy to send one message verbally, without knowing that at that very moment it is being contradicted by gesture, facial expression and voice tone. I know that I often murmur, "I see", when I am far from seeing whatever it may be, and my face has a puzzled expression. Which message is likely to be received by the pupil? For all sorts of reasons, he is likely to pay attention to the unintended non-verbal message rather than to the words used.

If we ask how an anxious or sensitive pupil is likely to react to this, we see just how easy it is to behave in a way which destroys his confidence in the counsellor. When a pupil is tense, the counsellor becomes tense too, making a remark such as "I do understand your feelings", in perhaps an embarrassed or business-like tone of voice. He is unaware of his physical signs of tension. But the pupil may well interpret these signs as anger. Then the counsellor begins to wonder why the pupil remains quiet. So he begins to ask questions, building up anxiety and resistance in the pupil still further. In this way, a lack of congruency between what he says and how he looks, between his inner feelings and his outer responses, brings something into the response chain which throws it off course. The counsellor realizes that there are other things which facilitate communication. Physical distance between counsellor and the pupil can be varied to suit the content of messages. If a pupil is discussing something private or hurtful, then it is a good thing to move one's chair closer to his. All these things go together to make for good communication.

#### 4. SENSITIVITY AND SKILL IN NOTING LOW LEVEL SIGNALS

We tend to rely on verbal messages so much in teaching that we miss other, less obvious cues. The anxious tap of fingers; the slight pulling back of the corners of the mouth or the lick of the tongue along dry lips; the way a girl sits on the chair; the look given to the door when someone passes; all these may be more revealing than the words, halting or fluent as the case may be. I recall the boy who was protesting that he was bored and who kept looking out of the window in a curious way. I ignored his statement, for all the signs were those of anxiety. Gentle persuasion helped him look at the behaviour and showed that the boy often felt like jumping out of the window in class. This sounds almost grossly unlikely, but the boy then went on to say that he had done this on a number of occasions. It was found to be true. There was one lesson and one teacher he disliked. The two unfortunately went together, and his last resort was to escape in this way. For reasons best known to himself, the teacher had not thought of reporting this until approached by the counsellor.

A counsellor needs to watch low-intensity signals such as voice quality, hesitations, facial expression, slight gestures and nervous mannerisms. Not to do this may be to miss some of the most important information in counselling. A good counsellor shows his perceptual sensitivity in other ways. He will recall details given earlier in an interview; forgetting or inaccuracy might well be interpreted by the pupil as indifference. He would adjust his manner to the pupil's mood and not behave in a stereotyped way. Put yourself in the position of a pupil who is depressed or facing what seems to be a crisis, and who is confronted by a counsellor who presents a front of heartiness or brittle cheerfulness. Then imagine your reactions!

One thing which can destroy communication is our need to be liked. We tend to ignore, whitewash, gloss over or deny the reality of feelings of hostility, boredom, unease and dislike of the counsellor which may appear in counselling. They should be discussed openly, without creating any sense of threat for the counsellor. We must see that every relationship includes positive and negative feelings and that we need to look at both. Big intellectual demands are made, for not only must the counsellor let the pupil get to the problem in his own way, but he must also accept the changes of topic which occur without having to impose his own structure on the interview. In other words, he must let the pupil lead the way, for if the counsellor decides that certain things are to be discussed this means he already knows the nature and meaning of the problem. In fact, this is usually what is not known. This is why the first phase of counselling, the expressive, downward and inward-looking activity is so vital in most cases. The very shifts of topic tell one much, and they can be discussed if desired. At least the counsellor is looking at behaviour occurring in the "here and now" where it can be shown to the pupil. Rather than impose structure, the sensitive counsellor allows it to develop, the most important thing in this being his ability to stop asking closed questions, and to put things in such an way that the pupil wants to elaborate and expand. Although counselling is often concerned with the reasons for behaviour, the most unnecessary question is "Why?". Not only does it revive memories of situations in which parents and teachers have faced one threateningly saying "Why?", but we don't know why we do many things. Some factory girls recently told me that when their foreman asked them why their production had dropped they felt miserable. They could not answer the question and it merely made them feel even more helpless.

*Role stress for the counsellor*

This brief analysis of counsellor role has not followed the usual pattern of examining norms or the prescriptions of behaviour attached to a role. As yet the role of the counsellor is amorphous, and no clear expectations exist. There is a great deal of opportunity for conflict, because of the very nature of the skills which have been outlined. They do stress self-knowledge and are likely to remove any comfortable confidence in our own adequacy (if we feel we possess it). When we consider the wide range of skills called for in efficient counselling within the school situation, we see that the counsellor is likely to feel himself under threat and in a state of considerable stress. In any situation where the expectations of others are ambiguous and the skills so wide, vulnerability to pressures exists. Many colleagues do view the counsellor with suspicion: careers masters and educational welfare officers often assume unjustifiably that he is a rival taking away their work, and heads and administrators fail to appreciate the nature of his work; whilst many colleagues see counselling as a soft option, and a retreat from the real work of the classroom. Fortunately, such reactions are diminishing or I would sympathize if the school counsellor felt he had to retreat to a position of isolation and take up a defensive position. This rarely happens, for a trained counsellor is aware of his dependence upon his colleagues; those trained in line with the active model see it as imperative that they should be fully integrated members of the staff. In fact, there is a fund of goodwill in our schools towards both counselling and counsellor, although we are somewhat slow to see it and respond. Many of the criticisms seem to come from a lack of knowledge or hasty and selective reading of the American literature.

Counsellors are extremely careful not to make unjustified claims for their work: they must certainly reject unrealistic expectations as to what they are equipped to do and can achieve. Although great changes in the climate of acceptance have occurred during the past three years, the fears mentioned earlier are still met. Such fears do not seem to be restricted to any age group or position within the school. They must be treated with respect, even though they may well reflect rigidity, a sense of threat or a lack of knowledge in those voicing them. The trained counsellor regards it as a first duty to explain clearly what he is doing, and also to provide his colleagues with relevant information which does not break confidentiality and which is helpful to the pupil. He avoids direct confrontations if possible, for these destroy communication and are not in the interests of the pupils who are being counselled. Perhaps the best remedy is the gradual involvement of such critics in counselling, although this must be taken slowly for it is fraught with many difficulties. A sense of sharing in the counselling process is an effective way of changing attitudes, but this is not the reason why the active model is advocated. It is put forward because it aids the transfer of skills into the everyday life of the pupil and is the most economical way of aiding a pupil's personal development and achievement.

One subtle type of role stress comes from the fact that school counsellors often have to interact with their counsellees as teachers as well as counsellors. As yet, a full-time counsellor is still a relative rarity, which means he has to teach. It is claimed that this places the counsellor in an impossible position, because he may have to punish the person whom he is counselling. A weaker form of the argument says that it is extremely difficult for a pupil to be open and honest with someone who has an authority relationship with him in another situation. Hard empirical research is needed to investigate this problem. It seems that several factors influence the degree to which this problem is likely to be severe. If the general tone of staff—pupil relationships in the school is poor, then there will be a far greater gap between the counselling situation and the daily life of the classroom. If personal relationships are generally good within the school, then the psychological distance between the two situations is diminished. How much part of the school organization the counsellor seems to be; how far he seems to be someone who deals with the seriously disturbed; how directive or non-directive his approach is, are questions which all have a bearing on this problem. The research by Moore and Fuller (1967) showed that pupils tend on the average to discriminate between the counsellor in the teaching situation and in the counselling one, making appropriate adjustments. Pupils after all are used to interacting with the same person in different roles: this is part of life. The teacher who is also a part-time youth club leader with the same children in the same building provides one example; the parent role combines both loving and punishing elements, caring and controlling: the child recognizes what is appropriate for each situation. The difference may be greater for the counsellor than for the child, and the argument could be an example of the projection of our expectations rather than an accurate statement about the way pupils feel. We may get ourselves into the position of the occasional writer on adolescence who stresses rebellion and the negative periods of adolescence, leaving one without the knowledge that adolescents mourn their parents if they die, want to live fairly close to them when they marry and can even say that they are fond of them. Pupils do trust teachers, they do confide in them. It depends upon the kind of teacher, rather than on the occupational role. When difficulties do arise, these can be overcome by frank discussions with the pupil and through self-awareness upon the part of the counsellor. I see such situations as potentially constructive, because they provide important learning experiences for the pupil which aid his growth. Just as the counsellor does not evade hostility or try to talk it away, but examines it as important behaviour, so it is profitable to tackle these situations of role conflict in the same way. There are real gains from teaching the pupil, because one knows him better, and the teaching experiences with him provide one with the chance of strengthening his self picture and providing unobtrusive support. The class room experiences provide valuable material for the counselling session.

## The counselling interview

### I. THE INTERVIEW AS A MARKET PLACE

It seems that the counsellor's personality is very important as are his skills, but all these are used in the context of something we call an interview. What is an interview? This word exchange directs us back to the simple feedback model in Chapter Two. This reminds us that not only is the interview a two-sided thing, composed of pupil and counsellor and a cumulative chain of responses, but also that there is an underlying process of bargaining and exchange. We have already seen that if the costs are too great or the bargaining not meaningful to the pupil he will not stay in counselling. Considerable warmth and support is necessary in the downward and inward phase, and the counsellor's skill at building up a satisfying system of communication is critical to eventual success. The aim of this exchange system is to develop the pupil's self knowledge, increase his capacity to make mature decisions, help him to solve particular problems which impede development and lead him to greater competence in interpersonal relationships. This is impressive, but we have to make it meaningful for the boy or girl who cannot plan ahead, and who has not the advantages of the middle aged, who can see the way things fall into place. Yet if we have nothing to exchange which the pupil needs, then the whole process becomes useless.

Firstly, we must see that the interview is a process of sending and receiving signals. Some signals are very rewarding, especially those which indicate that we respect the pupils for themselves and are not trying to impose upon them our ideas of what they ought to be like. We are traders, for we exchange the good picture of the pupil for his co-operation and honesty. The opportunity to make decisions, the positive expectations and the concern, together with the skills in problem solving and the supports we muster are all exchanged to compensate for the costs of coming and the efforts that will be asked of the pupil. One important fact is concealed here, namely that if we exchange goods we lose our superior position. We must learn to ask ourselves, when counselling seems to be failing, if the goods we offer in exchange are either not wanted by or are worthless to the pupil.

Sometimes, in these exchanges, counsellors begin to play the kind of game that Berne has described. There are a number of games which the trainers of counsellors observe as students learn to counsel. The first one might well be called "Down the Garden Path". This is the kind of exchange where reality is being ignored. The most striking example was where one highly imaginative (and eventually good) student concentrated on a boy's interest in pigeons. Remarkably interesting stories arose, but for six weeks the fact that this boy was in dire trouble at home and with the police remained undealt with, whilst counsellor and pupil were encapsulated in an unreal relationship. Counsellors who are tempted to play "Down the Garden Path" are warned that very strange fairies are to be found in the bogland at the end of the path.

Next comes one which many of us have played, including the writer. It is tempting, but destructive to play "Only I believe in you". It separates the pupil from others in the school and is liable to produce outbursts of resentment against both counsellor and pupil by staff who vaguely know that something is wrong. It is only a short step to playing the associated game of "I'm different from all the rest". One is then very close to taking a defensive position against other teachers. It reflects the counsellor's own needs. It is true that we like to be liked, but sometimes we can misuse this.

There is a danger of being loosely liberal or of losing a sense of direction in counselling. This can occur when the counsellor plays the "Me, too" game. In this the counsellor has identified with the pupil at a probably very infantile level; certainly adult responsibilities are being abandoned if this game develops. Two other destructive games are "I'm only trying to help you" and "The purpose is just to talk and understand each other". Both sound so very reasonable that it is easy to get trapped into playing them. The "I'm only trying to help" game is the cry of every incompetent counsellor, or those who are not prepared to make the emotional and intellectual effort to see things from the standpoint of the pupil. What they do is based on their own needs, rather than the adolescent's, and they are left to protest uselessly when their efforts are rejected. These counsellors do things with the best of intentions and the most destructive results. "The purpose is just to talk and understand each other" is nice to play, coming from a misreading of the literature on the non-directive approach in some cases, but it denies the purpose of counselling, devalues action and eventually leads to the impotence of the counsellor.

## 2. THE MARKET PLACE HAS BOUNDARIES AND ORGANIZATION

The image of the market place is still useful. Let us use the description of a social system provided by Talcott Parsons (1957) as it seems to aid understanding of the counselling interview as it occurs within the active model of counselling. Two people are engaged in this process of exchanging meanings, giving and getting rewards and the process we call counselling. As this happens a specific pattern of relationships is built up which becomes the basic structure of the counselling interview. We must see that this structure gradually develops and that it is dependent upon both parties. Remove the counsellor and put a new one in, and the whole pattern of interaction changes. The pupils are very different in personality and have different problems which causes the pattern of relationships forming the structure of the interview to vary greatly between cases. This is why experienced counsellors are always reluctant to answer questions such as "What would you do if so and so . . . ?" You cannot say, for what you do depends upon the structure of counselling which emerges, and this is not imposed and arbitrary, but one which is constructed during the course of counselling.

Let us use the image of the market place a little longer. It may be that the processes which go on in the market would be disruptive if they were taken into the department store. There is a market with boundaries and its own organization. It is obvious that some of the interaction and exchanges which go on within the counselling interview are very different from those of the classroom. The school counsellor must see the need to keep confidences, to remain frank and to develop a relationship of near equality within the counselling interview, otherwise tensions arise for both participants. Although the school counsellor is part of the total staff team, it is important that he keeps the type of interaction which is peculiar to individual counselling within the bounds of the interview. This is, one suspects, the reason for the insistence by some people that it is impossible to counsel and teach. It is also possible that it is an intuitive knowledge of the consequences of failing to observe these boundaries which causes some experienced teachers to feel that counselling may undermine discipline and teacher—pupil relationship. We have dealt with the exchanges over the boundary a little in Chapter Two, but this needs elaboration. The experienced counsellor is always asking about the *unintended* consequences of his intervention, and the impact of what a pupil is saying or trying to do in the classroom. If the exchanges with the classroom or school produced by the interview are negative, then the feedback is difficult to handle. Both pupil and teachers may become resentful. If the pupil leaves the counsellor in an excited or aggressive mood, then it is not too difficult to predict that both the counsellor and the pupil are going to meet unpleasant reactions from the staff. This can happen to everyone. I give a wry smile when I remember the result of an interview with an intelligent girl who was truanting and yet strongly desired to be a teacher. The consequences were looked at closely and the girl saw for herself the way she divided knowledge into things she was told and things she knew. In fact it was a very productive interview. Unfortunately, the girl left the interview thinking so deeply, that she absented herself from the remaining two periods. More skill would have anticipated this, but unfortunately I missed this possibility. It was not easy to explain this to a rather disbelieving staff.

What one has to be alert to is the fact that it is only too easy to allow the establishment of a pattern of transactions which are unhelpful and then difficult to modify. This comes for students in training when they are faced by pupils who have been sent to them and who come unwillingly, feeling that they are being "picked on". The student may not feel able to bring this out in the open so that a pattern of minimal co-operation and resistance occurs almost before one realizes it. Both pupil and student can get set into this type of interaction and it needs considerable effort to change it. The same thing occurs when the pupil is shy and inarticulate. The student may well become anxious, and then ignore alternatives such as the fact that drawing, simple games or the provision of some aid such as a picture will stimulate communication. For many pupils, not only is the interview situation unfamiliar, but it has unpleasant associations. With these children, an unskilled interviewer can create a situation of unnecessary silences, broken only by the slightly desperate questions of the counsellor to which the child often nods agreement, whether or not he has understood the meaning of the question. His main impulse is the urgent desire to escape from a threatening situation by compliance.

The counsellor has to be aware of negative feedback. The first diagram in Chapter Two drew attention to the fact that part of the output returns to the next interview in the form of reactions and comments both by the pupil and teachers. Negative feedback is the equivalent of a governor on an engine, or the automatic pilot of an aeroplane. The nature of negative feedback can be understood by the following illustrations. On one occasion I had spent considerable time in helping a rather colourless and inarticulate boy develop confidence. He did this, but suddenly began to express himself rather too exuberantly in the classroom. His form teachers began to see him as a nuisance and punished him. The resentment he brought back into the counselling interview was negative feedback which drew my attention to my own stupidity in not anticipating this development. I had allowed the counselling to "go off course" and it took a great deal of energy to put the situation right. In yet another case a twelve-year-old boy who was isolated from other pupils began to make a real friend in his form. Shortly after this friendship was established, his year tutor said he had noted signs of very real antagonism between the boy and the rest of the form who had ignored him prior to the formation of the friendship. This negative feedback was acted upon and I found that he was now spending his pocket money on sweets, sharing them with his new friend, but ostentatiously refusing them to other boys in the form. To restore the sense of direction to counselling, it was necessary to show him just how provocative this behaviour was.

These simple examples drawn from the counselling of two boys lacking in social skills gives some idea of negative feedback which is produced by actions of the pupil outside the interview situation. It can also occur within the interview when a boy suddenly shows that what the counsellor is saying or doing is unpalatable or threatening. When it occurs within the interview, negative feedback is shown by immediate signals of anxiety, by the sudden appearance of resistances, by aggression which cannot be explained, or even by the adoption of an appearance of stupidity or apathy. It has to be noted carefully; the counsellor must ask himself if perhaps the counselling is going too fast and a difficult area is being approached too quickly. The ability to become sensitive to feedback and use it constructively is an essential skill. A counsellor who does not pick the signals up is likely to be so firmly focusing on the task or goal that he does not see that he is harming the pupil by a clumsy approach. He could even be so wrong-headed as to convince himself that the signals of disapproval from colleagues meant that they were being difficult, instead of recognizing in their evidence that the boy or girl needs to work out the problems in a way better suited to the school. The active model certainly requires real sensitivity to feedback processes.

### 3. THE INTERVIEW AS A PROCESS OF SELECTING SIGNALS

We have seen that the interview is a process composed of exchanges and reactions as the counsellor and pupil interact. Now we need to look at a process of selection which goes on between them. Any policeman knows that the accounts of an accident will vary greatly even when the individuals concerned are trying hard to be objective. The work of Bartlett (1932) and Allport and Postman (1945) are very relevant to the counsellor, as is other work on person perception. In studies of the psychology of rumour it was found that two processes are at work, "levelling" and "sharpening". Sharpening is the focusing of attention on some details which are retained and reported. Levelling means that other facts are glossed over and forgotten. In rumour, the facts which are retained are those which are of particular interest to the reporter, facts which confirm their expectations and which help them structure the story.

Bartlett found certain mechanisms at work in the recall of information. The process seems to be one of (a) leaving out material which appears to be irrelevant, (b) creating a more coherent story, and (very crucially for the counsellor) (c) the changing of what is unfamiliar into the familiar. There was the tendency for certain incidents to become dominant ones.

We are seeking to explain behaviour. Yet we are often in a very ambiguous situation, where we cannot predict what will emerge. We may then be tempted to put early closure on the situation by giving it premature meaning. This is to be suspected when the counsellor says, 'this problem is just . . . " or "I knew what the trouble was as soon as he began". He may be correct, or the desire for clarity and certainty may have led him sadly astray.

What we have to understand is that we select. We pick up or respond to only those signals to which we are attuned. Sometimes we can concentrate so much on the verbal ones that we do not register contrary ones coming from the body of the pupil. Even with verbal signals, we discard or do not notice certain words or phrases because they do not fit our expectations or ideas of what should be meaningful. The inexperienced counsellor tends to regard quite important information as irrelevant, whereas the trained counsellor has a wider range of responsiveness, and has learned to use more information. Even with experienced counsellors there is always idiosyncratic selection, making the pattern of transactions which emerges vary according to the counsellor. Two equally competent counsellors who counselled the same pupil would probably build up different patterns of transactions, yet because they were scanning the evidence widely and were sensitive to feedback information the outcomes would be more or less the same. It is unprofitable to think that there is one correct way of counselling for everybody, because of the existence of this selectivity. The counsellor is always engaged in a search after meaning and he selects from the mass of signals which impinge on him those which fit his hypothesis about the situation.

In one way it is reassuring to know that the process of selectivity is so widespread, although the counsellor needs to be very aware of the possibility of distortion. Error is always possible when things are left out, whilst the constant coding and changing the unfamiliar into the familiar means that one is making judgements about the significance and import of statements. Although these judgements are not revealed to the pupil, they still shape the chain of responsiveness with which this chapter began. Many of the pupil's statements may contain several alternatives on which we could focus attention, but the counsellor may only respond to one, thereby shaping what happens. We need to know why and how we categorize, and this is something which no book can do for us. We can be responsive to a surprising degree to such ideas as those which associate red hair with violent temper or a square jaw with stubbornness, only seeing this when someone else questions the judgements. Pupils can be labelled as lazy because of their slowness of movement and other physical characteristics; I can even recall an occasion on which the labelling of a boy as sly by an adult was really a reaction to his particular bone structure and lank greasy hair. It was not until the phrase "snake-like" was used that suspicions were aroused. This is so surprising that it almost sounds implausible, yet it does happen. Then, once labelled, pupils begin to react to their labels. School counsellors and those doing pastoral work need to be aware also of "halo effect". This means that an implicit theory about which personality characteristics go together is at work. It is a kind of false psychological logic which says that if a person has Attribute A, then he should also possess Attribute B. We often tend to assume that a boy who has been caught stealing is delinquent in other ways. He may be, but we have no right to assume this is the case. A little more subtle is the situation when we are ready to believe that a boy who is aggressive to adults is also likely to be guilty of bullying. What is happening is that we are tending to say that bad goes with bad or good goes with good. It is not too hard to see in schools the assumption that a boy who is intellectually able is also one who is morally good. Therefore we dissolve into shock, making the remark, "I didn't expect that of an A Stream boy!"

*Basic structure of the counselling interview*

Now that some of the complications of interaction in the counselling interview have been presented, we can begin to explore the interview in a more straightforward way. The following simple points will ensure maximum co-operation and communication:

I. THE IMMEDIATE IMPACT ON THE PUPIL

Things can go wrong almost as soon as the pupil enters the door. Indeed, it seems that this moment is very important for setting the tone of the interview. A mistake can easily create a wrong impression, and though this is not revealed by the pupil, underneath, the misconception shapes his attitude and responses. The first thing that the counsellor must do is to give the pupil immediate signals of acceptance which show him that he is being treated as an individual and is welcome. The counsellor has to confirm without saying anything that this is not a disciplinary matter nor is the boy going to be punished. The very fact that a boy is sometimes sent for counselling is likely to make him feel vulnerable, particularly if the others criticize him. Last week a student reported that he had a pupil who was said by Head and teachers to be suspicious, remote and almost stubbornly antagonistic. On being asked what had happened, the student stated that the boy was open and friendly. The student had taken the trouble to get up when the boy came into the room, shake hands and give a pleasant greeting. This initial behaviour is signalling not only warmth, but also—perhaps more importantly—treatment as an adult, indicating the future pattern of the sessions. These simple courtesies are all too often neglected in our work, but they increase our efficiency. Sitting behind a desk is familiar behaviour to the teacher, but it is not necessarily the best thing to do in the counselling situation.

## 2. PACING THE INTERVIEW

The next step is to try and adjust the pace of the interview to the pupil. Each one of us has a different rate of talking, habits of hesitation when speaking and inserting phrases such as "You know" and a certain level of need for reassurance that a message is being accepted and comprehended. Some pupils are very dependent upon the grunts, the "ahas" and nods of the counsellor and dry up if these are removed. Others stop if one makes a sound or removes one's eyes from their face. Some demand a great deal of eye contact, whilst others avoid it and are put off their stroke when it is forced upon them. The first interview is the time in which the counsellor is learning these important things about the pupil and begins to make the necessary adjustments. His aim is to learn how to intermesh his responses with those of the boy or girl in such a way that optimal conditions for a real flow of communication are created. The first interview is spent in establishing warmth, the counsellor being highly responsive to the pattern of communication which seems to bring out the best in the pupil. Every attempt will be made to make the pupil feel secure and unthreatened, for it is only too easy to bring unrecognized and unintended threats into a counselling situation.

This assessment session can be combined with discussion of interests and hobbies, although this does not mean it will degenerate into aimless chat. It does mean avoiding a great mistake, namely the earnest determination to extract all the facts from the pupil. This is impossible: we do not know what the relevant facts are, and we cannot be sure when we have them. But—much more important—it is an unnecessary and probably destructive activity. If the developmental problem is to be tackled, then we need to look at the way the individual interacts with people, both of his own age and adults, assessing his skills in personal and social areas. A large part of his counselling will be directed to improving his interpersonal relationships and getting constructive communication established in areas where he is failing. The sensible thing, then, is not to be so concerned about the number of brothers and sisters or the father's job, but get something positive going between him and us.

We stress listening so much in training counsellors that we are almost in danger of forgetting that we are establishing a relationship which goes two ways. Indeed as every counsellor soon learns, if one relied on listening too much with some nervous pupils, communication would never get started. Not only are they unaccustomed to people listening to them, but they have little to say at first. Indeed, this is often part of the problem, meaning that they have little ability to express their feelings precisely. Blind feelings of inadequacy, resentment or dislike may be permeating their whole life, the pupil venting them in a haphazard way. Part of the counselling process is often concerned with making diffuse and amorphous feelings more precise so that they can be dealt with. Some inarticulate pupils and also the highly anxious ones will only give one something useful to listen to after this process of support and intermeshing has been done. Certainly the counsellor will have to use some of the aids to communication which will be discussed in the next chapter.

### 3. QUESTIONS IN THE INTERVIEW

Ask many children what a teacher does and they will reply that he asks questions. Yet in counselling we often use questions clumsily, or rely on them too much. Even very experienced counsellors have to question pupils. Both the type and the timing of questions are important in building up the two-way system. The great division is that between closed and open questions. Closed questions indicate that a *yes* or *no* answer or a brief reply is sufficient. They also tend to suggest the kind of answer that is expected. From this it is obvious that a counsellor has to follow up one closed question with another to gain the next response. This gives a feeling of interrogation which is highly disturbing to the adolescent, particularly if he comes from a poorer background where interview situations are usually closely associated with trouble or putting on a mask of social respectability. Open questions are those which do not suggest that a specific type of answer is desirable and do not shape or set any limits on the response. The most useful form of the open question is taking up a word or phrase in what has just been said, and then echoing it back to the boy or girl in a neutral tone of voice. This usually brings elaboration. Although it does not shape the actual response, it is an act of drawing attention to some element in the statement, thereby increasing its importance in the interaction. One must know why a certain part of the statement is being treated in this way.

The balance between open and closed questions calls for skill in the counsellor. The weighting between them should be a product of the stage of counselling and the anxiety and verbal habits of that pupil. In the latter stages of counselling, one does not seem to need to ask questions, because the pupil knows the need for certain kinds of information. Such questions as are necessary seem to be open ones. In the initial stages we may have to rely more upon questioning and the use of closed questions to get the process started, especially with nervous and anxious counsellees. Every question is a potential threat which can be seen as an attack by the pupil; probing is a process which should be restricted to surgeons extracting bullets and detectives solving crimes. No recipes can be offered, because it is a matter of adjustment. The situation is like that of pastry making, where you can be told the ingredients and how they should be mixed, but the actual mixing process is one learned only through experience. I hope that the reader will use this book to develop his own style, using the principles set out as a rough guide.

The technique of *funnelling* is one that is acquired with experience. This seems to work best by approaching known or suspected areas of tension with broad open questions, gradually making the questions more specific until the heart of the matter is reached. The broad questions help the pupil by giving a chance to talk around the edge of the problem without feeling overwhelmed, gradually gaining a sense of security. The counsellor is keenly aware of the danger of pushing, and is able to withdraw without too much difficulty if strong signs of anxiety emerge. Once he feels it safe to approach the topic, then the funnelling process begins. Closed questions can be used to provide a supportive structure when the pupil gets to the core of the problem. After it has been reached in this way, then it is useful to return to open questions to get the individual nuances and standpoint about the problem.

Not getting to the point can be more threatening than getting there. This is the case when such problems as bed-wetting or physical stigmata differentiate a child. I recall the gasp of relief, and the behaviour which seemed to say that a load had been shed, when I casually asked a fifteen-year-old how the bedwetting was. Everybody knew about it, but nobody talked to him about it. A warning is necessary: there was a good relationship between the counsellor and the boy, and a great deal of energy had been previously invested in sending him acceptable signals of worthwhileness. To broach such a topic without this basic good relationship seems to be extremely risky and to show lack of respect for the counsellee.

The counsellor must always keep the welfare of the pupil uppermost in his mind and not be tempted to try for early results, or allow himself to be pushed into applying distorting pressures on the counselling process. Certainly he will have to develop a different pace, style of questioning and communication for each pupil, for a stereotyped approach is death to the personal interaction which is at the heart of constructive counselling.

Skill and thought are essential. It is far too easy to ask a question in which alternative answers are presented, without seeing that one answer is so strongly contaminated by social desirability that it will almost inevitably be chosen. Sometimes it can be so attractive intrinsically that the pupil will almost always endorse it. The counsellor who remains oblivious of these things, then proceeds to complain that there are discrepancies between what this pupil says in the interview and his behaviour outside it, fails to see his responsibility for creating this situation by his questions.

### 4. ENDING THE INTERVIEW

If this is not done carefully much of the good work may be undone. Certain pupils may produce important material near the end of the interview. To explore it would cause emotional distress which could not be resolved before the end of the interview. The practical thing is to note this with the pupil, but delay investigation of the topic, unless it is clear that it must be dealt with immediately. If it can be left, then make sure that the pupil knows the date and time of the next interview so that he does not think that you are avoiding the topic. The exact strategy used will depend upon the pupil and the circumstances. It is a principle of counselling that it is wrong to send a pupil away in a state of distress, emotional elation, upset or confusion which might have serious consequences for him. To do this is to run the risk of putting him in a situation where he may do something stupid or hurt himself and others in some way. One way of reducing the last minute production of material is to adopt the habit of looking casually at one's watch and saying "We have only ten minutes left, I'm afraid". This slows down the rate of interaction, so that the interview can be brought to a constructive conclusion. A few pupils seem to need to produce important matters in the last few minutes. The counsellor's best strategy is to bring this into the open, trying to find out what this behaviour is about. It is necessary to show them how it makes the counsellor useless to them, allows them to avoid dealing with the topic and that it suggests there are some feelings about counselling which have not been brought out. It may be thought that the end of the interview is concerned with trivialities. This is not the case, for the pupil is encouraged to recapitulate what he has done, and to clarify his feelings and goals. Because of this, he leaves with a pleasant feeling of successful effort and a sense of something gained.

### Distortion within the counselling interview

#### I. LANGUAGE DIFFICULTIES

Social workers have sometimes been left with the uneasy impressions that although the client was affable and agreed with them, there had been no real communication between them and the client. This happened despite all their efforts at clarity and at allowing the client to formulate things for himself. There was always a feeling that the client was agreeing with the worker, but that they were really talking about very different things. It seems that counsellors have a very similar situation to meet in school. A child who has a restricted language code (and we should note that this does not automatically mean all the children in the school who are labelled as "working class" by the teachers) tends to make up his mind very early about a problem and then remains impermeable to persuasion and new information. Great reluctance to modify a standpoint once it has been taken seems a feature of these pupils. Some of them disappoint us because they display a superficial fluency of speech which is intensified by the accepting attitude of the counsellor. It is only after a little time that we see that the pupil is saying very little, and is essentially making noises rather than communicating, whilst his speech is repetitive and the statements essentially circular. We seem to be witnessing a situation in which a number of verbal formulae are being applied almost indiscriminately. Even more intimidating to the counsellor is the situation where we realize that there are vast verbal blocks and inadequacies, intensified by tensions. Stress develops, often leading to the hasty termination of badly needed counselling.

One thing which forces itself upon the counsellor's attention is the fact that these pupils are very uneasy about communication which asks them to make more than very limited and conventional responses. They seem able to do this only within the context of the family or with close friends, if at all. When we set out to talk to someone we usually try to shape the message so that it is acceptable and meaningful to that person, adjusting what we have to say to his capacity to understand it. These children seem to have a deficiency in coding for other people. This causes the counsellor grave difficulties at times and considerable effort is needed to adjust to the fact that they take the counsellor's ability to understand them for granted. We can fool ourselves that we have understood the pupil. Added difficulty comes from the fact that many pupils are more sensitive to *how* we say something rather than *what* we have said. They rely on the non-verbal cues rather than the content of the statement. Teachers will be able to think of children who are very responsive to voice quality, often disliking a teacher because "he shouts". Some of them pay more attention to the gestures and mannerisms of the teacher than to his precise words.

If the pupil has poor verbal skills, then the non-verbal elements in the counselling interview become more important. These are the things the pupil focuses on, and they become the elements around which he organizes his feelings. Such a pupil will need a more supportive relationship before he can respond to the counsellor's efforts. This factor of language is very important, for as Luria (1961) has suggested, language skill allows a person under stress to find ways of controlling the situation and reinforcing his own attempts at finding a solution. Some pupils may lack the language skills which allow them to sort out for themselves the sources of threat and anxiety, to see what is reality and what is not. They are deprived of a major tool in their attempt to cope adequately with their world, and the counsellor has to do something about this.

Experience forces the counsellor to realize that many pupils needing counselling come with such poor language skills that they find it difficult to shape their messages so that they can be understood by the other person. They are often frustrated, because they feel nobody is taking the trouble to understand them; it is little wonder that they become inarticulate. This is associated with a build-up of negative attitudes towards school, adults in general, and more specifically their teachers. Such adolescents not only see little need to send messages bearing the recipient in mind, but even when they are persuaded of this, they cannot achieve it without great effort. In practice, there is little difference between the messages intended for others and the way they code for themselves. What can the counsellor do beyond making extra effort to understand these pupils? The remedy seems to lie in deliberate planned attempts to increase the ability to take the standpoints of other people. Standpoint taking is more than just being able to see the viewpoint of another person; it is the ability to *reconstruct in imagination* the role of another person. If it were the boy's father whose standpoint was under question then the boy would need to understand the impact of his own behaviour upon his father, and to understand the things which make his father behave in certain ways towards him. Many pupils are very surprised at the differences between their own viewpoints and those of others when they begin the role playing and other techniques inducing this skill. Without inducing the capacity for standpoint taking in these pupils it is unrealistic to expect an increase in social skills and a growth of sensitivity. At the worst, such pupils seem to have very primitive conceptions of themselves and others, regarding other people either as obstacles to satisfaction or as a means of satisfaction. They see people as things to be used. The active model of counselling would see the counsellor as initiating a process which is given further shape in social education programmes. Role playing and simulation techniques would be used in counselling, group experiences following the individual counselling. As well as this, there could be special activities designed to help such pupils. The important thing is to identify and aid these pupils as soon as possible in the secondary school, avoiding submitting them to experiences of failure and rejection and trying to ensure that they are not alienated from the classroom activities.

## 2. PERCEPTUAL DIFFICULTIES

We have seen that counselling is a set of transactions which both partners in the interview build up. Complex feedback effects occur, and already some hint has been given that the way the pupil sees the counsellor and the way the counsellor views the pupil are very important. Counselling is intimately concerned with interpersonal perception. We are engaged in a search for meaning, and we wish to build up an orderly and coherent view of the environment and, above all, of other people. In order to achieve this, we have to go behind the surface behaviour of others and attribute motives and intentions to them. Heider (1958) claims that in our everyday interactions with other people, our perceptions are based upon a naive or implicit psychology which allows us to identify relatively stable dispositions and intentions lying behind the flux and confusion of everyday behaviour in those around us. We then focus upon dispositions and attributes and not the behaviour as such. This giving of motives and intentions to a pupil's behaviour is the process by which we make sense out of it. Consider an incident witnessed some years ago when I was a young teacher. A colleague was marking books during the lunch hour when a boy came up to him and told him a fairly amusing and slightly off-colour joke. The teacher laughed good humouredly and appeared to make a return joke. Just as he was finishing marking another lad came along and made a fairly similar joking remark. This time I was surprised to see displeasure and a hint of real anger. When I came down from my end of the hall to join my fellow teacher, he complained angrily to me about the cheek of the second boy. From the onlooker's position both behaviours seemed very similar, but the teacher had interpreted them very differently. The way we see things determines how we behave towards someone, and we all see things differently.

This last remark draws our attention to a major danger for the counsellor who works in isolation. The process of attributing motives to people and giving causal meaning to behaviour is very open to error. The halo effect has been mentioned, but even more serious is the way in which the needs and implicit personality theory of the counsellor can distort the idea he has of a pupil. Some check on perception of behaviour and motives is always needed. Unless the counsellor is integrated into the school and receives information from a number of sources, he is giving meaning to the pupil's action on the basis of minimal cues. Although we want to know what the situation looks like to the boy or girl, we would be foolish to make judgements based on his viewpoint without additional evidence.

We can now get to the basic dynamics of person perception in the counselling interview. It seems that the counsellor is engaged in a process of "reading" the pupil's behaviour to make sense of it. This "reading" is the product of two things. First there are the psychological concepts held by the counsellor; it could well be that these are either ill-defined or over simple. Next, it is through psychological processes in himself that the counsellor detects such processes in the pupil. The counsellor's own problems, tensions, need for recognition or to be liked, and sometimes his emotional deprivations, can cause him to see the pupil's behaviour in a light which reflects in his own inner state rather than what is actually there. Laing, Phillipson and Lee (1966) have given great attention to one aspect of this process. We have already discussed the way in which feedback is important when this comes back into the sessions from outside, but there is another type of feedback which is the product of the way in which a counsellor and pupil see each other. This is shown below:

### PERCEPTIONS CAUSING FEEDBACK IN THE COUNSELLING INTERVIEW

Counsellor's view of the pupil's view of the counsellor.    (iii)
Counsellor's view of himself/pupil's view of the counsellor.    (ii)
Counsellor's view of the pupil.    (i)

COUNSELLOR                                        PUPIL

Pupil's view of the counsellor.    (i)
Pupil's view of himself/counsellor's view of the pupil.    (ii)
Pupil's view of the counsellor's view of the pupil.    (iii)

We have, in counselling, a situation in which two people are constantly scrutinizing one another, each trying to assess what the other thinks of him. As Laing *et al.* show there are various levels to this. We often forget that the pupil is continuously assessing the counsellor and his behaviour. First, there is level (i) of the counsellor's view of the pupil and the pupil's view of the counsellor. This seems straightforward enough. The fact is that possibilities of mismatch and discrepancy exist, which if not detected and corrected lead to difficulties, particularly if the pupil has been sent to the counsellor and has not referred himself. The counsellor may view the pupil favourably, whilst the boy or girl sees the counsellor negatively perhaps as a source of punishment for having "done something wrong" as one pupil insisted. Even self-referrals sometimes have misconceptions about the role of the counsellor, whilst the teacher referrals may not only see him as a disciplinary agent, but as a "headshrinker". None of this may be voiced, but it will affect the responses of the pupil. At level (ii) comes the match or disjunction between the view of each about himself and the other's view of him. The pupil sees himself as tough, but the counsellor may see him as inadequate or as a bully, whilst the counsellor who sees himself as permissive and benevolent may be viewed by the pupil as "one of them", that is an authority figure of whom one should be suspicious and whom one should attempt to outwit.

The most important level is (iii) which Laing and his co-authors called meta-identity or "my view of your view of me". In this business of counselling there is complex interaction between (a) the pupil's view of the counsellor's view of the pupil, and (b) between the counsellor's view of the pupil's view of the counsellor. This will occur whatever method of counselling is adopted, and is the source of resistance, distortion and error at times. Sometimes only a little exploration is necessary to find out that a pupil thinks that the counsellor sees him as a real delinquent or as emotionally disturbed, and that he is reacting against this. The counsellor on the other hand may too lightly assume that the pupil sees him as someone who is trying to help and as a teacher with a special role. In fact the counsellor may have completely misinterpreted the boy's perceptions of him, and he may actually see the counsellor as a probing busybody who is associated with the probation or psychological services. Phantasy is often present even when the counsellor chooses to ignore it. A feeling that counselling is "not getting anywhere" has indicated to me the wisdom of looking for disjunctions in these three levels of perceptions. Usually something has been found which explains the failure.

In this business of perception there is a close relationship between these three levels of scrutiny and the pushing on to other people of feelings which we cannot admit exist in ourselves. The counsellor needs to recognize the times when a pupil projects his feelings not only on to other teachers and pupils, but also on to the counsellor. The pupil may well believe that others are always picking on him, when this is a projection of his own feelings of hostility. This feature of projection is not confined to pupils, for I have seen a number of examples in mature students. Some of these conscientious people often think that they are doing badly and that the counsellor trainer thinks this, when in fact they are being given signals of approval and acceptance. This projection is partially caused by the new demands of counselling and the high anxiety it creates at first, but it is interesting to see it operating in the student counsellors. Projection occurs in counselling, and when the irrational appears—and it almost inevitably will in counselling— then it is necessary to explore the projected feelings very cautiously and carefully. Although counselling is problem-centred and future-orientated, it is possible to wander into rather dangerous situations unless one is aware of these factors, knowing what can be done and when to refer pupils for more skilled help. This again shows the need for training, for it is impossible to anticipate when irrational and distorted emotions will surface themselves in counselling. Experience in training has caused me wry amusement by making me speculate about the proportion of counselling interviews in which projections and mistaken views of the counsellor's role have caused the pupil to be responding towards a counsellor who is largely an invention or phantasy of the pupil. The laughter fades, when I ask myself how many times I have been guilty of doing this myself to the pupil. It is fairly clear that developmental counselling is a situation in which perceptions are important, and there should be somebody in the school who has some skill and knowledge in this field.

### 3. TRANSFERENCE

Many discussions of counselling mention transference because this is something which the counsellor cannot evade. Most explanations of transference are phrased in technical language, and it is difficult to give a valid short description of a complex concept, but for our purposes we can define it as a special type of positive or negative emotional attitude felt towards the counsellor by the pupil. It is special in the sense that it does not develop from the current events in counselling, but from experiences and attitudes to important figures in the pupil's life. It is therefore a shifting of what belonged to other people (such as the pupil's parents, grandparents or other important individuals in his life) on to the counsellor. The personality of the counsellor and the particular problems and atmosphere of the counselling sessions allow transference to appear very easily, for it is encouraged by emotional and dependent situations. These last words should not be misunderstood. They merely mean that counselling is concerned with anxiety, a sense of threat, guilt and tensions. The emotions and attitudes shifted on to the counsellor do not represent the reality of present or past relationships, but the pupil's perceptions and phantasies about the people involved. Perhaps it can be seen that it is a spread of feelings towards the counsellor which is not justified by his behaviour and personality. Sometimes counsellors who take a non-directive approach find themselves overwhelmed by sudden intense positive feelings which are almost stifling in their quality. This is an indication that one has been counselling in an undisciplined way, and that the future-looking approach of developmental counselling has been lost. When massive dependency, levels of emotional involvement which seem unhealthy or irrational, and unmodifiable hostility persist, it usually means that one has taken on a severely disturbed child who should have been referred to the educational psychologist and the child guidance clinic. Panic must be avoided, although it is only too easy to panic: the best device is to discuss the problem fully with the psychologist or psychiatrist. The aim is to find a constructive way of getting out of the situation without doing the pupil any harm, and of guiding him or her towards real help. It would, of course, be grossly unethical and stupid to stop seeing the pupil abruptly, without getting proper advice. This is the kind of situation in which those using the active model find they have built up useful supports; indeed, with the active model it is much harder for these situations to develop. They are often a product of isolation from colleagues and a desire to show what can be achieved.

In selecting counsellors, universities try to eliminate those who seem unstable and likely to fall prey to their own emotions. There is, however, that thing called counter-transference. This means that all of us, even if we have sound personality and thorough training, still tend to take irrational attitudes towards pupils. We must know that we can do this, and then take steps to deal with it. Otherwise we are in the position of the man who believes illness will not strike him, and when it does, finds himself unprepared for coping with the situation. If strong likes or dislikes emerge very quickly about a pupil, then we should take stock of ourselves, because we may be responding to something very odd in our own make-up. Pupils have problems which often impinge upon unresolved and unrecognized problems of the counsellor, and his reaction is really to these and not to the pupil. We can take up roles in counselling which reflect our own parents' attitudes towards us. The counsellor of the adolescent often is of the age when he is dealing with the problems of his own adolescent children. This can cause him to slip into a quasi-parental role or even behave towards the pupil in the same way as he behaved toward his own children, even although this does not fit the current situation. Adolescence is a period of conflict between parents and children about vocational choices, further education, staying on at school, drug taking and other matters. It is an almost intolerable situation to be faced in one's work by the very problem which one is facing at home or has miserably failed to resolve. Again the support emanating from colleague participation makes for a much healthier approach.

### 4. OTHER SOURCES OF DISTORTION

In designing questionnaires and personality tests a lot of attention is given to avoiding distortion due to the influence of social desirability, and the counsellor is well advised to pay attention to this. It is easy to create an interview structure which produces pressures pushing boys or girls towards the production of socially desirable rather than true responses. This is coupled with the maintenance of a façade of compliance and passivity. This is a self-defeating strategy which appears almost unnoticed. One source of pressure is the type of referral. Sources of referral are parents, teachers, peers and the pupils themselves. It is tempting to try to rely on self-referrals; this, however, would be to avoid the more difficult situations where a pupil needs help, but is unwilling to admit it. Pupils who come for counselling on their own volition will be the least likely to feel pressures towards the production of conforming and superficial responses, whilst those who are referred by others are more vulnerable to these reactions because a sense of blame, failure or inadequacy is associated with the referral. When a friend brings a pupil these feelings are usually not present. Social desirability is a product of threat, and this enters counselling in many ways. Separation from a peer group which gives valuable satisfactions, the fear of being laughed at, called a ponce, nutcase or nark by friends strongly operates amongst some groups in the secondary school. This can provoke antagonism, but it can also lead to adoption of socially desirable responses in the hope of escaping a distasteful process as soon as possible. Just as some mental hospital patients learn to take up the good patient role to get away from the hospital, so can some pupils take up the part of the good counsellee in order to be released quickly. This response is usually a result of the counsellor emphasizing his separation from the school, the pathological nature of his counselling and the refusal to see that counselling is the right of all pupils. The answer is to link counselling with the pastoral care system and everyday activities of the school, resolutely reinforcing the link between counselling and teaching in every possible way.

One of the major sources of threat is the already mentioned "probing". This is a phrase beloved of many counsellors, but it is a form of intensive questioning which is not only alarming to the pupil, but very ineffective, because it produces inaccurate responses on many occasions. If one behaves like a surgeon probing for a bullet without anaesthetic then it is not surprising when the patients kick one. Probing should be unnecessary: if supports, concrete aids and the right level of threat-free interaction are provided the pupil speaks freely. A counsellor learns to look for unintended threats when the pupil misunderstands a remark. "I will ask Mr. Brown", or "I'll look it up in my files" are the kind of remarks we make thoughtlessly without appreciating that the boy or girl listening puts very sinister interpretations on them. It is very reprehensible to leave a file lying around with someone's name on it, for a pupil then wonders what is in his own file and whether the counsellor is equally careless with that.

A last source of distortion lies in unintended reinforcements. The pupil has us under acute observation. Then when we begin to show signs of more than usual interest or approval this acts as a reward and signal that we think what he is saying is important. Some of us perk up when a pupil begins to say negative remarks about his parents and other adults. If we begin to show interest then he will go on producing such material and shift the weight of the interview from positive things to destructive ones. It could lead to the curious situation in which a pupil felt he could best gain the approval of the counsellor by being negative about himself and others. The counsellor does not have to say anything; it is sufficient to lean forward attentively at these points or introduce a smile and general impression of greater attentiveness. Unless we are aware of these things it is sometimes a moot point as to what is being reinforced in the counselling interview.

### Summary discussion

This chapter drew your attention to the way in which the interview is composed of two-way transactions. It showed the inadequacy of talking about the pupil's replies as if they existed in isolation. The counsellor plays a great part in shaping the pupil's statements.

The counsellor's role requires him to adapt to each pupil and not to attempt to treat different pupils with different needs as if they were alike. He must adapt to each pupil. Next he must be intellectually alert and use his knowledge in a sensitive way to explain the behaviour and motivations of the pupil. He must maintain communication, which includes the proper pacing of interventions and questions, but also ensure that he is sending the same kind of messages by verbal and non-verbal channels. He must train himself accurately to note signals of anxiety, dislike and avoidance which are not easily recognized by the unskilled interviewer.

A number of role stresses exist for the counsellor, the most important being those of the conflict between the teaching situation and occupation of a counselling role. It was suggested that this conflict is often more important to the counsellor than the pupil, and that adolescents are capable of making realistic discriminations between the same person when he occupies different roles. It is possible to be both a teacher and a counsellor, provided one is capable of behaving appropriately in both roles, maintaining the boundaries between them.

The interview was presented as a situation in which the pupil and counsellor exchange many things, information, rewards, support and the teaching of social skills being amongst the goods which are exchanged. It is only too easy for counselling to become a set of destructive games unless the counsellor is aware of the quality of the transactions going on between him and the pupil. We must always be aware of the pattern of interaction which is developing, the output from the interview and the consequence of this. The interview is also a process of selection and coding and this can lead one astray. The process of levelling and sharpening which goes on represents a search for meaning and the desire to turn what is unfamiliar into the familiar; but this may also mean that the counsellor is distorting the whole thing.

The counsellor has to learn how to structure the interview, making sure that he ends in a way which leaves the pupil able to cope with the immediate demands that he has to face. He has to learn to use questions skilfully, mixing open and closed questions according to the needs of the pupil and the topic which is under discussion. He has to intermesh his responses to the pupil, so that the best possible flow of communication is established; this means that he will talk at different rates, and not always in the same way. The counsellor knows that language ability reflects the way in which a child is tied to or free from immediate experiences and concrete illustrations. He knows that pupils with restricted language ability will have more difficulty in taking the viewpoints of other people and that they will need more aids to communication.

The interview is subject to many sources of distortion, one of the most subtle being the influence of the counsellor's implicit ideas of personality. Counselling, like other processes of person perception, is concerned with the attribution of motives and intentions to the other person and this opens the door for the entry of grave errors. Socially desirable responses rather than true and honest ones can also distort counselling. Such responses often satisfy us as teachers, but they have little place in counselling because they do not aid development and change. Many unrecognized sources of threat exist in counselling and this causes a boy or girl to retreat to a position where they say what they think is the response that will please the counsellor. Lastly, it is important to keep in mind the three levels of perception of the counsellor by the pupil and the pupil by the counsellor. We then begin to see why things can go wrong, especially when "my view of your view of me" is inaccurate, in either counsellor or pupil.

## REFERENCES

Allen, T.W. & Whiteley, J.M. (1968) *Dimensions of Effective Counseling*, Ohio: Merrill Publishing Co.

Allport, G. and Postman, L. (1945) 'The basic psychology of Rumor', In Maccoby, E., Newcomb, T., and Hatley, E. (Eds. 1958), *Readings in Social Psychology*, Methuen.

Bartlett, F.C. (1932) *Remembering*, Cambridge University Press.

Carkhuff R.R. (1969) *Helping and Human Relations*, Vols. 1 and 2. New York: Holt, Rinehart & Winston.

Heider, F. (1958) *The Psychology of Interpersonal Relations*, New York: Wiley.

Laing, R., Phillipson, H. and Lee, A. (1966) *Interpersonal Perception*, London: Tavistock Publications.

Luria, A.R. (1961) *The Role of Speech in the Regulation of Normal and Abnormal Behaviour*, Oxford: Pergamon Press.

Moore, G.D. and Fuller, J.A. (1967) School Counselling: A Survey of the Roles of Counsellors who qualified in Reading in 1966', Guidance Unit, Institute of Education, University of Reading.

Parsons, Talcott (1957) *Economy and Society,* Glencoe, Illinois: Free Press.

# CHAPTER FOUR

# TECHNIQUES DURING THE FIRST PHASE OF COUNSELLING

### *The purpose of this chapter*

You are now introduced to some of the techniques which can be used during that part of the counselling process where the major emphasis is on the building up of understanding of the pupil. This is part of building up meaningful communication and encouraging the pupil to find a positive sense of direction and purpose for himself. We will be concerned with the picture of himself which is held by the pupil and the view of the world which he has gradually built up during childhood.

The techniques mentioned are quite simple. The imaginative teacher will find himself able to improve upon them and develop them in ways suited to particular pupils and his school.

### *The questions asked in this chapter*

Although it is mainly descriptive, this chapter answers certain key questions. The most important of these are:

(i) What is the significance of a pupil's self image in the counselling process?

(ii) Why is it important that we should understand the viewpoint of a pupil? Is this an unnecessary luxury?

(iii) "We get what we expect." What is the truth concealed in this statement and how does it apply to school counselling?

(iv) How can we find out the way in which a pupil sees his world and understand the kind of predictions he makes about his own behaviour and that of others?

### The stages of counselling

I have always felt it sensible to develop techniques of counselling based on my own skills as a teacher. This was economical, and it also had the virtue of not arousing resistance and alarm in pupils, because counselling was very close, in appearance at least, to the everyday activities of the school. Counselling can become seen as something meant for the deviant and the oddities of the school with surprising speed. Clumsiness and lack of sensitivity to feedback is the cause of this, but it is almost disastrous, for it impedes the development of self-referrals, and many pupils never get the help they need. To allow counselling to be labelled in this way is a self-defeating exercise. It should not only be related to the everyday activities of the shool, but *be seen* to be this. The way this separation can happen can be illustrated by the experience of students early in their training. They often bend forward and earnestly ask the pupil what his problem is, recoiling in a disconcerted and disorganized way when they get the firm answer, "I haven't got any problems". They may then make matters worse by trying to tell the pupils they are shutting the door on self-exploration. But this very pupil without any problems, will, when he feels safe, freely talk about his worries, the moments when he experiences panic, the feelings he has about lack of friends, and the times he feels like running away. He would still say, if asked, that he has no problems, because not only are "problems" things which other people have and he does not, but if he admits to problems he is putting himself into a special category. For many reasons, the category of "people with problems" is one with unattractive characteristics. To ask him to admit he has problems, is to ask him to identify himself with a negative group of people. All our techniques should be aimed at preventing pupils from defining themselves as different and deviant, and facilitating growth and development.

Some techniques are more useful in the first phase of counselling, whilst others are more effective in the later "task-achievement" phase of counselling. Let us remind ourselves of the differences and special purposes of each of these stages. In the first stage, which is described by Carkhuff (1969) as the inward looking, the job of the counsellor is to build up a communication system within which the pupil can express himself and explore his life situation. This is not so simple as it looks. Riden (1970) reports that the major difficulty of trained counsellors was dealing with inarticulate children, whilst the work of Bernstein (1965, 1971) suggests that many pupils are in a situation where they have to make constant translations of the demands and statements of teachers into a form suitable to themselves. Many never succeed in this task. In the first phase the counsellor's role is expressive and responsive, giving a sense of warm acceptance to the pupil, and the general emphasis is on the feelings and viewpoints of the boy or girl. If the counsellor is successful in this first phase, then he will come to understand very clearly what the world looks like to that individual. But even more important is that out of the pupil—counsellor interaction in this stage comes a sense of purpose and of definite aim. Targets are defined during the first stage, and these are actively striven after by the pupil, because they are created by him and not imposed. Counsellors are concerned with the development of controls by the pupil, rather than with external constraints, but this by itself is a cramping view of counselling. It could be a strait-jacket in which adolescent idealism and aims are confined for ever. If self-discipline is merely self-control and the inhibition of impulsive behaviour then it is sterile. As teachers and counsellors we are concerned with a model of *man in the process of becoming*—and good teaching and good counselling are trying to build up creative forms of self-discipline linked with the active pursuit of self-selected goals. Critics of counselling often complain that it is merely another step in the process of abdication of standards and the denial of hard work and initiative. We are not providing pupils with excuses, neither are we castrating them intellectually and emotionally. Far from it, because counselling is a process in which pupils develop real aims and purpose, and once these are defined, the counsellor helps pupils pursue them with energy and single-mindedness. The difference between counselling and other forms of support is that *the aims are self-chosen*, and once a firm choice is made, the counsellor refuses to accept the pupil as less than he can be.

High standards of striving, a strong sense of purpose and the expenditure of a great deal of energy mark the second stage of counselling. The active model gives equal weight to the second stage of counselling because it is here that we meet the crucial problem of transfer of training. We may, with hard work, achieve changes of attitude and produce new ways of thinking and behaving within the counselling situation, but we get rude shocks if we assume that this will automatically transfer to outside situations in the class, school or home. We have to take various measures to try to ensure that what is happening inside the counselling situation is given successful expression outside it. Most of us would take it for granted that choice of a job is a key factor in a young person's life, yet Hayes and Hough (1971) have evidence that young workers who have made bad first choices do not apply what they have learned to their second choice. They tend to repeat the original errors. If there is failure of transfer of learning in this area, then it is just as likely to occur in counselling. Indeed it was the need to ensure transfer which led to the development of the active model; and it is also concerned to build on the creative skills of the teacher. To introduce the word creative means to run the risk of being vague. I shall use the definition offered by Read (1943), although I am very appreciative of later work on divergent and convergent thinking. In Read's definition the creative process is one where form and order is given in a situation where it did not exist before; the definition also includes creating new order and structures to replace previous ones. It will be fatal to the liveliness of counselling if we see it as a diluted form of psychotherapy or as a purely talking therapy. It is therapeutic, but it is fundamentally developmental and often it includes little talking for the reasons mentioned earlier. We will here be concerned with concrete aids to communication, utilizing the teacher's capacity for inventiveness. The discussion will be suggestive and not prescriptive, however.

## The first phase of counselling

### I. THE PUPIL'S SELF IMAGE

In the first stage of counselling we try to see things the way the pupil sees them. One of the most critical aspects of this is, of course, the way he sees himself. As counsellors we have to be aware of the picture of himself which a pupil has built up during his social experiences, especially at home, in school and in relation to his age mates. We already know that people see *things* differently, and this is partly responsible for their behaviour, but we also have evidence from Rosenberg (1965) and Strang (1957), amongst many others, which shows that adolescent behaviour is also partly the product of the way a boy sees *himself*. We can say "I hurt myself", but it is also possible to say with meaning, "I hate myself" or "I like myself" and this has a potent influence on our behaviour. Self-esteem is very crucial in social behaviour and achievement. Much of our culture is still orientated towards the great ethical injunction of "Love one another as you love yourselves". A great truth is hidden in this: if we dislike, disapprove and devalue ourselves, then the results when we try to love others are likely to be somewhat disconcerting. Exploration of the picture of self is practical, for the picture of the self shapes the interpersonal relationships, and interpersonal relationships are usually the cause of the developmental difficulties leading to the need for counselling. The specific discussion here will be limited to self-esteem, but the self-concept is more than this: it is the total organization of a person's feelings about himself.

The self-image is built up by imagining how we appear to others, anticipating and guessing their judgements of us—a process of reflected appraisals, producing feelings of worth or shame, as the case may be. If we have continuous signals of failure or interpret signals inaccurately as those of failure, then gradually we build up a negative picture of ourselves and anticipate failure and rejection. A number of workers, including Rosenberg, report that low self-esteem is found in association with depression, rejection by those of the same age, psychosomatic illnesses, and negative judgements of others. We now know that the father—son relationship is a crucial factor in the development of self-esteem. Rosenberg found that adolescents who report close relationships with fathers are considerably more likely to have high self-esteem and stable self-images than those boys who describe their relationships with their fathers as distant. The supportiveness of the father seems a key factor and it is likely that boys with low self-esteem are in particular need of a warm relationship with a man who also provides them with a model of masculine competence. This means that it is important that there is a man available to counsel such pupils. Pupils with low self-esteem seem to be unable to initiate social relationships in a constructive way, feel awkward in group situations, react hypersensitively to real and imagined criticisms and adopt the negative attitudes towards others that they feel are adopted towards themselves.

The more uncertain a pupil is about himself, the more likely he is to respond with anxiety and withdrawal from group activities. Many pupils respond to feelings of inferiority and low self-esteem by creating a façade or false front. All their energy is invested in *saving face*, and they feel under constant threat because there is always the danger of exposure. This comes out very strongly in the field of masculine role activities, where boys feel compelled to put on a defiant front of toughness. Indeed, as Turner (1961) points out, such a boy often requires the condemnation of the teacher as a form of reassurance. Without this, he is uncertain if he is playing a tough role. This is not an outlandish type of response, but a fairly common one. Within the last week a student has presented me with an essay in which he describes the frantic way he was driven to sport and body building in an attempt to state his masculinity. A pretty face and a slight build stimulated very negative self-feeling in him. Looking back from the point of a successful marriage, he can understand it more completely, yet at the time he felt there was always danger of exposure. It is very common in the field of intellectual endeavour to find that the underfunctioning bright pupil sees himself very negatively and has opted out, whilst another pupil will strive desperately to eliminate all competition. Even when he comes first, he still anxiously strives for better results, neglecting other aspects of his life. The pupil with low self-esteem who is pressured by parents to do better than he is really capable of doing can work very hard; but the whole façade may suddenly crack. This is also true of pupils who come from very authoritarian homes, where they are subjected to suppressive discipline and an insistence upon rigid performance of duties. Such pupils are raised in an emotional climate which echoes with the words "without fail". Everything has to be done without fail; indeed such parents often use the phrase. But in school the front cracks, and sudden outbursts occur, or very real depression. Sometimes both are found in the same pupil. Counselling often has to consist of building up a sense of control and a tolerance of anxiety coupled with an improvement in the child's picture of himself, because such parents are unlikely to change their ways. The most constructive strategy is to help the boy or girl withstand the stress.

Pupils with low self-esteem are very vulnerable in interpersonal relationships: they assume that others do not like them, and they feel relatively lonely and isolated. Later the counsellor may attempt to include them in special counselling groups where peer relationships are very important. Low self-esteem will be important in school performance. It is a basic principle of remedial education that the first step is to build up a picture of the pupil as someone capable of achievement. What is interesting at the secondary stage of education is the evidence that pupils with low self-esteem are reluctant to enter into a power relationship either as a power holder or as a subject of power. This means they avoid leadership situations and competition and are motivated by fear of failure. Birney, Burdick and Teevan (1969) show the strategies used by pupils motivated by fear of failure. They tend to set themselves either impossibly high targets or ridiculously low ones. The psychological mechanisms are those of evasion and avoiding blame, for in the one case they can appear to be noble failures who should not be blamed, and in the other people are supposed to believe that they could do it if only they would try.

A few more points can be made before moving on. We can see that the more uncertain a pupil is about what he is like, the more anxiety he will feel. The counsellor must realise that anxiety is often linked with low self-esteem and an uncertain sense of identity. When pupils fail to respond to simple measures of reassurance and the concern of the counsellor and teachers, we should begin to look carefully at their picture of themselves. Sometimes our own rigidity prevents us from seeing anxiety where it exists. We need to remind ourselves that the boy who wants to be a welder or carpenter may experience just as much anxiety and be as full of self doubt about his capacities as the one who wishes to be a doctor or lawyer.

Sometimes group membership has an effect on self-image and produces conflict. This may be true of working-class pupils who are moving upwards in the social scale. It is true of other groups too. When qualities are admired within a group, but rejected outside it, tensions and confusion about identity can result. A student is counselling a Jewish boy, who is provoking rejection and creating hostility towards himself because he feels impelled to define himself as Jewish in a provocative and aggressive way. This appears to be a recent development, but it crystallized when pupils asked the form master why the boy did not go to assembly and religious education periods. The boy said, "I'd told them I was a Jew, but they didn't really believe it until the teacher told them it". The teacher had not behaved improperly, yet his statement had crystallized a situation. Now the boy seems to have a core identity as Jewish with high self-esteem attached to this, but he also wants to have a different identity with his class mates. He has maintained a front of a rather arrogant type with apparently high self-esteem, but he is beginning to reveal that beneath it lie uncertainty and a desire to belong to the peer group.

The first phase of counselling is concerned with attitude change, and attitude towards oneself is the basic attitude with which we are concerned in counselling. It is easy to talk about attitude change, but it is, in fact, a difficult thing to do. An attitude is basically a readiness to respond in a particular kind of way, as Allport (1954) points out. Fishbein (1967) brings out Allport's original insistence on the emotional nature of an attitude when he says that it is the evaluative aspect of a concept. He goes on to say that by a concept he means any distinguishable part of the individual's world. Nothing is more emotional than evaluation, because evaluation means not rational cognition, but a tendency to approach or avoid the attitude object and to regard it with favour or disfavour. He summarizes his argument by saying that an individual's attitude towards any object is a product of *his beliefs about that object* and *the evaluative aspects of those beliefs*. This is important for us to hold in mind when counselling. Attitudes are tendencies to approach and avoid and to evaluate; and the most crucial thing that is evaluated is the self of the pupil.

There are two important types of attitude concerned with the self-image which should occupy our attention in the first phase of counselling. *The ego instrumental attitudes* are those which serve to indicate to other people the sort of person that one is. We use dress, hairstyles, speech habits and many other things to build up a picture of ourselves. Each one of us carries around an "identity kit" which we use when necessary. This can be seen in the behaviour and dress of pupils who are beginning to opt out of the school situation, and this is why we begin to take action when pupils turn up without uniform. It is not that the wearing of school uniform is considered to be either good or bad, but that refusal to wear it has certain implications. The pupil may be rejecting the role of good pupil or of adolescent altogether and may be attempting to define himself as adult. This is seen in the pupils who are beginning to take up delinquent roles within peer groups. The denim jacket and Tee shirts are very important signals of a self-definition. We must remember, however, Sugarman's point (1967) that there is a world of difference between subscribing to a general system of symbols which identify pupils with a particular generation and culture, and the active playing out of roles in those groups. A certain hair style does not say anything about morality or behaviour, and we must be careful that our behaviour does not push an adolescent towards the active implementation of roles in teenage groups. Let us also adapt to the fact that many young people who are in the identity crisis of adolescence can only define themselves negatively, by what they are not. They appear to have little idea of what they really want to be like or are like. This negative definition of self is the starting point for the counsellor. His techniques will be aimed at gradually helping the pupil build up his own self-picture.

We must recognize and understand the attitudes which define the type of person the pupil is. Without this, little will be achieved; our attempts may even have the reverse effect to that we intended. If smoking is linked with a boy's picture of himself as tough and with his desire to be tough, then we should take note of what this means. To try to get him to give up smoking is to ask him to identify himself with a group which has very unattractive characteristics for him in relation to his self-image. He sees non-smokers as a group of people whom he dislikes or despises because they lack the toughness which is important to him. Until his needs for toughness are met and he feels secure enough to manage without being tough, attempts at changing his attitude are likely to fail. To attack smoking directly is, in his case, to attack an important part of his self-picture, and also an activity which is very valuable to him because it is part of his identity kit as a tough person. If drug taking is associated with a self-concept that one is somebody who has rejected conventional morality and the dreariness of the establishment for living dangerously, then we see that saying drug taking is dangerous or immoral can make drug taking more, not less, attractive, for it actually strengthens the underlying definition of self. This does not mean we have to abdicate our values or condone dangerous behaviour, but we must understand the true significance of that behaviour to the person indulging in it. The counsellor finds out the *meaning* of the behaviour and he does not unintentionally reinforce it by well-meaning moral statements. He tries to encourage development, so that the behaviour and attitudes are discarded.

Often it is necessary to provide a boy with evidence that his definition of himself is inaccurate and that he is deceiving himself. A very able sixteen-year-old boy was loosely attached to a group smoking cannabis and taking L.S.D. Little pressure was needed to shift him more completely into membership of this group and harden his identity as a rebel and outcast. He felt that his great need was to be creative, and he also believed that honesty and truth were virtues confined to the working class, whilst those from his middle-class background were inevitably shallow and hypocritical. It was pointless, indeed it would have been damaging, to attack his beliefs directly. Creativity and expression were important to him and some discussions began. By a lucky chance his paintings during the last two years were available, and these became the basis for discussion. He began to see for himself a dramatic decrease in vitality and sense of movement, and a loss of original content in these paintings; indeed he saw that they had degenerated into repetitive and stereotypical productions of the pop art school. This caused him to question some of his basic assumptions. (It is disappointing to have to record that other factors pulled him out of school, and therefore the process was left incomplete.)

*Ego-defensive attitudes* are those which serve to protect an individual from seeing his undesired qualities and facing unpalatable facts. We have met the false front erected by those with low self-esteem, but this is rather different: the possessor of the false front is often deceiving others and he fears exposure; the ego-defensive attitude allows one to deceive oneself. A recent example concerns a fifteen-year-old who held a clowning role in the form and who also felt that he was a good actor and playwright. Both these concealed ego-defensive attitudes, for he was unpopular with the boys although he did not believe this, and his skill at acting was very limited. The problem appeared during counselling: it was his anxiety about being short and rather plump on entry to the secondary school, inferior in games and late in entering puberty. He was defending himself against this negative body image. Once he understood this, it was relatively easy to teach him new social skills and self acceptance. If the counsellor or teacher shows the pupil he is valued for himself and he is allowed to reveal his feelings without punishment, then he may not only become aware of these attitudes, but desire to discard them. The fact that he *desires* to change does not mean that he is *able* to change without further support. As we have seen, ego-defensive attitudes can be illustrated by the pupil who hides his reactions to his physical inadequacies from himself or even more frequently deludes himself or herself about the nature of his relationships with the opposite sex. He may think he is attractive to girls when he is rejected by them, continuing to push his attentions on a girl until he is forcefully disillusioned. Probation officers know only too well the pseudo toughness of many delinquents which hides a basic uncertainty. School counsellors also know the need for sensitivity and care in approaching these ego-defensive attitudes.

Where ego-defensive attitudes are strong, great pains must be taken in the first phase of counselling to ensure that a sense of security is established. In later stages the team approach is essential in helping these pupils, because it is only too easy to reinforce these attitudes unwittingly. A number of teachers may have to collaborate with the counsellor to provide the good experience and the new positive sense of self and achievement which have to be given before the need for such defensive attitudes will disappear. In some cases, it is a profitable exercise for a team of teachers to examine the pattern of daily interaction between teachers and the pupil, and evaluate it in terms of these two basic attitudes and the impact on self-esteem. Many unnecessary situations may be found which produce threat and anxiety, provoking defensive responses and calling ego-defensive attitudes into operation. It is never a negative process, for there is constant searching for opportunities of building up a positive sense of self.

## 2. VERBAL TECHNIQUES

The discussion on the self-image was necessary to prevent us from being in the position of a cook who has the ingredients for a recipe, but who knows nothing about the process of mixing and cooking, and cannot visualize the end product. We now begin to look at the verbal techniques used in counselling during the first phase, although these are only of major importance when language skill is well developed. The simple technique of having paper, felt pens, charcoal or a lump of plasticine on the table has much to commend it. We all talk better when we have something in our hands, and the presence of these everyday things does a lot to reassure a pupil.

We have discussed questioning earlier, but the counsellor needs additional techniques to understand the situation of the pupil. These are provided by *reflecting back* and *confrontation*. It is necessary to allow a pupil to elaborate responses if one is to build the communication structure. *Reflecting back* involves some restriction of the counsellor's own verbal responses, and therefore the first thing to learn is when to be silent. A teacher often feels the equivalent of a moral obligation to interrupt and possibly correct what a boy or girl is saying. That is death to counselling. What is proper in the classroom is not necessarily right in the counselling interview. Reflecting back means that, instead of asking a question, a sentence, phrase or word used by the pupil is repeated by the counsellor in a tone of voice which brings out further responses. This sounds passive, but in fact it demands intellectual alertness and constant judgements about what is salient and what is not. Direct questioning shapes the pupil's answers too much, and it can arouse a sense of threat, causing him to shift to another topic. If we are skilled at reflecting back, then we get a wealth of material from the pupil. Caution is necessary, for if one uses the wrong tone of voice in the first interviews before a relationship has been built up, an anxious pupil can interpret a questioning tone as an implicit criticism. This makes him modify his original statement rather than elaborate on it. Warmth of voice and the ability to smile is essential: counselling is anything but a dreary process of interrogation.

Reflecting back involves clarification. This has two dimensions, for it can be directed towards the counsellor or the pupil. We need to admit to ourselves that we do not understand the significance of what is being said and that we have been working on our own assumptions. I find that I have to say that "I'm a clot . . . I'm sorry, but I did not see what you meant". This does not destroy counselling, although it may be easier to say, "I'm not sure that I follow this" or "I wonder if this means you . . . ". Care is needed, for too great a reliance on this can make counselling artificial, may make the pupil feel that he cannot communicate, or more healthily, make him feel irritated because the counsellor appears unable to understand simple straightforward statements. Everything which occurs in the counselling interview is grist for the counsellor's mill and we should not gloss over or ignore this feeling. Exploration of it will not only make him realize that adults of goodwill still find it difficult to follow him at times, but looking at his own irritation deepens the relationship and brings more into the open. It can be the first step in providing the skills essential for better interpersonal relationships. It is wise to leave clarification until the boy or girl feels that he knows the counsellor. When clarification is used to help the pupil, the counsellor believes that things are being said of which the pupil has not seen the significance. Sometimes there are unnoticed contradictions in his statements. It is at this point that we see we cannot rely on verbal techniques alone, for we may find it useful to write these things down on a pad, draw cartoons which express the contradiction or devise an impromptu diagram. Better still, get the pupil to do this himself. It is a basic principle that counselling is just as much an activity of the pupil as the counsellor. Counselling should also be full of humour and fun when possible; the cartoon approach is a good thing.

Clarification is therefore a type of constructive confrontation. One way in which this can be achieved is to keep a small tape recorder available, switching this on and recording the statements, then letting the pupil listen to himself. In training students I find it useful not only for them to do this, but to have a second tape recorder. They then listen with the pupil to the first recording and ask him what they should have said, or if what they said was helpful. This invitation to the pupil to criticize what we are doing aids communication and even an inarticulate pupil is prepared to do this. Perhaps even more important is the fact that it makes it clear that the process is pupil-centred, and essentially a partnership. In using tape recorders we must be clear that the pupil will always ask himself what the counsellor is going to do with the recording; therefore I have found it useful to teach them how to erase a recording. It can be put that this is something useful they can do as the equivalent of cleaning the blackboard.

If one uses *confrontation* with a pupil, it should occur towards the beginning of the interview. Producing a confrontation at the end is not helpful, unless it is urgent. This may mean that the counsellor has to extend the interview. The counsellor gradually acquires understanding of the way in which a pupil communicates, picking up some of the subtle overtones in a way which can rarely be detected in the classroom. He begins to recognize phrases and images which appear to be of special significance for that pupil. I remember one very tough pupil who often referred to medieval castles and a chasing game ending in jumping a gap. This was used in counselling because the ideas were very meaningful to him and related to phantasies. There was no attempt at interpretation of the kind used by psychotherapists, but we were able to draw castles, look at defences and see the relation of the castle to his view of the world and relationships with other people. Because it was a meaningful image coming from him, it was possible to use it in counselling as something on which he could project ideas and associations which would have been hard for him to tackle directly. The chase image revealed his anxieties, especially those about hurting himself, and the feelings he had about his peers. Much was done. Yet it was all eminently practical, and concerned with what he was doing in his daily life. It is all too easy to start producing superficially plausible depth hypotheses, but the counsellor lacks the training for this. As soon as possible the boy was moved into the second phase where he was given essential skills which helped him gain his O-Levels and prepare himself constructively for a craft apprenticeship. The skilled counsellor gradually incorporates such images into his own statements to the pupil, although he never does this until he has understood their meaning for the pupil.

This process of individualized communication cannot be hurried, but if the climate is one in which the pupil feels safe and central, then he usually talks freely even if it is with aids, and it is possible to become steeped in his style of thinking and his significant phrases. This is not advocating the use of slang or gaining acceptance by using speech habits found in the pupil; it is a stress on the need for the counsellor to learn to code messages explicitly for each individual pupil. The burden of realistic adaptation belongs to the counsellor, and part of this is sensitive coding. Sixth form pupils who are becoming alienated from school, and who are moving into sub-cultures which emphasize world-rejection and inner experience will not respond unless one uses their images and modes of thought. It is a stimulating exercise because these are based on philosophy and sociology and involve exciting concepts. Conscious adaptation by the counsellor is needed to provide the ground for communication upon which new ideas can be accepted and incorporated into his thinking by the pupil. These simple verbal techniques begin the important process of increasing a pupil's ability to take the standpoint of other people, simply because they allow the pupil to modify what may have been very rigid and almost impermeable ways of thinking and viewpoints about life. This is made clear by the case of a fifteen-year-old who was referred to a student counsellor by the headmaster as a grave discipline problem marked by outbursts of a violent type in class. Episodes of window smashing in the school were also the cause of concern. The very imaginative and able student found that the boy had the following labels attached to him, Scarf: Haircut:

Transfer: Junior. These were nicknames used about him by either staff or boys. Scarf related to the fact that he wore a college scarf belonging to an elder brother to school. Transfer stemmed from his demands for transfer to another school whenever he was bullied in the first form. Haircut came from the fact that he was wearing long hair and staff constantly referred to this. Junior referred to his smallness. These labels did not emerge at once, but when the counsellor discovered the significance of Junior he asked for others and got them. Out of this emerged, amongst other things, counselling which centred on his feelings of being the baby in the family and in his peer group, his reactions to a limp caused by an operation, the high expectations of his mother which involved unfavourable comparisons between him and his siblings, and finally, conflict of the norms of his delinquent peer group with those of his family. The counsellor did good work here, but the point is that it was the sensitivity to key images which led to the discovery that in contrast to what might have been expected this boy could work very constructively at the symbolic level. In describing a window smashing episode he said, "I was drawn like a magnet", and was then able to take up the idea of a magnet usefully in the sense of things which attract and those which repulse. This counselling was most successful, largely because of the counsellor's ability to see that this pupil could work with these images.

### 3. CONCRETE AIDS TO COMMUNICATION IN THE FIRST PHASE

In discussing these aids we shall deal first with those which are related to the process of self-exploration and stimulate knowledge of the self-image. These are then followed by techniques concerned with a pupil's predictions of the consequences of his actions and the sources of threat or help which exist in his life space. It has been pointed out that the counselling situation must contain activities which parallel those of the classroom because pupils are intimidated by any hint of a clinical approach or signs that they are being treated as deviant. An incomplete sentences instrument is one useful technique. This consists of sentence beginnings, set out in the following way:

I like  ...............................................................................

Boys in my class...............................................................

I think fathers ................................................................

I worry  .........................................................................

Girls say I  ....................................................................

I enjoy ..........................................................................

It always seems to happen that............................................

My clothes ....................................................................

If only ..........................................................................

My face  ........................................................................

I work ..........................................................................

I'm happy  .....................................................................

In using this technique you should include both positive and negative sounding beginnings to the sentences. They should be presented in mixed order, avoiding putting the positive sentences into one part and the negative into another. These are some pupils who will enjoy writing these, whilst others are happier if the counsellor gives the initial statement and they complete it verbally, the counsellor writing the responses down. An alternative approach is to record the responses, and then listen to them together. Be clear that this is not a test, but just a way of increasing communication. It does not provide one with answers nor does it give one objective information. Sometimes it is difficult to prevent teachers training as counsellors from turning it into a sterile information-seeking process. After all, what has one really gained by knowing that father drinks too much or that sister Ann is not all she might be morally? What is important is the pupil's view of himself and his interpersonal relationships, which means we are interested in sister Ann only to the degree to which the pupil is respond-ing to her behaviour. The same holds for the father's drunkenness or unemployment. Sometimes it seems as if teachers who are counsellors feel compelled to get hold of all the facts, feeling failures if they don't achieve this, and yet not knowing what to do with the facts when they have them. In the incomplete sentence technique, the first step is to ask the pupil if some responses seem more interesting than others. Then once he has discussed this, it is possible to draw his attention to responses which interest you or which link with things which have been done before in the counselling sessions. In compiling the incomplete sentences instrument, it is useful to have in mind areas which you wish to tap, e.g. anxiety, body image, peer relationships and family reactions.

Each one of us has a picture of himself as he is and another of himself as he would like to be. Sometimes we have a harsh picture of ourselves as we ought to be. The ideal and actual selves of a pupil are important in counselling. It has been said that an extreme distance between ideal and actual self is indicative of maladjustment, although there is some evidence that a gap between ideal and actual self is creative and healthy in adolescence. The work of Wylie (1961) draws attention to the fact that many ambiguities exist in the concept of the actual and ideal self. Certainly the ideal self seems to have a tighter organization and to reflect cultural demands, but experience also shows that even those children who see themselves as doing badly in school and who have rejected the norms of the school still endorse responses in the ideal self which indicate a desire to do well. We are concerned to use the ideal and actual self scales as a means of discovering more about the pupil and stimulating discussion. We are looking at what is important to the pupil in his self-image and at discrepancies between the actual and ideal self without imposing premature meaning on these. Any value the instrument has depends upon the counsellor's skill in using it. The form I have found most useful covers five areas:

> School performance and activities
> Body image and personal appearance
> Peer relationships
> Maturity
> Confidence.

Items from each section are given below in the format used in my own counselling.

| | Like me | Not like me | Don't know |
|---|---|---|---|
| Get my homework done on time | — | — | — |
| Good at games | — | — | — |
| Strong and tough | — | — | — |
| The right size for my age | — | — | — |
| Always with a group of people | — | — | — |
| Get on well with most of the class | — | — | — |
| Save up for the future | — | — | — |
| Choose my own clothes | — | — | — |
| Tackle most problems that come my way | — | — | — |

The ideal self is similar to the actual self but instead of the headings above it has "I want to be like this" and "I don't want to be like this". It is best to let a pupil do the actual self scale before he does the ideal self scale. Any teacher will think of appropriate items, the skill coming in the use of this aid. When a pupil is doing it, important information is given by his hesitations. Sometimes he will hover over an item rather anxiously or uncertainly and this is worth mentioning later. He should not be kept passive during the discussion, but can be given the opportunity to draw up a picture of himself by listing what he sees himself as being and what he sees himself as not being. The don't know endorsements merit special attention. The version used by my students is split into sections with a separate form giving a discrepancy score between actual and ideal self for each section. This aids discussion, but always has the danger that a spurious precision can be attributed to these scores, when in fact the meaning differs for each pupil. It is useful to discuss the picture of himself as given by the school section and its relation to what he thinks is the role of the "good pupil". Often under-functioning pupils have very odd or demanding ideas of what it is like to be a successful pupil. The counsellor will also look at the relationship between his view of himself in the various areas and the evidence about these which has been gathered from colleagues and other sources. To discuss this automatically would be very destructive, but sometimes it is possible to begin to deal with these discrepancies at a later stage.

Another version of the "like me/not like me" technique is to prepare a list of adjectives and get the pupil to tick them under the appropriate heading. Such a list might include:

|  | Like me | Not like me |
| --- | --- | --- |
| Strong | — | — |
| Miserable | — | — |
| Happy | — | — |
| Small | — | — |
| Serious | — | — |
| Argumentative | — | — |
| Friendly | — | — |
| Lonely | — | — |
| Attractive | — | — |
| Tough | — | — |

Again the list can be built up, but no exact significance should be attached to the endorsement of responses. We look at the responses as a starting point for discussion, bearing in mind that many adolescents find it easier to say what they are not than what they are. The fear of rejection and being thought to be "big-headed" will often deter them from giving too favourable a picture of themselves. Drawing can be linked with these approaches towards self-understanding and this usually leads to real interaction between counsellor and pupil without any sense of threat being present. I often begin with the old parlour game of squiggles in which I draw two or three differently shaped lines and ask the pupil to turn it into a picture. The use of a stop watch turns this into a game. We sometimes build a story around the completed drawing; this is intended to stimulate communication, not as an imitation of psychotherapy. The counsellor should resist any temptation to read too much into these drawings. Even if he does speculate on the significance of the pictures and stories, he is well advised to keep his thoughts to himself. Another way is to give pupils "two minutes to draw yourself as you are today" which is then followed by the request to draw himself as he thinks he would be in five years' time. A great deal of information comes from asking a pupil to draw himself as he thinks he looks, followed by drawing himself as he thinks his mother sees him or as his father sees him. These drawings can be done on a piece of paper folded so that he can eventually look at all three drawings and compare them. Without being questioned, he will begin to talk and the counsellor can get to work. This device is one of the ways in which a counsellor can encourage a pupil to look at himself from the standpoint of another person.

It is very useful to ask a boy or girl to draw the nicest thing they know, followed by the nastiest thing. Such simple expedients prevent the counselling interview from becoming a situation of interrogation or being full of uneasy pauses in which anxiety rises sharply in the pupil. The list of activities based on drawing could be extended, but what I have mentioned seem sufficient to indicate that the counselling interview is full of activity and humour, and that a sense of direction will emerge from all this activity when these techniques are used by a creative teacher.

In the first phase of counselling we are building up the communication structure, understanding the pupil's view of himself and changing his self-image when this is necessary. Before we can go into the upward and outward phase it is very important that we should have some picture of his life space. By "life space" I mean the relationships between him and other people with whom he has to live. We can ask the pupil to imagine himself in the middle of groups of people who matter to him in his daily life and say what is important in the way they behave towards him. One such life space diagram drawn up by a fourteen-year-old boy looked like this (p. 127):

----

This picture of his life space was both negative and accurate; further counselling revealed that this represented almost exactly the kind of relationships in Paul's life. It was possible to help him decide what

| Father | Mother |
|---|---|
| Impatient and rough. Wants me to leave school. Gets angry if I do little things wrong. | Gives me plenty of pocket money. Fusses me too much. Wants me to do well and stay at school. Seems to be always doing things for my young sister. |

$-\nwarrow\searrow-$    $+\swarrow\nearrow\pm$

**Paul**
Well dressed. Better at lessons than others in class. Not good at games. Bullied by tough boys in the class. Wants to get out of the class and do harder work.

$-\swarrow\nearrow-$    $-\nwarrow\searrow-$

| Teachers | Classmates |
|---|---|
| Don't stop others from hitting me. Don't praise me when I get things right. Don't give me enough time and help. | Bullies. Rough. Haven't got any brains. Make fun of me. |

needed to be changed in each area. Counselling lasted about nine months, but real changes began to occur. Paul worked out many simple drawings and diagrams to help him see his own behaviour and the steps needed to change this. The lines and the symbols indicate the weight of the relationships as either positive or negative. It may be interesting to know that the counsellor worked very closely with both parents and the teachers in helping Paul. Paul did gain promotion and a great deal of time was then spent in helping him understand why he annoyed other boys. This preparation was begun as soon as it was decided that Paul was to be promoted. Part of his trouble was his inadequate stock of behaviours for dealing with the teasing and horse-play of earlier adolescence. The change of class made Paul very receptive to the counsellor's teaching of appropriate behaviours. The arrows in the diagram remind us that the flow of relationships is two-way. In Paul's case, a great deal of time was invested in changing his attitudes towards other people, showing him that as he changed, so did they respond differently towards him. It is a matter of pride to record that the first area to respond to change was that between Paul and his teachers, probably because the counsellor carefully explained what he was attempting to do, allowing them a real part in reinforcing the positive changes in Paul. Certainly the teacher support was excellent and without it little could have been achieved.

It is useful to draw up one's own life space diagrams about a pupil based on the information available to the pupil. Sometimes there will be striking differences between these diagrams and those produced by the pupil. It can be very productive to introduce parts of these diagrams into the counselling sessions, discussing the discrepancies with the pupil. Care has to be taken, for too blunt a use of this technique may make him feel threatened or helpless which is the reverse of the desired effect. Another use is to look on life space diagrams as snapshots which can reflect growth and development. It has been found rewarding to show a pupil a life space diagram of himself at intervals in counselling, letting him see where progress has occurred. He will usually begin to make suggestions about tackling the other areas without prompting by the counsellor. I have found that, when development is slowing down more than seems desirable or when the process seems to be stale or stagnant, the device of getting the pupil to draw his life space diagram before he began coming and as it currently is, will stimulate further effort.

#### 4. THE PUPIL'S SYSTEM OF PREDICTIONS

There is one more element in this first phase of counselling with which we have to deal if development is to be successfully stimulated. We must know what a boy or girl predicts will happen if new behaviour does occur. Change of behaviour is often a major aim in counselling, but we often are uncertain how this can be achieved. This is where Kelly's (1955) construct theory is of great utility. The suggestions which are made below can be criticized as a gross dilution of Kelly's own instruments, although I hope that it is still in line with his creative theory. The school counsellor not only helps a pupil see the tasks, but has to help him mount an effective attack on them. A developmental approach to school counselling is, in fact, an approach which emphasizes the strategies of coping used by the pupil in dealing with the tasks and discontinuities which form part of adolescence. If we are to understand why a pupil cannot take certain courses of action which appear obvious from our viewpoint or why he will not discard inefficient ones, then we must understand the system of predictions about the consequences of change. Any teacher with experience of deprived and disadvantaged pupils has had to battle with the fact that such pupils may see themselves as relatively helpless, predicting failure rather than success for themselves, often passively relying on luck rather than actively striving after realistic goals. A first step in developing more effective ways of coping is to understand the predictions that one makes, but this is followed by the realization that it is possible to develop more positive sets of expectations. We have to understand the world view of a pupil which is shaped by a complex system of expectations which have been built up over the years. It all seems to be crystallized in the phrase, "We get what we expect", for our expectations determine our behaviour. The practical counsellor therefore has to take note of his pupil's systems of expectations.

Kelly says that every man is a scientist, for the key quality of the scientist is to make predictions about the possible courses and consequences of events. As we live we build up systems of constructs or predictions which enable us not merely to respond to our environment, but to *represent* it, thereby being able to anticipate and to gain some measure of control over the environment by taking appropriate action. Constructs are predictive and they are being validated continuously during everyday life. It is crucial to understand that each pupil who comes to us for counselling brings with him a set of constructs which actually determines his behaviour. It determines his behaviour because it is responsible for his anticipation of positive or negative consequences, and in effect is the factor which decides what is suitable behaviour for that individual. Those of us who are concerned with counselling or pastoral care recognize this, for we often meet pupils whose lives seem dominated by predictions of failure, rejection or attack. The fact that constructs determine behaviour makes it imperative that we consider the theory in school counselling. There is also the equally important fact that Kelly's work seems to suggest that a person's current interpretations of the world are subject to revision and replacement. Counselling is a process which facilitates the modification of constructs in order that the pupil may deal more efficiently with his life situation. To examine the way in which a pupil construes those sectors of reality with which counselling is concerned is a major point in the first phase of counselling. Without this, we may be unable to understand the behaviour of the pupil. Kelly is saying something very close to, although not identical with, the statement that behaviour is determined by the environment as perceived by the person indulging in that behaviour. Sometimes we have been puzzled by the failure of remedial teaching in reading, but Ravenette (1967) has shown that reading can have surprising meanings for individual children, and that it is not until these are discovered that we can devise appropriate remedial steps. This element of subjective meaning, so important in remedial situations, is at least as important in counselling; time spent in discovering this idiosyncratic meaning is time well spent.

Kelly's approach supports the model of school counselling suggested in this book because it states that the determination of behaviour comes, not from external events as such, but from self-erected mental structures which not only form the spectacles through which a pupil interprets those events, but also determine his reaction to them. This means that we are subscribing to the model of personality where a pupil is not seen as merely a reactive being, but as someone who is potentially able to control and modify his environment. Perhaps you can now see why the first phase of counselling is so important. Unless the counsellor understands the way in which the pupil views the world, he is unlikely to be able to develop this sense of emergent direction.

Let us be clear about what is being said. Kelly is not implying that a situation of confusion exists; rather the reverse, namely that individuals always act in an orderly and predictable way. The laws of action which guide a pupil's behaviour are self-erected, springing from his construct system, which he has developed over time. It is crucial that we understand that the basic outlook of an individual is a very real phenomenon and an essential part of the data of counselling. It does not matter that it seems to represent reality inaccurately from the viewpoint of the counsellor and his colleagues, it still determines the reaction of the pupil. Without understanding the viewpoint produced by the construct system, we will be unable to build up the communication necessary for real co-operation and the emergence of a definite sense of purpose. Anyone who has counselled will know the feeling of bewilderment and sense of frustration which can overcome him, until he recognizes the way in which a boy or girl interprets the actions of people and events—such as answering questions in class or changing for games. Once this is achieved, real counselling begins.

A simple illustration may help. There are certain super-ordinate constructs around which other constructs are organized. We often need to identify the key constructs around which a boy organizes his life. I recently met a pupil who was quiet, obedient, intelligent and well dressed; he seemed to possess all the attributes of the ideal pupil, except for the fact that he was failing in school. During his first three years in the secondary school he had been regularly demoted. Various approaches intended to relieve his anxiety were tried without result. Then a simple construct approach based on a number of situations was tried and it became clear that an unsuspected construct seemed to dominate this boy's life. This was the construct of things one *had* to do or was *made* to do, and things where this did not apply. This construct was central in the life of this apparently compliant and inhibited pupil. Discussion then led to disclosure of his burning resentment about having to do things, including being counselled. He was given the chance of discontinuing counselling, being given time to think this over. He eventually decided to continue. It became clear that he predicted failure and rejection in the activities falling into the category of "things I am made to do". It is impossible to detail the course of the subsequent counselling, but it is noteworthy that after three years of steady demotion, this pupil's performance dramatically increased and he was promoted to a higher form. The improvement seems to have increased during the last six months. Without the construct being detected, much of the counselling would have been ineffective and might well have reinforced his tendency to organize his world in the way described.

Constructs and concepts are based around ideas of similarity and difference. To avoid confusion with logical ideas of difference, it is usual to talk of contrasts rather than differences. A construct is bipolar; just as the idea of good necessarily involves the idea of evil, without which it has no meaning, so does a construct have a contrasting pole. Each one of us organizes his life around these constructs, but remember that the opposite pole does not necessarily represent a logical opposite in the dictionary sense. We have to *discover* what is associated together rather than *assume* what goes with what for a pupil. Kelly says that much of this process of construing is unknown to the individual, for many of the patterns of equivalence and difference may never reach the level of speech. The function of the counsellor in the first phase of developmental counselling is that of detecting such patterns and their consequences in behaviour, and then, by drawing the pupil's attention to them, help him to modify behaviour. Considerable intellectual alertness is essential, but it is a process which provides real satisfaction for both parties. There is no substitute for the original work by Kelly, although the work by Bannister and Fransella (1971) is an admirable introduction. The repertory grid tests seem overelaborate and beyond the skill of the school counsellor, but less complex variations of the technique are possible which retain the creativity of Kelly's original work. In passing, it is worth noting the link between Kelly's work and Freud's insistence on free association which revealed unexpected associations and links in a patient's perceptions.

In our everyday life our predictions are concerned with people or specific situations, a fact which makes picture forms of construct tests of potential value to the school counsellor. School counsellors might find these introductory suggestions useful. Collect about fifteen to eighteen pictures of persons of the same sex as the pupil, ensuring that they cover

various ages and levels of social class. Most pictures should be somewhere within five years of his age. The right type of picture is one which
suggests character and mood, avoiding stereotypes and the obvious.
It is surprisingly hard to collect these. Pictures cut from mail order
catalogues, for example, are instantly recognized for what they are, and
they also emphasize clothes too strongly and crudely. Sometimes such a
set is useful, but experience is necessary before using them. After carefully mounting and numbering the set of pictures you then proceed to:

(i) Present the pictures to the pupil in combinations of three. As
you do so say, "In what *important way* are two of these people
alike and one different?"

(ii) Record the answers on a duplicated form which has the following headings: *Pictures Construct Contrast* Record the "alike"
response under Construct and the "different" response under
Contrast on the record form.

After a certain point I find it useful to let the pupil choose his own
groups of three, dealing with them as before. A blank figure or outline
can be included which represents the pupil. This is then included into
the sorts of three pictures presented to him. The activity also includes
asking him to choose the figure he likes best and likes least, the picture
he thinks is most like him and the one which differs most from him,
and finally the one he would most like to be. The counsellor can easily
gain elaboration of this material by asking a few open-ended questions.
Indeed my experience has been that the wealth of material coming
from so-called inarticulate children is almost embarrassing and one has
to learn to control the flow. Though the beginner may find that very
obvious differences and similarities emerge, only very little skill is
necessary to elicit more subtle responses, which often provide evidence
of unusual constructs and associations.

The counsellor next has to attempt to analyse the responses. This
calls for the ability to suspend judgements and scan material thoroughly.
For the sake of integrity, it is important to realize that we are not getting
scores or the ultimate truth, but merely an indication of the way in
which a pupil sees things. Kelly's work needs constant reading and re-
reading, if we are to gain sensitivity to this. One thing that emerges is

the fact that similar constructs appear in a number of responses. Each construct has a range or area of events to which it applies, and in some cases, such constructs as "being picked on" may have a wide area of application and be very important. Sometimes the constructs which appear are simple and crude, not only reflecting the true nature of things, but the ineptness of the counsellor. Even so, we often find that neither counsellor nor pupil had recognized the importance of these constructs. We must remember also that the pupil has to have practice to gain familiarity with this approach.

A number of further possibilities suggest themselves. A set composed of figures of persons of the opposite sex can be useful, particularly when heterosexual relationships seem very important in the social problems lying behind counselling. Sets composed of both males and females also yield illuminating results. The type of picture used is determined by the needs of the pupil and it is essential that these techniques are imbedded into the counselling process rather than being applied in a rigid way to every pupil. When the counsellor has understood a response and the construct associated with it, then he discusses it very thoroughly with the pupil, sometimes asking him to imagine that he is with these people in a particular situation.

A number of snags exist. It is very easy to confuse persons and situations, especially if there is a background which strongly suggests some activity. Careful mounting after cutting out the figures can prevent this. Without mounting, one can never be sure whether the pupil is responding to the person or the situation. We must see that we have to interpret the meaning of the construct and this means we have to discuss the responses thoroughly with the pupil. This is not time wasting, for out of this arise strategies of constructive action which work in line with the prediction system possessed by a boy or girl. What works for one individual does not work for another. Construct theory reminds us that one man's meat is another's poison, or one man's deviance is another's custom.

We can construct similar forms of the test which deal with everyday life situations. We must ensure an adequate sample of situations. A P.E. enthusiast once produced a set of pictures in which almost 50 per cent of the pictures were concerned with games and athletics—and he was completely oblivious of the bias. Another approach I find useful is that of writing the names of role holders or situations on cards. The card approach is very easily done and means that one can quickly produce sets of material designed for individual pupils. Care is essential, for one's hunches have a habit of getting out of control at times, leading to the construction of sets of cards which confirm the original intuition. Such self-fulfilling prophecies produce a warm feeling in the counsellor, but do little for counselling and the pupil. One set of situation cards I used during the last week included:—

Writing an essay
Talking to your father seriously
Getting up
Answering the telephone
Sunday dinnertime
Swimming
Going to the dentist
Coming home late
Going to church
Using apparatus in the gym
Getting a haircut
Visiting relations
Being interviewed for a job
A party where you don't know many people.

These simple situations produced a wealth of material which aided understanding between counsellor and pupil. Another set which has to be used with greater caution involved:

A time when you feel really bored
A time when you feel very peaceful
A time when you feel like crying
A time when you feel very adult
A time when you can't stop laughing
A time when you feel very annoyed with someone.

Such a set means that the counsellor has to write down the situation which produces that feeling on a card. It is these cards which are then presented to the pupil in the way described above. The answers to the first three might be:

When the history teacher talks for an hour
When I'm by myself on my bike in the country
When my mother says nice things about me.

If the names of role holders are required then it is as well to be cautious. If you ask a pupil for the name of a teacher whom the pupil dislikes, not only may a colleague be alienated but the pupil may have an odd idea of your motives. Colleagues can misunderstand these techniques, seeing them as subversive, if not actually encouraging direct misbehaviour. Some enthusiastic counsellors may feel irritated by this prudential approach, but the object of the activity is to find out what needs to be done to gain a sense of purpose and direction in the second part of counselling and here the support of colleagues will be at least as important as your own contribution. It is self-defeating to destroy goodwill by ill-considered actions which only reveal information which is obtainable without direct questioning. The greatest danger in this first stage of counselling seems to be unwitting seduction into playing the counselling game entitled, "Only I understand you". This is not only probably untrue, but it separates the pupil from other teachers. I have watched myself take the first steps in such a game on many occasions and some ruthless self-discipline has been necessary.

Examples of the instruments which can be devised are given below. The life space play has been included because it draws your attention to the way in which counselling can be linked with teaching. Once the teacher-counsellor starts to make his own tools for facilitating communication with the pupil, he will quickly see the relevance of his professional background.

### Summary discussion

This chapter has been concerned with building up communication in the first phase of counselling. Techniques have been suggested which aid self-exploration. The emphasis has been two-fold. We have seen the

ACTUAL AND IDEAL SELF SCALES

NOTES FOR THE TEACHER-COUNSELLOR

A caution:

1. Please do not think of these scales as tests which yield scores having a precise significance, although the lay-out of the scales may give you this impression. They are intended to help a pupil become more aware of his self-image, but also of the discrepancies which may exist between what he is and what he desires to be. A great deal of sensitivity is needed if you are to help a pupil discuss his concept of himself.

2. The Ideal Self Scale is an exact replication of the Actual Self Scale except for the instructions and the headings of the columns which are ticked. These are reproduced for you at the end of the Actual Self Scale.

Administration:

1. Always give the Actual Self Scale first. Allow a few days to pass before giving the Ideal Self Scale.

2. Allow the pupil to fill in the record sheet, but do not let him see it until he has completed both Scales.

3. If the Scales have been given to a group, then it is advisable to work through the recording of Section A with the pupils. They will then understand the scoring procedures and be able to proceed on their own.

Interpretation:

1. The difference scores have meaning only in relation to a particular pupil. Do not attribute arbitrary meaning to them. The significance of discrepancies between the Actual and the Ideal Selves varies with the individual.

2. Areas covered are:

   (a)  school performance
   (b)  body image
   (c)  relationships with peers
   (d)  maturity and anticipatory adult behaviours
   (e)  confidence

3. First look at the section which has the largest discrepancy score. Discuss this. Then look at individual items which the pupil feels to be important. Again discuss these. It is important these discussions lead into plans for behavioural change if possible and necessary. The pupil could explore:

   (i)  the items where he wants to change, evaluating the costs and consequences of this.
   (ii) items where he feels change is possible or it seems to be too threatening to attempt.

If used sensitively, these Scales lead the process towards planning for constructive behaviour modification.

ACTUAL SELF SCALE

Pupil's name ........................   Date ....................
Counsellor's initials   ........

WHAT TO DO:

Below are some important statements about people of your age. By
the side of each statement are three boxes. The boxes in the first
column are ticked when the statement describes someone who is .like
you. The boxes in the third column are ticked when the statement
describes someone not like you. If you can't make up your mind, then
tick the box in the middle column, but most people of your age find
it possible to decide whether they are like the person described or
not.

Here is a sample item which has been done for you.

|  | Like you | Don't know | Not like you |
|---|---|---|---|
| Like to fight a lot | ☑ | ☐ | ☐ |

Please remember this is not a test, but a way of finding out about
yourself. Only you and the counsellor will see what you do.

SECTION A:

|  | Like you | Don't know | Not like you |
|---|---|---|---|
| 1. Good at school work | ☐ | ☐ | ☐ |
| 2. Get my homework done on time | ☐ | ☐ | ☐ |
| 3. Near the top of my class | ☐ | ☐ | ☐ |
| 4. Always try to do my best at school | ☐ | ☐ | ☐ |
| 5. Not often away from school | ☐ | ☐ | ☐ |
| 6. Usually answer questions in class correctly | ☐ | ☐ | ☐ |
| 7. Good at practical subjects | ☐ | ☐ | ☐ |
| 8. Good at written work | ☐ | ☐ | ☐ |
| 9. Get things right easily | ☐ | ☐ | ☐ |
| 10. Do as I am told in school. | ☐ | ☐ | ☐ |

SECTION B:

|  | Like you | Dont'know | Not like you |
|---|---|---|---|
| 11. Try to look older | ☐ | ☐ | ☐ |
| 12. Attract girls | ☐ | ☐ | ☐ |
| 13. Fashionable | ☐ | ☐ | ☐ |
| 14. Fit | ☐ | ☐ | ☐ |
| 15. Good looking | ☐ | ☐ | ☐ |
| 16. Hard | ☐ | ☐ | ☐ |
| 17. Neat and tidy | ☐ | ☐ | ☐ |
| 18. Slim | ☐ | ☐ | ☐ |
| 19. Strong | ☐ | ☐ | ☐ |
| 20. Tall | ☐ | ☐ | ☐ |
| 21. Usually on the go | ☐ | ☐ | ☐ |

SECTION C:

| 22. Make friends easily | ☐ | ☐ | ☐ |
|---|---|---|---|
| 23. Join in things others are doing | ☐ | ☐ | ☐ |
| 24. Get on well with girls | ☐ | ☐ | ☐ |
| 25. Take charge of things | ☐ | ☐ | ☐ |
| 26. Usually on my own | ☐ | ☐ | ☐ |
| 27. Start new things | ☐ | ☐ | ☐ |
| 28. Go along with the crowd | ☐ | ☐ | ☐ |
| 29. Help others | ☐ | ☐ | ☐ |
| 30. Often lead a group of friends | ☐ | ☐ | ☐ |
| 31. Keep things to myself | ☐ | ☐ | ☐ |

SECTION D:

|  | Like you | Don't know | Not like you |
|---|---|---|---|
| 32. Save up | ☐ | ☐ | ☐ |
| 33. Stay out late | ☐ | ☐ | ☐ |
| 34. Plan ahead | ☐ | ☐ | ☐ |
| 35. Buy my own clothes | ☐ | ☐ | ☐ |
| 36. Act like my older friends | ☐ | ☐ | ☐ |
| 37. Do a part time job to get extra money | ☐ | ☐ | ☐ |
| 38. Know what I am going to do before I go out | ☐ | ☐ | ☐ |
| 39. Smoke | ☐ | ☐ | ☐ |
| 40. Go on holidays with my parents | ☐ | ☐ | ☐ |
| 41. Go around in a fast car | ☐ | ☐ | ☐ |
| 42. Bit of a rebel | ☐ | ☐ | ☐ |
| 43. Swear quite a lot | ☐ | ☐ | ☐ |

SECTION E:

| 44. Always try to be myself | ☐ | ☐ | ☐ |
|---|---|---|---|
| 45. Keep my head | ☐ | ☐ | ☐ |
| 46. See things through | ☐ | ☐ | ☐ |
| 47. Relaxed | ☐ | ☐ | ☐ |
| 48. Often the centre of attraction | ☐ | ☐ | ☐ |
| 49. Meet new people | ☐ | ☐ | ☐ |
| 50. Stand by what I say | ☐ | ☐ | ☐ |
| 51. Tackle most things successfully | ☐ | ☐ | ☐ |
| 52. Always in control of myself | ☐ | ☐ | ☐ |
| 53. Go to new places on my own | ☐ | ☐ | ☐ |

IDEAL SELF SCALE

Pupil's name ........................... Date ................
Counsellor's initials     .......

WHAT TO DO:

This looks exactly like the scale you did before, but there is an
important difference.  In the last scale you described yourself
as you are, now you HAVE TO SAY WHAT SORT OF PERSON YOU WOULD LIKE
TO BE.

Please tick either the box which shows you want to be like this,
or the box which shows you do not want to be like this.  If you
can't decide then tick the middle box, but please try to make a
definite choice.

Here is a sample of what has to be done.

|  | I want to be like this | Don't know | I don't want to be like this |
|---|---|---|---|
| Always polite and thoughtful | ☑ | ☐ | ☐ |

Please remember this is not a test, but a way of finding out about
yourself.  Only you and the counsellor will see what you do.

IDEAL/ACTUAL SELF SCALE - RECORD SHEET

NOTES:

1. You have gained a great deal of important information about how you see yourself, and what you would prefer to be like. This can be very helpful to you, but it must be clear where the differences lie between your actual and ideal self. This form makes this clear.

2. Enter below under the correct item number a + when you ticked either LIKE YOU or I WANT TO BE LIKE THIS, and an x when you ticked either NOT LIKE YOU or I DON'T WANT TO BE LIKE THIS. This shows the difference between your ideal and actual self.

3. Then count up the number of items where you have a + and a x for the same item. Enter the total of these items for each section where it says DIFFERENCE SCORE.

Each section should look like this when you have finished it :-

| Item No. | 1 | 2 | 3 | 4 | 5 | 6 | 7 | 8 | 9 | 10 |
|---|---|---|---|---|---|---|---|---|---|---|
| Actual Self | + | + | + | x | x | + | x | + | + | + |
| Ideal Self | + | x | x | x | + | + | + | + | + | x |

DIFFERENCE SCORE = 5

4. Be certain you enter the Actual and Ideal scale scores in the correct row.

SECTION A:

SCHOOL ACTIVITIES

| Item No. | 1 | 2 | 3 | 4 | 5 | 6 | 7 | 8 | 9 | 10 |
|---|---|---|---|---|---|---|---|---|---|---|
| Actual Self | | | | | | | | | | |
| Ideal Self | | | | | | | | | | |

DIFFERENCE SCORE =

SECTION B:

YOUR BODY IMAGE

| Item No. | 11 | 12 | 13 | 14 | 15 | 16 | 17 | 18 | 19 | 20 | 21 |
|---|---|---|---|---|---|---|---|---|---|---|---|
| Actual Self | | | | | | | | | | | |
| Ideal Self | | | | | | | | | | | |

DIFFERENCE SCORE =

SECTION C:

YOUR RELATIONSHIPS WITH PEOPLE OF YOUR OWN AGE

| Item No. | 22 | 23 | 24 | 25 | 26 | 27 | 28 | 29 | 30 | 31 |
|---|---|---|---|---|---|---|---|---|---|---|
| Actual Self | | | | | | | | | | |
| Ideal Self | | | | | | | | | | |

DIFFERENCE SCORE =

SECTION D:

YOUR DESIRE TO GROW UP RAPIDLY

| Item No. | 32 | 33 | 34 | 35 | 36 | 37 | 38 | 39 | 40 | 41 | 42 | 43 |
|---|---|---|---|---|---|---|---|---|---|---|---|---|
| Actual Self | | | | | | | | | | | | |
| Ideal Self | | | | | | | | | | | | |

DIFFERENCE SCORE =

SECTION E:

CONFIDENCE

| Item No. | 44 | 45 | 46 | 47 | 48 | 49 | 50 | 51 | 52 | 53 |
|---|---|---|---|---|---|---|---|---|---|---|
| Actual Self | | | | | | | | | | |
| Ideal Self | | | | | | | | | | |

DIFFERENCE SCORE =

YOUR NOTES:

THE SORT OF PERSON I AM

NOTES FOR THE TEACHER-COUNSELLOR

1. This is a very useful way to start a pupil on the process of self-exploration.
2. It can be used as a written exercise or you can adopt one of the two methods mentioned in the instruction. Other possibilities will suggest themselves to you.

Using it:

1. Let the pupil discuss it at once. You may need to start him off by asking:

    (i)  Which one did he find most difficult ?
    (ii)  Which one seemed the easiest ?
    (iii)  Which sentences seem to go together ?

2. Keep him active. Avoid obvious questioning and probing. You can get him to write out the numbers of sentences which:

    (i)  Are concerned with pleasant feelings.
    (ii)  Mention worries and unpleasant feelings.
    (iii)  Tell him what other people think of him.
    (iv)  Say something about his desires and aspirations.

Link responses up with the activity of drawing. This leads to really useful work.

3. Please avoid any temptation to draw dramatic conclusions from this instrument. It is merely an aid to communication.

THE SORT OF PERSON I AM

To Help you:

1. Your name: _____    The date: _____

2. THIS IS NOT A TEST. There are no right or wrong answers.
   We hope that doing this will help you find out useful things
   about yourself.

3. WORK AS FAST AS YOU CAN. Correct spelling and very neat
   writing are not important in this situation. PLEASE PUT DOWN
   THE FIRST THOUGHT THAT COMES INTO YOUR HEAD.

4. Please finish the sentences below. Sometimes you can record
   the whole sentence or your teacher will write your replies
   down after he reads the first part out to you.

5. You will be able to discuss your sentences as soon as you
   have finished.

1. I like _____

2. I am good _____

3. My mother _____

4. I want _____

5. It is _____

6. I want to grow _____

7. I can't _____

8. It's fun _____

9. Fathers _____

10. I worry _____

11. People think _____

12. I wish _____

13. In class _____.

14. My face _____

15. It seems difficult _____

16. I work _____

17. The others say _____

18. I hate _____

19. It always happens that _____

20. If only _____

We have tried to think of interesting beginnings for your sentences,
but we may not have put the ones you wanted to use. Would you like to
write two complete sentences of your own below ?

1. _____

2. _____

A SITUATIONS INSTRUMENT

INSTRUCTIONS FOR THE TEACHER-COUNSELLOR

The purpose:

These situations introduce you to the use of construct theory in
the way described in Chapter Four. You should explain to the pupil
that the activity will aid his understanding of himself and of his
"way of looking at the world".

What to do:

1.  Write the situations on separate cards giving each the
    number allotted to it in the list.
2.  Explain the purpose of the activity to the pupil.
3.  Present the situations to the pupil in groups of three and ask
    the question "In what important way are two of these alike and
    one different ?" You will have to decide on the actual groups
    of three presented, but you should be aware of the reasons behind
    your selection.
4.  Record the reasons for the similarity under the appropriate
    column and then do the same for the differences under the
    contrast column. Enter the numbers of the situations in the
    second column.
5.  Always ask a pupil to explain a little more clearly or give you more
    information if you feel this is necessary. There is no need to
    accept superficial replies.
6.  You can ask a pupil to think of situations he would like to
    include. Write these on cards and include them in your sorts.

Discussion and use of the results:

1.  Examine the responses and try to detect the major themes which
    appear. Draw the pupil's attention to these.
2.  Look for unusual associations and bring these into the discussion.
3.  The activity of analysis and exploration belongs to the pupil.
    If you wish to analyse the responses in the way suggested by Kelly
    then you should consult your educational psychologist.
4.  Divide the situation cards into three groups - 1 to 11; 12 to 21;
    22 to 32; then ask the pupil to pick the one that gives him
    most pleasure or satisfaction. Discuss these three situations.
    After this ask him to pick the one in each group which he finds
    most distasteful. Again compare the three and discuss them.
    Other variations and activities will suggest themselves to you
    as you begin to use the technique.

## BASIC SITUATIONS

1. Waiting outside the head's room.

2. Being interviewed.

3. A row with my best friend.

4. Riding my bike without brakes.

5. Trying on new clothes.

6. Coming home late at night.

7. Taking a big part in a play.

8. Doing my homework.

9. Having a shower.

10. Doing something secretly.

11. Jumping on a trampoline.

12. Washing up.

13. Lying on the beach.

14. Going up a dark lane at night.

15. My first day at work.

16. Having a hair-cut.

17. Waking up.

18. Visiting somebody in hospital.

19. Riding a horse.

20. Answering questions in class.

21. Travelling on the bus without paying my fare.

22. Saying I am sorry.

23. Taking a purse I found to the police station.

24. Going for a walk by myself.

25. Waiting to go out with my friends.

26. Watching a funeral.

27. Having to meet a stranger.

28. Cooking.

29. Dancing at the disco.

30. Knowing my hands are sweaty.

31. Losing my temper.

32. Doing an exam.

SITUATIONS TEST

RECORD FORM

| SORT | SITUATIONS USED | SIMILARITY | CONTRAST |
|---|---|---|---|
| 1 | | | |
| . 2 | | | |
| 3 | | | |
| 4 | | | |
| 5 | | | |
| 6 | | | |
| 7 | | | |
| 8 | | | |
| 9 | | | |
| 10 | | | |
| 11 | | | |
| 12 | | | |
| 13 | | | |
| 14 | | | |
| 15 | | | |
| 16 | | | |
| 17 | | | |
| 18 | | | |
| 19 | | | |
| 20 | | | |
| 21 | | | |
| 22 | | | |
| 23 | | | |
| 24 | | | |

LIFE SPACE PLAYS

Notes for the teacher:

1. This is one way of using drama in counselling. As the pupil makes his play he reveals very important attitudes and values which can be discussed afterwards. This is an example of the indirect approach to problems.

2. You should duplicate lists of characters and "starter" sentences. Two examples are given. Note that the pupil should always be able to choose his characters.

3. You only want the main elements of the plot, although it is useful for a group to act it after you have discussed it with the pupil.

For the pupil:

1. Choose three or four characters from the list. Give each one you choose a name.

2. Choose a part for yourself and build the play around that character. You may want a character not included in the list. We have left a line for you to describe him.

3. The first sentence is often the hardest to write in a play. To help you we have provided three sentences from which you can choose one. Only use it if you feel you need help in getting started. Your own sentence would be better.

4. Your teacher will let you tell, record or write the outline of the plot. Later, you may be able to act it.

## LIFE SPACE PLAYS

CHOOSE THREE OR FOUR CHARACTERS ONLY.  CROSS OUT THE ONES YOU DO NOT WANT

| THE CHARACTERS | THE ACTOR'S NAME |
|---|---|
| Someone who tries very hard | .............................. |
| A boy who feels he does not get a fair deal. | .............................. |
| A helpful adult | .............................. |
| Someone who is very successful and clever | .............................. |
| A nice girl | .............................. |
| Someone who is often ill or unwell | .............................. |
| A boy who likes excitement | .............................. |
| .............................. | .............................. |

Starting sentences you might like to use:

1.  It was just as I expected .....................................
2.  It was one of those dull days which make you feel fed up, but ..................................................
3.  At last something happened.
    ..................................................
    ..................................................

| THE CHARACTERS | THE ACTOR'S NAME |
|---|---|
| A person always in trouble | .............................. |
| A gang leader | .............................. |
| Somebody who uses their brains | .............................. |
| A boy people like very much | .............................. |
| Somebody who has a secret | .............................. |
| An honest and courageous boy | .............................. |
| Somebody who can't help doing silly things, but doesn't mean to | .............................. |
| A person who makes you laugh | .............................. |
| .............................. | .............................. |

Starting sentences you might like to use:

1.  It was very quiet and still when ..............................
2.  Honesty pays because ..............................
3.  Quite by chance the two boys met that evening and ..............
    ..................................................

## THE JOB I WOULD LIKE

### NOTES FOR THE USER

1.  This questionnaire is typical of the simple aids to vocational counselling that can be devised by any teacher. It is concerned with some of the social and psychological factors that are crucial in work satisfaction.

2.  It is useful to write each statement on a separate card. When the pupil has filled in the duplicated questionnaire he can lay out the cards under the headings of "very important" and "not at all important". This allows him to see what has gone into either category. It is useful to get him to rank the "very important" items. A great deal of thought and discussion usually follows this.

3.  A few pupils may not understand the different implications of item 2 and item 8. Check this.

4.  Take the "fairly important" group and ask what would make them become "very important".

THE JOB I WOULD LIKE

What to do:
1. This form lists a number of things that are found in different jobs.
   It will be very helpful to you to know which are important to you.
   Your counsellor or teacher will explain why.
2. These statements are below together with three columns headed
   "Very Important", "Fairly Important","Not at all Important".
   Read each item and then tick the column which shows how important
   that job quality is to you.

|  | Very Important | Fairly Important | Not at all Important |
|---|---|---|---|
| 1. Lets me meet a lot of people. | | | |
| 2. Has a good pension. | | | |
| 3. Where I can be my own boss one day. | | | |
| 4. Gives me a chance of promotion. | | | |
| 5. Be near home. | | | |
| 6. Be always new things to do. | | | |
| 7. Gives plenty of money straight away. | | | |
| 8. Where it is hard to get the sack. | | | |
| 9. Where I have to take a lot of responsibility. | | | |
| 10. Lets me use my hands. | | | |
| 11. Where somebody tells my just what to do. | | | |
| 12. Lets me work on my own at my own rate. | | | |
| 13. The same as my father/mother * does or very like it. | | | |
| 14. Makes me think a lot. | | | |
| 15. The same every day. | | | |
| 16. Something skilled. Learning a trade or getting trained. | | | |
| 17. Where I have to talk to people a lot. | | | |
| 18. Be in a big firm. | | | |
| 19. Be useful to other people. | | | |
| 20. Be in a little firm. | | | |

* Delete the alternative you do not wish to use.

need to improve the self-picture of the pupil, helping him to see himself more positively and as a person of worth. Next we need to understand his world view or what he predicts will happen when he does certain things. Underlying this chapter is the idea that it is the way that people see themselves and the outside world which determines how they behave, rather than forces which are outside them.

A number of techniques have been suggested which are capable of development by any imaginative teacher. The aim is that of building meaningful communication between pupil and counsellor—meaningful because it develops to suit the pupil, and does not come from the preconceived ideas of the counsellor about the problem. We are dealing with the ideas and perceptions of the pupil which operate to determine the coping strategies he uses and his reactions to stress and problem situations. Let me clearly state that we are not trying to devise home-made projection tests designed to reveal unconscious feelings and conflicts, but merely instruments which aid a pupil's self-understanding. This talk of projection tests has been necessary because we must rid ourselves of any idea that school counselling is for the abnormal. We must be clear in our own minds, and make it evident to both pupils and colleagues, that our concern is with helping individuals tackle developmental tasks common to all adolescents. Although they may not be succeeding by themselves, the fact that help is needed does not make them abnormal.

If the line is reproduced which represents the first phase of counselling, then the techniques in this chapter break it at two points:—

(i) *Concern with "what is"*. Understanding things as they are, e.g. the self-image or the pupil's picture of himself and others.

(ii) *The meaning of this*. The meaning of what is present in the pupil. The predictions he makes about his own actions and those of others

You can see that the first step is concerned with self-image and finding out what is present, rather than imposing our own notions about what ought to be present. The next, very logical, step is discovering the effect this has upon the pupil's view of the world and behaviour. All the techniques we use are based upon the idea that the pupil must be an active participant in this process and work to produce the information, and not the passive partner in a process of questioning. Not only should he be kept active, but we should also make it clear that this information is always for his use and not for the benefit of the counsellor. Without this, the question, "What is he going to do with this?" enters to distort the counselling. Only when the pupil is certain that counselling is for his benefit will the sense of threat implicit in it be removed. The techniques which are outlined are not only means which lead to change of behaviour and the acquisition of more effective coping strategies: they also help young people gain a sense of positive identity and a sense of direction and purpose.

---

## REFERENCES

Allport, G. (1954) *Handbook of Social Psychology*, (Ed. G. Lidzey). Vol. 1, 43-45. Reading, Mass: Addison–Wesley Co.

Bannister, D. and Fransella, F. (1971) *Inquiring Man*, London: Penguin.

Bernstein, B.B. (1965) "A socio–linguistic approach to social learning", in *Penguin Survey of the Social Sciences*. Ed. Gould J.B. London: Penguin Books.

—— (1971) *Class, Codes and Control, Vol. 1*, London: Routledge & Kegan Paul.

Birney, R., Burdick, H. and Teevan, R. (1969) *Fear of Failure*, New York: Van Nostrand–Reinhold Co.

Fishbein, M. (Ed) (1967) *Readings In Attitude Theory and Measurement*, New York: Wiley.

Hayes, B. and Hough, P. (1971) *The Perception of Other Work Roles: Implications for Job Change*, Leeds: Dept. of Management Studies, University of Leeds.

Kelly, G. (1955) *Psychology of Personal Constructs*, New York: Norton.

Ravenette, A.T. (1967) "Everyone His Own Scientist", *Newsletters,* London: Assoc. of Educational Psychologists.

Read, H. (1943) *Education Through Art,* London: Faber & Faber.

Riden, D. (1970) *D.S.C. Dissertation,* Swansea University College.

Rosenberg, M. (1965) *Society and the Adolescent Self Image,* Princeton, N. J.: Princeton University Press.

Strang, R. (1957) *The Adolescent Views Himself,* New York: McGraw-Hill.

Sugarman, B. (1967) "Involvement in Youth Culture. Academic Achievement and Conformity in School", *Br. Jr. Sociol.,* 18, No. 2, 151–164.

Turner, R. (1962) "Role-Taking: Process Versus Conformity", in Rose, A. (Ed), *Human Behaviour and Social Processes,* London: Routledge & Kegan Paul.

Wylie, R. (1961) *The Self Concept,* Lincoln: University of Nebraska Press.

# CHAPTER FIVE

# TECHNIQUES IN THE SECOND PHASE OF COUNSELLING

*The purpose of this chapter*

The specific focus is on three of the many techniques which are available, but the general purpose is to demonstrate the need for the counsellor to analyse the coping strategies used by a pupil in response to the situations which cause him to react by feeling stress and tension. These techniques have been selected for discussion because they relate very closely to those used in teaching, reinforcing the emphasis in this book on the link between teaching and counselling. They also reflect the developmental emphasis of counselling in schools because they fully involve the pupil by making him active and are intended to put him in control of his life situation to the greatest possible degree. The general theme in this chapter is that of the development of viable coping strategies and of "life-planning" skills. The discussion again underlines the dependence of the counsellor on his fellow teachers, stressing the valuable contribution they can make to the counselling process.

Other relevant techniques which could be used in this phase are mentioned, but the discussion is kept brief because many of them require considerable training and, if mishandled, could result in damage to the pupil.

### The questions asked in this chapter

The questions raised in this chapter are capable of much more thorough exploration than can be undertaken in this book. They are:

(i) What are the uses of role playing? What dangers are inherent in this technique?

(ii) What is the significance of coping strategies? How can a counsellor help pupils develop more effective ways of coping?

(iii) Is there a place for the use of simulation in counselling? How can it be used to stimulate development in adolescence?

(iv) The central question is: Can we do anything to ensure that the new attitudes and aspirations are transferred from the counselling interview into behaviour in the real life situation?

### Structuring your reading

Because it is so familiar, the material of this chapter may seem deceptively simple. You may find it useful to read the summary first, before beginning on the main subject matter.

---

### The second phase

School counselling is a very practical activity. This practicality however is based upon the ability to give due weight to the first phase of counselling which allows us to understand a situation before we rush into action. As we get to grips with the first phase, a sense of direction and purpose emerges in which the pupil decides upon the goals and targets that he wishes to reach. We have the responsibility of looking at the feasibility of these, and also of assessing the skills which will have to be acquired if he is to attain his goals. Quite serious deficits of intellectual and social skills are often revealed during the first phase of counselling, and it is part of the counsellor's task to remedy this situation during the second stage of counselling.

We are faced with the equivalent of the old problem of transfer of training. We can get a change in self-perception, new attitudes and new levels of aspiration in the face-to-face counselling interviews, but we need to ensure that a pupil can successfully put these into practice in his everyday life. Without this, counselling is almost a waste of time. In the following sections we shall be discussing such essential social and intellectual skills as role-taking and standpoint-taking, which means that we must use role-playing and simulation techniques. There is no reason why the second phase of counselling should be confined to individual counselling, for it *may* be more effective to use group counselling at this task-orientated stage. The counsellor always has the responsibility of evaluating the situation and then of deciding which is the most efficient strategy. We also need to face the fact that our role may change radically during the final stage of counselling because our isolated efforts will be ineffective. We will often need to call upon our colleagues and ask them to take the active participant role outlined in the second chapter. The efficient school counsellor therefore possesses the capacity to adapt his own role according to the circumstances and the stage of counselling, often handing over the major responsibility for action to his colleagues, becoming a mobilizer and co-ordinator of resources.

### Role-playing

Attention is now being shifted from the pupil's thoughts and feelings to his actual behaviour in school and class. Role-playing is an important technique, springing from the seminal work of Moreno (1951), which helps behaviour and intellectual processes as well as feelings. It may be difficult to connect role-playing with intellectual activities, but a moment's thought on the need to present and analyse a situation from several viewpoints in, for example, a good historical essay provides a clue as to the link. If role-playing is wisely used, then a pupil will gain increased ability to take the standpoints of other people and predict how they will behave in the situation under examination. Perhaps more importantly, it can enlarge the pupil's picture of himself because it provides him with new ideas of what are possible kinds of behaviour for him. We can use role-playing as a way of enlarging the pupil's construct system in areas where this is necessary and of changing the predictions he associates with certain situations. Failure in a subject which is not due to lack of ability provides one example. Recently a school counsellor gave me an example of the use of role-playing to prepare a boy to take examinations in the company of other boys. For several years this pupil could only take an examination in a room on his own with the invigilator. Through role-playing he was able to anticipate the panic he felt when examined with other boys and to come to terms with it. It should be scarcely necessary to point out that role-play was only one weapon in the counsellor's approach to this problem. The whole question of the boy's self-concept and his relationships with peers and his parents were involved in this counselling.

Role-playing is one method of breaking into the stereotypical responses to situations which are often presented by pupils with limited language ability, or by those coming from rigid homes where initiative has been suppressed. It gives tools for building up new relationships with others. It is useful in counselling because it is "make believe", providing the anxious pupil with protection. To push him into premature action would be irresponsible, and to tell him of all his deficiencies would be destructive; but through role-playing he can gradually come to terms with himself. Role-play is not only preparation for the inadequate pupil, it is protection. The element of "play" and the fact that it is one step away from reality is a safety device for both counsellor and pupil. Once role-play begins the counsellor may learn a great deal about the fears and attitudes of the boy or girl and these may alter his approach to the situation. It is possible to build up a list of situations for role-playing once the second phase of counselling is entered, but in my experience the best way is to allow the actual role-playing to arise out of the counselling.

Although the counsellor has analysed the situation and made some decisions about the skills that will have to be taught through the activity, it is best to wait for an opportunity to arise in the sessions. Pupils will then see the point of the role-playing more clearly and will be enthusiastic about it. This also leads to the next essential step. Just as one does not force the role-playing upon pupils, so does one not embark upon it without adequate discussion. I always explain why it would be useful and what the technique can and cannot do. Without this discussion, role-playing becomes an imposed activity which is foreign to developmental counselling and to the principle that the pupil should be encouraged to become actively responsible for himself, and it will almost certainly be abortive. The discussion should clarify the situation and indicate the possibilities for alternative action. I find it useful to write down the ideas produced by pupils on a sheet of paper or on the blackboard. In a situation concerned with bullying, it was possible to get from the boy who was being bullied some ideas about the way in which he provoked the bullying, the signals he sent to others of being different from them and of his reactions to being pushed about. This then led to very constructive role-playing where new possibilities were put forward by the boy. Preliminary discussion seems to be essential if precious time is not to be used up without result. It has also proved useful to tape record the role-play, and then listen to it together. At this point it is sometimes very useful to introduce a form of peer counselling in which a friend of the pupil or several of his classmates are invited to discuss the effectiveness of the tactics he has used and the general response they think he would draw out from others.

Standpoint taking is central to role-playing, and it is also the key to better interpersonal relationships. Once you are able to take the standpoint of others, then it is possible to anticipate their reactions to your own behaviour and to modify it. The essential thing in role-playing is that role *reversal* must always be included. In role-playing a father-and-son situation, the pupil should play both roles—father and son—in turn. Without this the impact is lost, and the discrepancies and similarities between the viewpoints of father and son will not be clear. I find it helpful to limit the role-playing to a very precise situation which has occurred recently, and to record both episodes. We then listen to it immediately and discuss very thoroughly. It is then very useful to ask the pupil to play the role of the counsellor, and in effect act as his own counsellor. This means the counsellor has to play the role of the pupil, and this makes it necessary to discuss the validity of the counsellor's interpretation of the pupil's viewpoint at the end of the performance. Sometimes I encourage the pupil to halt the role-playing when he feels my rendering of his role is inaccurate. When pupils play the counsellor's role it is not uncommon to find them giving very authoritarian advice or suggesting lines of action which would be disastrous. This is extremely valuable because the counsellor then explores this in subsequent discussion and a great deal of useful learning occurs. Perhaps it is now clear that role-playing is conceived as a real process of learning, rather than a single episode which somehow or other drastically changes a situation. It is always followed by discussion in which further alternatives and refinements are examined and the consequences and costs of the behaviours are evaluated. Further re-enactments occur, and usually a great deal of valuable learning takes place. But role-playing works with some pupils and not with others, and there is no point in continuing if it does not yield results. Sometimes it works and sometimes it doesn't; I am unable to say why.

Although a well-planned series of role-playing episodes widens the pupil's concept of himself and his understanding of other people and provides him with new possibilities of behaviour, it can be a very dangerous tool. Perhaps most destructive is the danger of implying to the pupil that there is a certain way in which he *ought* to behave, or that certain emotions and responses are required of him. If we let this happen, then role-playing becomes a highly authoritarian technique in which the pupil is being manipulated by the counsellor to come to the conclusion that certain modes of behaviour and action are more desirable than others. This does not deny the morality of counselling, nor does it deny the fact that in the second phase of counselling we do not accept the pupil as less than he can be. Real standards exist, but the way in which these standards are achieved are not dictated by the counsellor, for if this happened they would be external rather than willingly accepted. You will recall that our aim is to build up controls from within the pupil. If we want to impose rigid ways of behaving on a pupil, then it would be easier to surround him with sanctions and punishments. The aim of role-playing is to provide an approximation of the situation and the behaviour, letting the pupil decide for himself whether these strategies and ways of behaving suit him, and to try to anticipate the costs and effort involved so that he is prepared for this when he has to face it in real life.

I have mentioned the importance of the mask of make believe. Apart from providing protection, it also operates to prevent the teaching element from becoming too restrictive, because the counsellor does not appear to be demanding that the pupil should change in any particular way. This relates to the transfer of behaviour from the role-playing situation to real life. Role-playing presents an over-simplified picture because it lacks many of the constraints and difficulties of reality. However carefully we devise and work through a situation, many factors have to be omitted or are not anticipated, and it can be only too easy to stimulate a very suggestible pupil to attempt something for which he is not yet adequately equipped. An excitable pupil can be rushed into impulsive action due to the stimulus of role-playing. In both cases these pupils may meet gross failure and have their previous predictions about negative consequences of such actions confirmed. This does not mean that failure can always be prevented, but it is wrong to produce it through ill-thought-out role-playing which pushes pupils towards action without consideration of the consequences. Indeed role-playing can and should be used to inoculate pupils against the experience of failure, so that they continue to try despite initial lack of success. It now becomes clearer why role-playing should be followed by very thorough discussion, and should not be used as a technique in isolation. In this stage of counselling we use role-playing to show a boy the possibility of alternative behaviour and to give him a glimpse of new and attractive perspectives of himself. But we realize that he needs time to think about this. Unless such new vistas become part of his picture of himself, it is unlikely that there will be any worthwhile transfer from role-playing to everday life. Premature attempts at transfer can cause dismay, self-doubt, and, as a reaction to this, the hardening of original attitudes and behaviour. This leads to my insistence on the need for care and sensitivity in using the technique.

Role-playing can be used to deal with situations as they arise in counselling. There is also another way it can be used, which is derived from the work of George Kelly. In this variation, I adopt the following technique when the pupil is becoming clear about his aspirations for change. I go away and produce a character sketch of the sort of person he seems to want to become. This is then brought to him, and we discuss it together. We ask questions about the reality of the sketch—is this person credible? Does the way he behaves seem right for a boy of his age? How will adults and friends view such a person? I then ask the pupil to produce a modified sketch of this character in his own terms. This does not necessarily mean writing, because after some discussion it can be recorded and we discuss the recording. After this preparatory work, we then begin to discuss actual behavioural change in the pupil. He then writes or records a sketch of himself as he wants to behave. This is carefully structured and broken down into reasonable steps so that he is not faced with impossible amounts of change. The next step is that of implementation of the behaviour. He is asked to try to behave as nearly as possible like that person for a short period, preferably about three days, after which we discuss what has happened and modify the sketch. Continuous support is necessary at this point, and the counsellor must be available. Colleagues will have been informed about this and their support obtained so that a climate favourable to success is created. Even so, many difficulties may arise and it is crucial that one maintains the trial or experimental atmosphere to prevent undue reactions to failure and unanticipated difficulties.

The procedure which has been outlined has been found to be very productive in my own counselling, but it does demand a great deal of thought and expenditure of energy by the counsellor. The involvement of colleagues is crucial, and although the use of a counselling conference provides structured support, informal contacts can be just as useful. Let us be clear that this is a process of experimentation in which constant modifications of behaviour and the trial role occur. Role-playing is linked with the real life situation. Pupil and counsellor become partners in a joint enterprise, but the façade of make-believe is maintained as long as is necessary. Usually this is discarded without either partner noticing what is happening. This technique can be used with groups where some common problem such as underfunctioning is the focus of the group counselling. In this situation pupils can work in pairs, but the method can be used in a number of ways, the group providing not only support but also constructive feedback about performances.

In the more usual forms of role-playing subsequent activity need not be confined to direct discussion, for pupils can be encouraged to record stories about similar problem situations and characters. It is possible to involve the drama specialist in this, using his special skills and sensitivity. In these activities the counsellor gives feedback and supplies reinforcements which accelerate development.

Behind this brief description of the use of role-playing in counselling lies a concept of role as a flexible pattern of behaviour which is modifiable by the individual, rather than as a firmly prescribed set of behaviours or a static set of rights and obligations. We are concerned in education with a process of role-taking and role-making, and with the way in which a pupil interprets his various roles. This is important, for example, we can hold a rigid idea of the role of the ideal pupil and be impatient of deviations from this narrowly defined way of behaving. The developmental approach to counselling requires that the counsellor should see the role—of pupil, son or daughter or adolescent—as somthing which is created and played out according to the individual's predictive system, rather than being totally imposed on him from outside. It is closely associated with the adolescent's skill in understanding the standpoints of other people. We have to train ourselves to think of roles as partly a product of the way *we think* that the people with whom we work and live see us and react to our behaviour. The crucial words lie in the phrase "we think". This underlines the need for the counsellor to appreciate the link between a pupil's perceptions and his behaviour. If a boy feels that he is being treated unfairly or is discriminated against, then he behaves as though this were the case, even when it is obvious to the impartial observer that this is far from being true. He may eventually produce a situation where he is in fact treated in this way, confirming his own role as scapegoat or victim.

In making use of role-playing in counselling, there are two major tasks we have to keep in mind. We have to persuade the pupil that it is important for him to understand the perspective of the other person and we must help him to make the effort to understand this. This is more easily said than done, when the viewpoint to be understood is that of the teacher, and the pupil is one who has rejected the values of the school and who is unaccustomed to trying to make himself clear to other people. Next we have to train him to make accurate discriminations about the attributes of certain role holders. This can be understood when we look at the reactions of certain pupils to the role qualities associated with the police. Some of us will not only see the punitive side of the policeman's behaviour, but will see a protective element and attribute positive qualities to him. Others will only see the negative and constraining elements. This has a very serious implication for role-playing in counselling. We need to help a pupil express as clearly and fully as he can his existing views of teachers, policemen or his peers before we attempt to extend them. To omit this step is to feed new information into an unknown set of ideas and can create further confusion and misinterpretation—rather like the well-meaning adult who attempts to answer a young child's ideas about sex and birth without allowing him a chance to express his own phantasies: the adult's factual information is then mixed up with the child's phantasies about anal and oral birth and very strange confusions indeed are created.

In an earlier chapter we saw that counselling is an exchange of benefits, and that if these exchanges are too costly pupils will opt out of counselling. We make difficulties when we fail to estimate the difference between the behaviour tried out in role-play and the reference groups of the individual. Reference groups are the groups from which he takes his values, and from which he derives his major standpoints. Teachers and counsellors often feel impotent in the face of peer group pulls and pressures. Yet it is often easy to confuse shadow with substance. Often what we are reacting against is only symbolic, in the sense that hair style and dress are symbols of a sense of belonging to a particular group which provides an identity. Many pupils wearing skinhead hair styles and clothing are not drawn into the brawls and aggressiveness which have become associated with that movement. They merely talk about it. The position is more serious when pupils are actively taking up roles in delinquent or anti-school groups. Yet we need not be paralysed and passive. People choose their reference and membership groups because they meet certain personal needs. The pupil gives these groups meaning and interprets the significance of membership according to his own construct system; the group does not impose an identity upon a passive pupil. Once we have seen that a boy is not the creature of his reference or membership group, then we can ask what basic needs are met in this group and what definition of self is offered by the group which seems important to him. We can see how this works if we consider the case of the youth who needs to see himself as tough, and who is only sure that he is tough when he has called out the condemnation of the teacher and gained the applause of an appropriate peer group. We then deal with this need for toughness, which may cover uncertainty and the need for success and status. If we cannot provide satisfying alternatives then we are going to be of little service. Role-playing and creative drama can help such pupils by giving them the chance to express their needs as well as learn new role behaviours. Role-playing activity which indicates that a boy is expected to sever himself from these essential groups without any alternative supports being available will only cause anxiety and anger, leading him to reject counselling. We have two lines of attack. We can help people change their ideas about the ways in which their needs can be met and the groups which will do this, and we can provide new experiences of satisfaction by incorporating them into new groups. The importance of group counselling methods is clear from these remarks. The essential step is to realize that the contrasts in behaviour must not be too sharp, or role-playing becomes threatening: the whole process is a gradual one. The peer models we offer both through role-playing and group composition must not be so different that the boy cannot accept them. At first I often tried to attach a not too bright working-class boy to a very able and successful middle-class boy, but as the years passed I have learned caution. The demands made were too heavy for both of them. Now I would tend to attach such a boy to a group of stable and achieving working-class boys, where there is a common language for communication.

Role-playing can be used to shift a pupil from one reference group to another, as his sense of purpose and direction emerges. During the last year I have also used it in other ways. In one case it helped an able boy from a poor background to understand his parents' resistances to his ambition to go to university, and it provided him with the means of coping with their anxieties and fears that he "was over-reaching himself". In another, a bed-wetter was helped to realize the reactions of his peers to the smell that came from a lack of washing; this was followed by very practical steps. It was possible for another pupil to discover how he provoked teachers and pupils into attacking him, and to learn new behaviours which gave him the attention he wanted. More generally, I have found that role-playing allows pupils to realize for themselves the nature of the curious egocentrism of the identity crisis of adolescent. They seem to feel that they are unique and that nobody else has ever experienced the emotions and feelings that beset them. Sometimes this produces a feeling of isolation which is harmful, and group role-playing allows them to see that they are not alone. They can also see that their feelings and experiences can still be understood by the middle-aged.

## Coping strategies

Our discussion of role-playing has already touched upon the need for coping strategies. Many pupils have a problem which forms the core of the counselling process, and the solution of this problem is necessary for well-being. The work of Lazarus (1966) provides a valuable guide to the school counsellor. In dealing with developmental problems the counsellor is dealing with situations which provoke stress, reactions to stress and to the important idea of threat. In the task-orientated phase of counselling we begin to ask precise questions about which situations, events or persons provoke stress reactions in a pupil. We recognize that we must not impose our own idea of what *ought* to be stressful on to someone else. We will have gained some ideas of this during the first phase, but now we have to attack the subject vigorously. Once we know which situations, events or persons provoke stress for a boy, we investigate the way in which he usually deals with the stress. We note such clear trends as avoidance through illness, or aggressive attack. Our approach is to link situations and reactions of stress by using the concept of *threat*. In practical terms, threat means that a pupil anticipates harm to himself. This seems so obvious that it hardly merits description, yet in working with pupils we often fail to recognize sources of threat for them. Different pupils see different things as threatening, and sometimes this threat can reside in very ordinary situations. Most of us when at school may have coped with undressing for gym or answering questions in class, yet these can be very threatening to some pupils. I have had to learn that some children think of people and events as dangerous when most of us see them as not at all threatening or even look forward to them. Sometimes I have totally failed to comprehend the nature of the threat until very late in counselling. Often the boy has been unsure himself about the source of threat, and until it was located, we made little progress. Sometimes the problem the pupil comes with is not the real problem: sometimes it is in fact this obscure sense of unidentified threats which has impelled him to seek support. It is easy to understand varied perceptions of the same situation as threatening if we look at the reaction of the supporters of opposing teams when a player is sent off in a football match. The supporter of the disciplined player's team interprets the situation as one of bias and unfairness and therefore threatening, whilst the other feels that the situation is fair and just.

This consideration of threat may seem dramatic, but in fact is practical, for unless we understand what it is that is seen as threatening, we cannot understand the way in which he tries to cope with the situation. When something is threatening to a pupil, he is predicting that he is going to get hurt unless he takes certain steps. We have to spend time in understanding his idiosyncratic process of appraisal which defines certain objects and events as potentially harmful.

Lazarus (1966) produces a complex and sophisticated two-stage model of the process of appraisal and coping which more than amply repays study. Here I offer a crude version, which is adapted to the needs of the school counsellor who is concerned with the coping strategies of adolescent pupils. To see threats means that the pupil has had to scan the situation. This scanning is what Lazarus calls the *primary appraisal process*. In this scanning the pupil registers certain cues which produce a sense of threat in him. This is not objective evaluation, but a highly personalized process to which many factors lying in the past history and personality of the pupil contribute. This process determines whether he perceives danger or threat. The school counsellor is not concerned with those factors which lie in the past or are beyond his competence, but with the fact that there is threat in certain situations for that boy and that he is reacting to it. We can see that again it is the interpretation the individual places upon events that is crucial. Once the pupil detects threat, he brings into play his methods of coping. This *secondary stage of appraisal*, as Lazarus calls it, is concerned with more precise specification of the agent of harm, followed by an assessment of ways of coping in terms of their costs and the outcomes they produce.

This will perhaps seem self-evident, yet it does have important implications for the counsellor in the second phase of counselling. We will want to help a pupil see his reactions are unjustified when the harm he detects is unrealistic, and we shall want to put him into control of the situation so that he does not continue to react blindly. In helping pupils make more realistic appraisals of situations, I have found a good first step is to get them to draw out their reactions in a diagrammatic form. Sometimes, I then get them to draw out in the same way the coping strategies which would be used by an admired friend or adult so that they begin to see alternative possibilities. This is particularly important with the less academic pupil who can deal with these problems provided they are made personal and not put in abstract terms. Sometimes the question, "how do you think I would behave?" produces surprisingly accurate responses. We then go on to discuss whether or not this way of coping is possible for the boy and the modifications which would be necessary. We often end up with a sheet of paper which contains the following information:

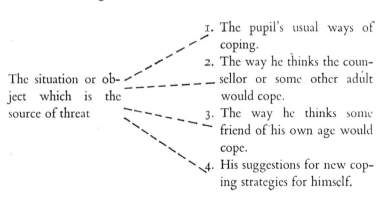

The situation or object which is the source of threat

1. The pupil's usual ways of coping.
2. The way he thinks the counsellor or some other adult would cope.
3. The way he thinks some friend of his own age would cope.
4. His suggestions for new coping strategies for himself.

The object of all this is to put him into control of a situation which seemed to him to be out of hand and make him aware of the possibilities of alternative ways of behaving. He is not told about these, but discovers them through his own activity. We then proceed to draw up diagrams which tell us about the costs and consequences of his suggestions for new ways of behaving, comparing them with the old situation. I have found this particularly useful with able boys who are failing in school and with those who are uncertain whether they want to stay on to take examinations as well as with those who are concerned because they seem to be getting into trouble either with the law or with teachers. In most cases, this is a productive device when we really begin to work out the ways of reaching the goals that the boy wants to attain. These goals, we should remember, are social and emotional as well as academic.

If we ask when a pupil is most likely to feel threatened we see the importance of the first phase of counselling. The strongest sense of threat comes when important aspects of the self-picture seems to be challenged by a situation or person. Threats to his status with peers, any apparent questioning of his masculinity or of his vocational aspirations produce severe reactions in the adolescent boy. As well as listening and becoming sensitive to the cues which trigger off threat reactions in the pupil, we have to make him active so that he can begin to make sense out of what is happening to him. A catalogue of situations and cues which produce the sense of threat is built up, and the common elements identified. The counsellor's role will include alerting other teachers to the pupil's reactions and gaining their support so that his new strategies are likely to succeed. We can split the task into two parts based on a division between what is happening within the boy and what is going on in the environment. We may need to concentrate at first on helping him modify his perceptions of what constitutes a threat and change his belief systems about the general nature of the transactions between himself and others. Adolescents do sometimes view the world as a jungle. They may see themselves as victims, and they may be acutely suspicious of those in authority without any objective reason. But, even in the most depressing circumstances, there are resources, and there is help available. The pupil may not be able to recognize the resources, so the counsellor draws his attention to them, adopting a strategy which is aimed at removing the sense of helplessness which can overwhelm the adolescent under pressure.

The method is simple, building on the teacher's skill in breaking down subjects and the curriculum into small steps. We identify the sources of threat, and then evaluate the strategies developed by the pupil to cope with threat. Next, we use diagrams, including the life space diagram, to make clear the relevant factors in the situation. Then we begin to assess the resources available which could be used. I often build up a balance sheet with the pupil, which puts all this clearly for him. We can then decide on our objectives in terms of behaviour. We can use some of the findings of the behavioural therapists, and make a list of tasks we intend to accomplish. It is best to rank these from the most difficult to the least difficult, and to begin to deal with the easiest. This is not always possible, for some situations may be urgent and immediate action may be necessary. The counsellor and pupil then together produce simple diagrams which specify the routes to a certain goal and the changes in behaviour which will be necessary. We pay great attention to the costs and to the possibility of failure. We carefully work out the first steps in the counselling session. These are then implemented with the knowledge and support of colleagues. Role-playing is used in the way described above as a preliminary.

A caution is necessary. We must relate what we do to the pupil's general style of coping, for problem-solving techniques must always be related to the person who is going to use them. An effective instrument in the hands of one person becomes a blunt tool when it is used by another. Perhaps we understand this most easily by looking at our acquaintances. Some of them tend to cope by conformity and by immediate compliance to the wishes of others: some may use aggressive attack as their general coping strategy. There are those who deny the fact that they possess even those weaknesses common to the human conditions, whereas others flaunt their frailties as a reason for evading the responsibilities that should be accepted as part of adulthood. This is, of course, an oversimplification of the situation and it denies many subtleties, yet it may help us grasp what is meant by a general style of coping. I recall pupils who always tended to emphasize success and avoid seeing any failures, whilst others concentrated on their failures, sometimes to the extent of devaluing their very real successes. If we suggest strategies and behaviour which conflict to an extreme degree with a boy's usual way of coping, then we probably arouse resistances and create unnecessary stress. This is avoided by involving him fully in the process and by treating him as a mature person.

### The use of simulation techniques

There is a great deal of overlap between the techniques of role-playing and simulation and it is only honest to say that the distinction may be more useful in exposition than in practice. Role-playing seems to be concerned with the development of the skills of empathy and standpoint taking, whilst simulation stresses the learning of behaviour and the social skills, such as bargaining between participants. Yet skills are undoubtedly learned during role-playing, whilst simulation does require anticipation of the responses of others in the development of standpoint taking. It is the weighting towards social learning and the rules of behaviour which differentiates simulation.

The teaching element in simulation is considerable, for we need to abstract from the selected situation the rules of interaction. We will describe the permissible actions, the obligations and expectations found in the situation, and the penalties for breaking the rules. If we are going to use simulation usefully in developmental counselling, then I believe we need to take a slightly different approach than is customary. The pupil should be actively involved in *working out* the simulation, rather than the counsellor devising a situation which is then presented to the child. In counselling we get a number of two or three person situations based upon transactions over clothes, pocket-money, staying out late, helping at home or completing homework. A pupil (or a group of pupils) can build up a simulation, perhaps beginning with one of these situations. He can emphasize the bargaining and negotiation strategies involved and note their limits. It is often possible to proceed to the next situation and after this has been devised and enacted, the links between the separate situations can be discussed. One recent simulation which was devised as part of counselling concerned the behaviour of a boy who was occupying a clowning role in a form. He was split between his desire to do well in class and his desire to maintain prestige with his classmates. It is interesting to note that he was in a form taking a mixture of C.S.E. and O Levels where the teachers' expectations were mixed: some saw the boys as academic, and some tended to despise them. Little was needed to tip this boy either towards allegiance to the school or towards integration with a group intending to leave school as soon as their parents permitted. The form teacher, who also taught them two subjects, was anxious not to be forced into a punitive role, but at the same time was also anxious about a breach in discipline. There was another boy who tended to use the first boy to act out for him, stimulating him into misbehaviour, whilst preserving his own respectability. A simple simulation was worked out by the boys involved and the counsellor in which the aims and intentions of each participant were specified and a great deal of change of behaviour seemed to occur in the group. Certainly there was a surprising appreciation of the viewpoint of the teacher. Most of the gains seemed to spring from devising the simulation, rather than from its performance. It seems best that the simulations used in counselling should come from the actual problems which exist. One useful field for simulations derives from the choices made by younger secondary school pupils in various situations, e.g. when they are selecting a football team. Questions about why pupils are chosen for a particular side, what happens when someone is not chosen for the side he wishes to be on and many others open the way up for a great deal of social learning within a meaningful context.

It is useful to look at simulation more closely, although good discussions exist such as that of Tansey (1971). We begin by noting that simulation is, by logical definition, an attempt to replicate reality. Obviously it can never be a perfect replication for then there would be no difference between reality and the simulation. The fact that simulation always means a selective simplification of reality is no bad thing for it allows us to focus on the crucial relationships. The teacher-counsellor identifies the consequences which follow real life behaviours, proceeding to build simulations in which strategies can be rehearsed without the penalties actually falling on the pupil, although he is made aware of them. It has been mentioned above that simulation is concerned with the rules and norms of interaction, which makes it an ideal technique to use with those pupils who lack social competence. When pupils are seen to lack skill in the usual processes of mutual exchange and social bargaining, or seem to be able to accept authority only when they are strongly coerced because they do not understand the complementary nature of role behaviour, then we need the active technique of simulation.

We begin by asking ourselves what is the objective of this simulation. Once we have a clear answer to this—and it is surprisingly difficult to clarify our objectives at times—the next step is to break down the simulation in a way which approximates to the following:

1. THE TOPIC

   (i) Decide on the general situation which is the basis for the activity and then work out the main requirements. Decide whether you wish to emphasize the vocational, personal or social aspects of the situation.

   (ii) We then proceed to narrow the situation down into more specific aspects of the situation, e.g. we might work from the general vocational aspect to a problem of work adjustment. We then see that we are setting the problem in the context of authority relationships in work and finally decide to use a situation related to immediate supervision in work.

2. THE PROBLEM

   (i) Next specify a particular situation which provides the core of the interaction.

   (ii) Once this has been done it is possible to delineate the setting in which the incident is to occur with precision.

3. THE OUTCOMES

   (i) This is the area where muddles will reduce the efficiency of the simulation. There are two types of ending to a simulation.

We can have a single solution which represents the "right" answer or an end point where the pupils are left with a number of possibilities. The developmental school counsellor would usually subscribe to the latter approach, seeing the value of encouraging pupils to search continuously for further possibilities.

(ii) Examples of outcomes which could provide the core for counselling simulations are:

(a) The provision of experiences which make pupils desire to investigate a situation more completely.

(b) Creating awareness of major attitudes and opinions held by various sections of the public about that situation which is the basis of the simulation.

(c) The making of implicit attitudes and ideas overt.

(d) The development of social and emotional skills as well as intellectual ones of cognitive analysis.

We can easily build simulations which degenerate into pleasant activity and merely occupy time which denies the purposive and action orientated nature of developmental counselling. When he suspects this is happening the counsellor will find it helpful to ask himself the salient questions below:

Can simulations increase negative attitudes towards learning or reinforce stereotypes and prejudice?

Have we unwittingly built in self-defeating strategies which prevent us attaining our objectives? Have we, for example, overtly stressed co-operation whilst using procedures which are emphasizing the value of competition and winning? In other words, we must scan the simulations we devise to check that there are not implicit objectives inherent in the procedures and rules which conflict with the explicit objectives. This is the equivalent of situations in family communication where an overt message from parent to child is contradicted by a latent behavioural message.

After these simple questions have been answered—and as usual we will find that the answers are complex—we can then proceed to ask the following:

, Which of the three models of personality are we building into the simulation? Is it man in the process of becoming or man as a reactive being? In the simulation construction it is a fact that there are many temptations to stress the idea of man as merely responding to incentives. I have found it only too easy to build in concepts of personality which reflect the nineteenth century idea of a rational economic man who is devoting his energy to maximizing his gratifications, but are adolescents like this and are people really concerned with hedonistic gratification of such an obvious type? Is there no place for altruism?

What is the impact of losing on some pupils? Have we not only seen the need to think about this, but prepare ourselves to intervene constructively?

Have we considered our responsibility to assess the relationship between the personality of the individual and the role he takes? There can be unintended consequences from putting a boy who is uncertain about his masculinity into either strongly masculine roles or asking him to take a female position in the simulation.

Have we thought sufficiently about our actions in allocating roles in certain situations? Consider the impact of a family based simulation on a pupil who has recently been bereaved.

It could be argued that this section misuses the Socratic method by raising questions without dealing with them. This is quite deliberate because we have to answer such questions in our own way and in relation to the school in which we work. I am anxious to avoid giving ready made mixtures which are not applicable to the reader's situation. In planning a simulation I find it best to begin by drawing up a schema which incorporates the following:

1. A description of the basic event.

2. The role holders in the simulation.

3. The basic social relationships which are supposed to hold between these characters and the general nature of the interaction between them—competitive, supportive, antagonistic.
4. The rewards and punishments which are to be simulated.
5. The barriers to the attainment of the outcome.
6. The nature of the outcome.

Once this has been done it is helpful to try to anticipate the sequence of events, paying especial attention to critical incidents which may appear or that you wish to introduce. Critical incidents, for my purposes, are defined as those which could cause the sequence of events to be modified, halted or even reversed. The examination of the rules comes next and we need to be practical for there is little point in producing simulations which have rules too complex to be comprehended by a group of players. We need to examine:

1. The clarity and effectiveness of the rules.
2. The way in which we make it clear to the participants that these rules can be found in their own social world.
3. Many simulation makers divide rules into the following categories which show their function:

   (i) those which are concerned with the procedure and provide essential order in the simulation.
   (ii) those which operate when a situation of conflict or *impasse* arises.
   (iii) those which specify the responses of the players to one another.
   (iv) penalty rules.
   (v) those which say how a particular goal may be achieved.

It may now be obvious to the reader that the planning of simulations is a very stimulating exercise for both counsellor and pupils. Sometimes there are pressures in education which cause us to pay more attention to the content of what we teach than the processes by which pupils learn. We look at both the skills of thinking and of interaction in simulation which can, if rightly used, help the development of autonomy in the pupil. Counselling is the activity of the pupil just as much as it is that of the counsellor, whilst the last thing we want to produce are docile and convergent thinkers, although let me stress that counselling is not concerned with rebellion. It is concerned with change in education and the growth of constructive dialogue between pupils and teachers. If pupils are given experience of simulations and then taught how to make their own, we are providing them with a valuable tool with which they can understand life. It is a noteworthy fact that I have found that even groups of pupils who have been labelled as "hopeless" are capable of producing really good simulations and begin to develop questioning attitudes towards life. I have found that I have learned much from pupils as well as learning with them.

It is wise to scrutinize any simulation that one constructs asking about the costs of the procedures. A type of balance has to be achieved between the style of the simulation and the cost it involves. If we make it very close to life, then many complicating factors will have to be assimilated. This means that playing it becomes very difficult and demanding because so many considerations have to be held in mind by each player. The rules also become very complex. If we make it very simple and easy to play then it gives a false picture of reality, although this is overcome if we gradually increase its correspondence to real life. It is very tempting to devise simulations which are not only absorbing but contain elements of excitement and thrill. We then run the danger that the wrong things are being learned, or worse still, the excitement destroys learning. If we earnestly insert a great deal of material or information which has to be learned then it is boring and too much like a lesson. This may not show up in the first few simulations because the novelty produces a favourable reaction in the pupils. Those who are interested in developing simulation will find a detailed discussion of the possibilities and the difficulties in Boocock and Schild (1968).

It is often convenient to use chance cards or some other device to represent the contingencies of real life, yet these can be very distracting to the players. We have to relate any such devices very carefully to the main aim of the simulation if this is to be avoided. Perhaps a final caution is warranted. Some pupils fear the limelight or dislike playing roles and we must ask if we have any right to persuade them into such activities as simulation. What we may consider helpful to individuals may be very distasteful to them. The best way to protect pupils against unintentional harm is to teach them to plan their own simulations—not only is this the best way of learning to understand unknown and ambiguous situations—but it also seems true that pupils are not so threatened by an activity which they have helped to create.

This approach to the use of simulation in counselling probably reflects my preferences in teaching method, but the aim is that pupils should be given every possibility of understanding the rules of inter-action and the ways of reaching the goals they set for themselves. Understanding comes from constructing the simulation rather than from merely enacting a prepared situation or game. Evaluatory studies of simulation techniques in the U.S.A. generally conclude by suggesting that there is little evidence of transfer of skill from the simulation to other situations. It is likely that the approach advocated here will still suffer from this limitation, although this whole chapter is based on the need to ensure transfer from the counselling session to everyday life. The insistence on the need to allow pupils to participate in the con-struction of simulations which are related to their immediate problems is an attempt to create conditions in which this can happen. I have, however, no statistical or experimental evidence to support me here: all that can be said is that it appears to help. It has seemed important, too, that in counselling the link between the simulation and real life should be explicitly reinforced by the counsellor although the whole teaching team has to help here. The viewpoint put forward by Krumboltz and Thoresen (1969) underlies this chapter. They stress that although the aim of counselling is self-realization, self-realization is very vague and almost meaningless. The teacher—counsellor accepts these global goals, but then has a responsibility to break them down into meaning-ful steps dictated by the needs and personality of the individual pupil, presenting them in ways which are likely to lead to success. Role-playing, simulation and any other method the counsellor devises can be helpful, but transfer is unlikely unless the teaching team becomes actively involved in the counselling at this point. It would be worth-while to return to the second chapter and read the discussion on coun-selling conferences and the team approach in the light of Chapter Five.

## The development and use of games in counselling

In the second phase of counselling we are searching for methods which satisfy the pupil's need for activity and independence. We must not blind ourselves to the implications of the fact that the traditional tool of counselling—the interview—is often contaminated by associations of "trouble" for many pupils. I have found that this feeling is alleviated by simple games which can be played by small groups of pupils. This activity gives them real satisfaction and is a method of moving towards group counselling.

These games can be very simple or quite complex once the teacher-counsellor has acquired the skills required for constructing them. A student making games for the first time devised one which provoked considerable thought in the players. It could be played by six to eight pupils. Each player was given a "starter" card which had a small photograph of a young person and a sentence such as "Mike rides a Honda" or "Susan works in an office". The rest of the pack or cards bore statements about people which reflected common stereotypes about the characters represented in the "starter" cards. Players picked up one card at a time from the pile and then had to decide whether or not this card was compatible with the character on his "starter" card. To allow bargaining to begin immediately, each pupil had been given one statement card when he drew his "starter" card. If he decided it was inappropriate he could try to persuade someone to exchange with him or someone else could offer him a card. The point is that they had to give reasons for rejecting the card and those offering another player a card had to explain why it was suitable. When decisions could not be reached another pupil who acted as an independent judge was called in. He was also required to justify his decision. The game continued until each player had collected a full set of eight statements about his character. Group discussion then followed on the validity of the statements. After experience with this game the pupils began to build their own sets of cards based on self-selected characters.

This reveals the possibility of starting useful discussions. Any teacher can devise successful games provided that he is prepared to acquire the necessary conceptual framework which leads to purposeful games. Some writers have described games as sets of transactions between players which lead to predictable outcomes, but this seems unhelpful to the teacher-counsellor. The most useful type of game is that which presents players with a number of situations containing possibilities which they have to evaluate. The counsellor should therefore devise games in which the discrimination of alternatives is coupled with assessment of their costs. We have to see the players as decision makers and present them with a number of choice situations in which they have to verbalize the reasons for their choice. The idea of moves only takes on real meaning when it is part of a long term strategy in the game. I try to present players with situations where their moves have repercussions on others, whilst the moves of others have a similar effect on them. You can see the possibilities when we think of the situation in which a small group is asked to take the position of a group of young people who have limited money and transport and who have to plan the way they would spend an evening outside their own village. In this way it is possible to compensate for a lack of experience in making decisions, whilst the games aid the development of relational thinking by forcing the player to decide in the face of possible counter moves.

In the second phase of counselling we need to continue the task of helping pupils become aware of the kind of judgements that they habitually make in social situations. We can apply the principle of graduation of complexity which is part of our teaching method to these counselling games. We can begin with a simple situation with minimal rules and then add further complications and constraints as they understand the elements of the situation. Pupils can add further rules and situations themselves once they have mastered the elements of the situation. A complex structure therefore evolves from the simple beginning.

The first step in planning is to be clear about the objectives of the game and define the situation which forms the basis of it. Next one decides on the decision points and the range of alternatives incorporated at these points. An important constraint is found in the roles which have to be taken by the players. The most useful type of counselling games have some idea of the character and role of the person whose viewpoint is being taken by the player. Without this, we lose an opportunity to stimulate standpoint taking. These activities give us an enjoyable means of encouraging pupils to think from the standpoint of other people. In thinking about a game we should specify quite clearly the kind of interaction—negotiation, co-operation or competition—that we intend to stimulate.

Games imply rules and the section on simulation dealt with this, so here we are mainly concerned with penalties. If we include penalties over and above those implicit in the consequences of choosing a specific course of action then we must be clear about their purpose. They may obscure the aims of the game to the players and reduce their effectiveness as aids in developing social skills. There seems to be little point in arbitrary penalties in counselling games such as "if you fall on a blue square go back six squares". It is possible to argue that this represents the chance forces found in many human dilemmas, although it seems to me to be more valuable to build in such devices as a referee to whom appeals for a decision have to be made at critical points.

In thinking about the "pay-off" attached to the strategies in a game we can take a rigid position because we assume that this always means that one person wins at the expense of the others. The "winner take all" ending to a game can be less helpful than one which leads to a relative balance of gains and losses. One important educational function of games is to lead young people to recognize the existence of situations where all the participants gain. This can be seen in the productivity agreements which are now associated with industrial disputes over pay.

The best way of building a game is to pilot it on a group of pupils and gather their comments and suggestions. In this way a meaningful game can be evolved gradually. Perhaps it is not as clear as it should be that the most productive games for counselling are those which are devised to suit the needs of a specific group rather than the elaborate game requiring an undue investment of time in making it and explaining the rules.

*Other approaches in the second phase of counselling*

It will be clear to the reader that this book makes no pretence at attempting to give an exhaustive description of counselling techniques. Many other methods than those described here are to be found in the literature. It is important that we do discuss the contribution that social modelling theory and other forms of learning theory can make to counselling. These relate counselling practice to the skills of the teacher in a very direct way. Bandura and Walters (1963) demonstrated the impact of exposure to models on the behaviour of children. Children who saw models in a film who were rewarded for aggressive behaviour were found to imitate this behaviour at a later time. In one experiment the influence of this was sufficient to overcome the resistances of boys to adopting the kind of behaviour usually associated with girls. If one recalls that there are very strong prohibitions in our culture against boys behaving like girls then the strength of modelling can be appreciated. It was found that the consequences to the model coupled with the perceived power of the model seemed to account for the imitative behaviour. The teacher-counsellor should examine the type of models available for a pupil at home and school and try to correct any deficiencies if this is possible. If a boy or girl is surrounded by aggressive models then it may be important for the counsellor and his fellow teachers to present non-aggressive, yet competent models to these adolescents. The interested reader will find a detailed account of social modelling and its relation to behaviour modification in Bandura (1969) whilst a very readable account of behaviour therapy can be found in Wolpe (1969).

This indicates the possibility of exciting developments in counselling. The use of videotapes for presenting models of behaviour that have been denied to some pupils and which leads them to the evaluation of alternative ways of coping is one potential development. Irrational resistance can be aroused by the words "behavioural techniques" because it is assumed that this means the manipulation of the pupil. This ignores the fact that the same ethical principles are applied to every approach. Sometimes these methods are dismissed as being mere conditioning, which is not only inaccurate, but ignores the fact that without conditioning, walking downstairs or shaving would be major operations. We have a responsibility to scrutinize new developments carefully whilst maintaining a balanced attitude of openness to new ideas.

We may receive a rude shock when learning theory causes us to question ourselves about the nature of our reinforcements in classroom and counselling. We may find that they are distorted towards the negative because we are directing the pupil's attention to this side of his behaviour or that many unintended reinforcements are present in our interaction which compete with our stated intentions. If we link some of the ideas of the behavioural therapists to the production of a positive self-image in pupils, then many of our teaching methods can be severely criticized as contradictory in nature as well as ineffective. The difficulty for the teacher-counsellor is that the behavioural approach to counselling and therapy is described in connection with abnormal behaviour such as phobias, tics and other neurotic symptoms. This obscures their relevance in dealing with normal developmental tasks. A snare is that many of the published expositions of the techniques are given in a straightforward way which hides the skilful adaptation made to a particular client by a therapist. We then assume that it was all much simpler than it actually was.

We are beginning to see the need to provide pupils with systematic programmes of decision making and life planning skills. Education is moving towards individualized programmes for pupils and this tendency is reflected in the counselling movement by the provision of material which helps a pupil explore and assess himself. A series of activities and scales lead the pupil to the position in which he can make his own decision about important situations. An example is provided by the work of Fox (1970) which consists of a small book of questionnaires and activities which help a pupil reach a decision about his preferred career. Hansen (1970) further illustrates the trend when she describes computer-assisted guidance. It is easy to dismiss this as utopian because of the cost of assembling an adequate data bank, yet these do exist in the USA and Canada. It is worth noting that a government sponsored working party is currently evaluating the possibilities of this approach in Britain. As a preliminary step we can develop individualized methods of guidance in our schools through the building of simple guidance carrels which supplement the work of the counsellor and pastoral care team. Synchronized slide-tape systems and other forms of teaching machine can be used in these carrels to help pupils develop the skills of decision making and planning. This would be just one facet of an integrated approach to guidance and counselling and part of a resources centre for guidance. The carrels could be built in the woodwork shop and I have recently seen some very useful slide-tape vocational information programmes produced by fifteen-year-old boys under the leadership of an enthusiastic careers master. This draws our attention to the ways in which we can involve pupils in the manufacture of guidance and counselling materials.

The valuable function of the behavioural and social learning theorists is that of forcing us to consider the importance of the pupil's total life space rather than restricting ourselves to the counselling interview. They remind us that we need to modify the environment for the benefit of the pupil rather than try to make him adjust to what chances to be there. The problem of transfer of attitudes and aspirations has had a large part in the earlier discussion and these workers provide us with useful hints for tackling this systematically.

Social learning theory suggests that the task of the educator who is concerned with development requires that he assesses the nature of the models of behaviour available within the school. We learn not only to ask the negative question about the costs of counselling, but the positive one which delineates the rewards which are meaningful to a pupil. If we do accept that it is proper to shape behaviour through the conscious application of the principles of reinforcement we must have strong ethical standards. Certainly the counsellor needs to examine the impact of classroom interaction upon a pupil, working with his fellow teachers to modify this when the results are harmful. It is useless to talk about rewards and reinforcements if we fail to see that the Chinese Box concept of counselling contains the idea of the school functioning as a signal system which conveys vital information to the pupil about his worthwhileness as a person. No rewards will be acceptable if they are given in a social system which devalues those who are expected to strive for the rewards. Yet this is the lot of many of our less able or disadvantaged pupils. The counsellor has to work with colleagues to change the signals about himself which impinge on a pupil and destroy his self respect.

We have seen the need to eliminate unnecessary and harmful threat in the lives of pupils during the earlier discussion in this chapter. Now we see that effective coping strategies can only be developed with the active support of colleagues in the actual classroom situation. Counselling does influence teaching method because it is often a process of re-education which involves the pupil in discarding habits and reactions which are maladaptive or which are rigidly applied to situations where they are inappropriate. If anxiety and threat are generated in the classroom then the counsellor who is a teacher has a moral responsibility for tackling this.

We end by seeing the need to have not a single counsellor, but a team of concerned individuals who act as multiple sources of positive information for the pupil who has a sense of inadequacy and provide him with what he needs. Strangely enough, it is not the single looking glass, but the combined effect of the reflections from many human looking glasses which produce a stable and healthy picture of oneself. The team produces a unified policy which gives a pupil what he, and he alone, needs for successful resolution of his developmental problems. In an atmosphere of teamwork there will be less danger of diverting blame from the school organization on to a hapless pupil by labelling him as inadequate or disturbed.

### Summary discussion

The second phase of counselling is task-orientated, and is concerned with the achievement of the targets which have emerged from the first stage of counselling. In this stage the skills of the teacher are very relevant to counselling because the counsellor needs to break down distant goals into a series of more immediate ones and specify the steps which have to be taken by the pupil. Many pupils lack the ability to plan ahead and to see the consequences of their actions. These skills often have to be taught.

The major techniques which can be used in this stage are those of role-playing and simulation. Role-playing allows pupils to develop the ability to see things from the viewpoint of other people, allowing them to anticipate the behaviour of others. It also stimulates them to communicate more effectively with others. Simulation can be used to teach them the rules of social interaction, the behaviours involved in important situations and the sanctions used for breaches of rules. The basic concern of the counsellor in the second phase of counselling is with the coping strategies which have been developed by a pupil. He brings these into play when he experiences stress or threat. Unfortunately these are often inefficient, if not self-defeating, because they deny him basic satisfaction. If we relate this chapter to the line indicating the action orientated nature of this phase we see that it is interrupted by these techniques:

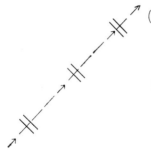

(iii) Involvement of colleagues as active participants who provide supports, reinforcements or even take over the counselling.

(ii) Role-playing / simulation / behaviour modification techniques/ games.

(i) Examination of the coping strategies used by the pupil.

We should remember that the line represents a rough model of the process and that in practice we move between the three points according to the needs of the pupil. Note also that the techniques used and the basic requirement for transfer of training not only indicates that group counselling may be more important than individual, but that counselling really becomes an activity carried on within the classroom and school rather than being confined to the interview situation.

## REFERENCES

Bandura, A. (1969) *Principles of Behaviour Modification,* New York: Holt, Rinehart and Winston.

Bandura, A. and Walters, R. (1963) *Social Learning and Personality Development,* New York: Holt, Rinehart and Winston.

Boocock, S. and Schild, E. (1968) *Simulation Games in Learning,* Beverley Hills: Sage.

Fox, J. (1970) *Inside Information on Solving Career Problems,* London: Dickens Press.

Hansen, L. (1970) *Career Guidance Practices in School and Community,* Washington: National Vocational Guidance Association.

Kelly, G. (1955) *The Psychology of Personal Constructs,* New York: Norton.

Krumboltz, J.D. and Thoresen, C.E. (Eds.) (1969) *Behavioural Counseling,* New York: Holt, Rinehart and Winston.

Lazarus, R.S. (1966) *Psychological Stress and the Coping Process,* New York: McGraw-Hill.

Moreno, J.L. (1951) *Sociometry, Experimental Method and the Science of Society,* New York: Beacon House.

Tansey, P. (Ed.) (1971) *Educational Aspects of Simulation,* London: McGraw-Hill.

Wolpe, J. (1969) *The Practice of Behaviour Therapy,* New York: Pergamon.

# CHAPTER SIX

# GROUP COUNSELLING AND GROUP GUIDANCE

*The purpose of this chapter*

We now proceed to look at the way in which group methods can be used in counselling, noting that not only do they have the advantage of economy, but that they also have certain intrinsic advantages, especially with some pupils. The discussion underlines the utility of group work in helping with the problem of transfer which has already occupied us; the way in which other teachers can be given a part in group counselling; and the link between group methods and creative education.

*The questions asked in this chapter*

The following questions lie behind the exposition of group methods:
  (i) What are the criteria on which the counsellor forms a counselling group?
 (ii) How do we make a distinction between group guidance and group counselling?
(iii) What stages exist in group counselling and what techniques and considerations are important at each stage?
 (iv) How can we use group guidance methods in the secondary school?

*Group guidance and group counselling*

The earlier discussion stressed two things. Firstly, that a pupil's behaviour is largely a product of the way *he sees* the school situation, whatever the reality may be. The counsellor must understand the viewpoint of the pupil as it emerges in the first phase of counselling, treating it as part of the basic data of counselling. Secondly, it has been argued that effective counselling requires the counsellor to be a full member of the school staff. Group methods of guidance and counselling provide a valuable bridge between individual forms of counselling and normal teaching activities, thereby not only aiding acceptance of the counsellor, but integrating counselling into the daily life of the school. Indeed the last chapter has suggested that at certain points group methods may be more effective than individual ones. This not only comes from the techniques employed, but from the fact that boys and girls will accept group counselling as part of the daily life of the school, although they interpret individual counselling as something which isolates them from their fellows.

Doubts have often been raised as to whether or not it is possible to combine the teacher and counsellor role. The argument against combining them states that the teacher occupies an authority role and that this would inhibit communication and the development of trust between the counsellor and the pupil. This view ignores the presence of warm trusting relationships between many teachers and pupils, and also denies the existence of real authority in the counselling relationship and therapy. It does not give the adolescent credit for being able to discriminate between the behaviour of the same person in different situations, and fails to see that he adjusts to this as part of normal living. Many teachers already act as leaders in informal activities in youth clubs at night, teaching the same pupils formally during the day without tensions or difficulty. We should keep an open mind and be prepared to experiment with the dual roles, finding ways which work within the organization of a particular school. My argument is that there is no inevitable conflict implicit in the combination of teaching and counselling roles. The relevant question may be not, "Does the councellor teach?" but "What does he teach and how does he teach it?" It could be an inefficient use of resources for a skilled counsellor to have to undertake some types of teaching which are not related to counselling. This brings us to the discussion of group methods of guidance and counselling.

The distinction which is now made between group guidance and group counselling indicates the existence of two different, but equally valuable techniques. Group guidance is a process which can be very exciting and which may include many opportunities for innovation. In it the counsellor's major task is the provision of information, the leading of discussion or some activity which *reinforces the objectives of the school,* or helps in the achievement of some goal common to the group. The normal unit for group guidance is the form. Group counselling differs because there is no assumption of any specific common goal beyond the resolution of personal difficulties. Wrenn in his introduction to the book by Mahler (1969) on group counselling pointed out that group counselling is a derivative of individual counselling, complementary to it and needing at least as much training and skill. It can be dangerous, because we can assume without any justification that group processes are necessarily helpful, when in fact I suspect that we have not given enough attention to the way in which group processes can create casualties amongst those whom it is hoped to help and the way in which negative behaviours and identities can be developed. At its best, it is a process in which a skilled counsellor uses group interaction to facilitate deeper self-understanding and self-acceptance. It can provide a climate within which the individual can explore and define his feelings safely, learning to control them in the process. The aim of such groups is to help the members sharpen their sense of identity in a positive way, providing them also with the skills which enable them to cope with the developmental tasks of adolescence. Group counselling is more economical, making the services of the skilled counsellor available to a larger proportion of the school population; it appears to be more easily integrated into normal school activities; but it also has certain intrinsic advantages. These come from the fact that each member is given access to a number of viewpoints, together with the provision of immediate feedback about his behaviour from a very potent source, namely his age mates. We can also utilize the techniques outlined previously more effectively. The realization of these claims depends upon the counsellor's ability to adjust to the specific group. A group of boys aged from thirteen to fifteen will need very different handling from a group whose members are in the later stages of adolescence. In early adolescence the establishment of a firm sense of identity and living up to their view of their sex role will be a major pre-occupation of some members. The quality of parental relationships during this period and the need to emphasize their independence may well cause some of them to thrust off attempts at too close a contact. The counsellor adapts to this, adjusting his approach to each group. Again let us be clear that whilst a good group provides support, group counselling can get out of hand, and be both damaging and frustrating for all the participants including the counsellor.

### Group counselling

The most immediate problem is that of deciding the purpose of a specific group and its composition. Little can be said about the purpose of any counselling group because the possibilities are so varied. Each counsellor has to work this out clearly for himself, taking into consideration the size of the group, the suitability of each member and the nature of the problems which are to be tackled. A reasonable number is from five to twelve members, although I find eight seems to provide the optimal number for communication and creative interaction. If the counsellor is inexperienced, then it seems best to begin with the lower number, because this makes observation and construction intervention easier. This does not mean the interaction is less complex, but the counsellor has more chance of understanding the meaning of what is happening.

The need to pay attention to the relationship between what occurs in the group counselling and the classroom is greater in the group situation than in individual counselling. It is only too easy to release aggression, stimulate hostility unintentionally and to allow the expression of negative emotions, thereby encouraging behaviour which brings the pupils into unnecessary conflict with other teachers. I have met group approaches where the "lid" has been taken off prematurely, and this has been very disturbing for the pupils. On one occasion I met a group who had experienced so-called group counselling which had reinforced their paranoid and egocentric tendencies to such a degree that they felt the school was totally uncaring and that all teachers were useless. This was a distortion of reality, for in fact the school contained an exceptional number of teachers who went beyond the usual limits of duty in trying to care for pupils. The counsellor was, of course, in the worst kind of collusion with the pupils; indeed he was retarding development rather than encouraging it.

Some pupils are not suitable for group counselling. There are pupils who are so aggressive that they would absorb too much of the counsellor's attention, and they would constitute a real threat to other pupils. Others may be too inarticulate to be able to participate. Others might be so tense and nervous that the experience would be intolerable for them. These considerations suggest the need for flexible thinking about the purpose and nature of a group, indicating the kind of difficulties that have to be considered in forming the group, and that certain pupils will benefit from inclusion in one group but not in another. We must always try to relate individual and the group. The counsellor must assess the pupil's suitability in a careful individual interview, explaining the purposes of the group and the way in which he hopes it will be of use to the boy. This interview is crucial, for pupils often have ideas which need instant refutation, otherwise they distort his participation in the group. Particular attention needs to be given to making it clear that the pupil is expected to respect others in the group and not misuse the situation. Leakage of information is only too easy in the group and if the counsellor is not satisfied that the pupil can hold his tongue, then he should not be included. The soundest policy is to select pupils who seem likely to respond, rather than devote scarce time to a few very difficult cases who have been left without help. The constructive strategy is early identification of pupils "at risk": this is discussed later. The good counsellor is one who knows what he cannot do, and who tries to obtain specialist help for those beyond his aid.

The composition of the group poses many questions. Should the members have similar problems, or should there be a range of difficulties? Is the age range to be wide or narrow? Similarity of problem in the members has attractions, for it eases the task of the counsellor in devising role-playing, problem solving and simulation techniques. Yet it can deprive the pupils of exposure to wider viewpoints about the difficulties, and the group could be reinforcing each other's maladaptive responses, stunting, or otherwise preventing change. A mixture of developmental problems is more stimulating, but thought has to be given as to what may happen. A dramatic problem may occupy the attention of the group, causing equally important problems to be ignored, whilst some members may use the situation to divert attention from themselves. A wide age range seems to have possibilities because it provides older models and can be stimulating, yet relatively small age differences are important in adolescence, and the presence of age differences can inhibit communication. Although there are different rates of development, which means that chronological age is in some ways unimportant, we have to see that the developmental tasks of the older adolescent are very different from those of younger pupils. This may already indicate the need for clear thinking by the group counsellor who has to sit down and work out his objectives, state his criteria for inclusion in the group and specify his proposed methods very clearly on paper for each group as an essential preliminary step. Group counselling cannot be entered into without due thought and preparation by the counsellor.

Heterosexual groups can be introduced with profit at times, yet they also produce problems. Girls mature more rapidly than boys and have different outlooks on work and relationships. The boys will sometimes react adversely to the presence of girls, seeing their presence as a signal for the display of compulsive masculinity. Errors in the composition of the group complicate the task. Too much homogeneity in the group leads toward sterility, in the sense that there are few forces within the group which push members towards seeing the need for standpoint taking. This would force the counsellor to become over-dominant in an attempt to correct the situation. I have been tempted to form groups composed of pupils with low language ability and communication and those who are skilled in these fields. Yet although it was sometimes beneficial, if the differences were too extreme and included values apparently related to social class, then the unskilled showed resentment and aggression which undid much of the work. I suspect that even if the differences were not too extreme, and the numbers were about equal, one might have two psychological groups who merely happen to share the same physical space. We have little firm knowledge about all this, despite the increasing amount of work on group dynamics, but the counsellor must be aware of the possibility of such factors as those mentioned impinging upon his group counselling.

Knowledge of group dynamics is essential, and there is no substitute for reading the standard research. Leadership is important to group counselling in two ways. First is the general style of leadership, whether it is that provided by the counsellor or that which emerges within the group. There are two broad types of leadership, the first being the type which helps the group attain the goals set for it, and is sometimes called task leadership. The other type is concerned with the reduction of tension, the easing of difficulties in relationships and it operates to prevent undue disruption of the group. This has been called socio-emotional leadership. The counsellor notes which members tend to take up these broad leadership styles, for most of us have a preference towards one or the other. He examines the way these roles develop as the group progresses, stepping in where necessary to supplement either type of leadership without taking away the role from the pupils. The mose useful way of looking at leadership seems to me not to be in terms of personality, but in terms of the functions the leader is performing for the group. In most situations the leader has a skill which is particularly relevant, yet we know that other group members also possess that skill. It is enlightening to find out why one person takes over at a particular moment, whilst others who are just as capable do not. I often pose this as a question for the group to explore. The counsellor has to deal with a situation in which different people assume leadership roles as the group develops. It is important that the members try to understand what is happening.

Just as the counselling interview can be seen as a bargaining and exchange process, so the group counselling situation can be viewed as a similar process, leadership roles being a by-product of these exchanges. This makes much that would be otherwise incomprehensible clearer to the group counsellor. Leaders only exist in as much as they meet the needs of the followers, and if we can see what needs are being met our contribution is then more relevant. Leader and followers exist only in relation to each other, and it is a fact of group life that the follower is not the passive occupant of a position in a frozen social structure, but is an active participant, deriving real benefits from the follower position. Followers possess a great deal of power. The counsellor has to learn to analyse the situation in terms of this exchange process. As this happens, one becomes aware that the leader's status is dependent upon his ability to meet the expectations of his followers, which explains why leadership varies from one situation to another. Once we have assessed these expectations, we must look at their rigidity or flexibility. Behavioural change often results from the clarification of these expectancies by the counsellor. Pupils then see what they are doing, and they may decide that they don't really like it, or that the game is not worth the candle.

We are often concerned about conformity to the peer group in adolescents, and sometimes feel, as was discussed earlier, that we can do little to modify the peer group influence. Hollander (1964), in a discussion partially relying on previous work, has shown an interesting relationship between conformity and innovation which is useful to the group counsellor. Conformity to the peer group and culture brings many rewards, but in the group it is more useful to see it as a process leading somewhere. Status in a group is based upon a kind of credit or a series of credits which are given to a pupil when he meets the expectations of members or when he contributes to the group in a way of which the members approve. We can see that conformity creates status. Eventually, however, a boy has accumulated enough credits through conformity so that he is able to depart from the group expectation or to innovate. The counsellor will see this as an opportunity for change and may use such members as they reach this status level as the spearhead of change. In any case, we should help group members read their status in the group accurately, for some not only misread the expectations of others, but either overestimate or underestimate their stock of social credits. Bringing this to the attention of pupils in a constructive way will help them achieve social competence, and this itself aids the positive development of the group.

This discussion emphasizes the leadership which emerges among the group members, but the counsellor is the formal leader. We have to make decisions similar to those made in individual counselling about our role. No clear evidence exists as to the superiority of any one style of leadership by the counsellor, although evidence from associated areas suggests that a democratic style will be most effective. I would hesitate before attempting to transfer into the secondary school, the type of group process marked by the absence of adult leadership. We should adapt to the level of maturity of the participant and the nature of the problem. To try always to withdraw and be neutral, handing over responsibility to the group members, may be to use as a technique what is actually the objective of the group counselling. The aim of counselling may be the development in pupils of the ability to take responsibility for themselves and to press this prematurely on individuals may prevent them from learning mature behaviour. If we fail to provide real structure and containment in a group then we may be guilty of creating conditions in which pupils have little chance of achieving a firm identity and making realistic decisions.

The group counsellor will find it useful to think more deeply about the comparison process which has already been mentioned when we looked at the costs of counselling for pupils. We look at it in groups because it is closely related to the clarification of identity which is a major developmental task. Groups can be dangerous here, although we have to make constructive use of the comparison process. Each one of us needs to be able to confirm our own viewpoint and to have a setting in which we can test out our conceptions of ourselves and other people. Group process is often a process of adjustment by the members and of convergence of viewpoints. Let me illustrate by reference to the work of Sherif (1948) which led to many experimental studies. If we view a point of light which is actually stationary in a completely dark room, it appears to move. This is a situation of illusion in which there is no clear point of reference. In such a situation people are very responsive to the suggestions of others. Sherif's work showed that people will conform to a previously agreed upon and arbitrary assessment of the amount of movement of the light when it was firmly put to them by confederates of the experimenter. As judgements were made, in fact, a norm began to emerge to which the group conformed. Judgements in the group counselling situation are rather like this, for they are largely determined by the social influence of the group, rather than being the product of the individual. The group counsellor has to be aware of this, making sure that group pressures and comments aid the growth of realistic identity in a boy. In the group situation counselling can degenerate into a process of unintended reinforcements in which pupils unthinkingly adhere to the group viewpoint. The group counsellor has to be sensitive to the fact that a group may be shaping a pupil's behaviour in a way which, although ostensibly desirable, inhibits real growth. We learn to watch for pressures which force a boy to change his opinion of something which may be very important for his aims. Such pressures may be very indirect and difficult to detect. Our success in building a group with high cohesion is sometimes dangerous, for this means stronger pressures towards conformity. Groups can force a false identity upon pupils, getting them to "behave in a proper way" when they do not or cannot behave honestly in that way. The counsellor disciplines himself not to do this in face-to-face counselling and he should not allow the group to do this. Counselling groups can become so important for pupils that they provide them with a ready-made identity, rather than allowing one to develop. Imposed identities are of little relevance to creative counselling and education.

We have to be alert to a basic process within the group, i.e. role-sending. This can be positive or negative, but the core idea is that members of a group send signals to particular individuals which indicate that the recipient is expected to act in a particular way. The counsellor is alert to this, pointing out what is happening. One of the most common forms of negative roles sent in a group is that of the scapegoat. He is given a negative role in the group because the others push out on to him the feelings and attitudes they cannot accept in themselves. The scapegoat is never entirely without blame, for he always offers the group by his behaviour some plausible reason which allows them to attribute the bad qualities to him. He may differ significantly from them in some way, perhaps in physical development or in social class, and he may flaunt these differences. We can see that it is possible for the scapegoat to get rewards from his position. He may get attention which would be denied him without this or he may even be satisfying a need for punishment. Be this as it may, it is not healthy for a group to be allowed to react to their own role-sending by isolating and rejecting the scapegoat. Not only does it create guilt and anxiety in the members, but it shows that something is wrong in the group. Sometimes we have created a climate in which pupils feel criticized or have set the standards impossibly high. If the group is to serve its purpose, the counsellor has to help the members accept the things actually belonging to themselves which they are projecting upon the scapegoat. We must not fall into the trap of thinking that every situation of rejection means that scapegoating is present, for some pupils deserve the signals that are sent to them by others and we may have to help them see why this occurs. Another form of role-sending which occurs is that of the wise man. This happens when one member, who is usually articulate, allows himself to be persuaded that he holds the answers to the problems of the group and its members. This is a device by which pupils refuse to shoulder responsibility for their own development. I have had to take myself to task on occasions for inflating myself into this role, although I know it is self-defeating. All group counsellors have to guard against a process developing which leads to the evasion of responsibility by the members. These two examples show the mechanisms which make the life of the group counsellor an exciting one.

Some writers have detected definite phases in group counselling such as those in the unstructured groups described by Bion (1961), but we should also be aware of the phases in problem-solving groups investigated by Bales and Strodtbeck (1951). No one theory or descriptive account of a group can be transferred with confidence to other groups, but the counsellor should have some idea of the stages which may occur in group counselling. Groups differ so much that no precise description is likely to be valid for all groups. The important point is that we should recognize that phases occur in the group which have

certain consequences. Some pupils are more useful and active in expos-
ing and analysing a problem, some are better at producing creative
solutions, whilst others are at their best when we need to get the group
back on a stable footing and reduce tensions. We have to see that the
amount of participation and activity by pupils will probably change
as the group develops and we must adjust to this, not expecting the
same amount of activity from the same boy throughout the group. I
find it useful to draw up charts based on Bales' (1968) suggestion that
it is possible to assess an individual's social interaction within a group on
three dimensions. These are (i) the power or the degree of ascendancy
he has over others, (ii) the pleasant or unpleasant quality of the feeling
which he engenders in the group, and (iii) the extent to which he
facilitates the achievement of group goals. It may be helpful if I say I
assess power by giving the usual sociogram based on liking and then
reversing the arrows:

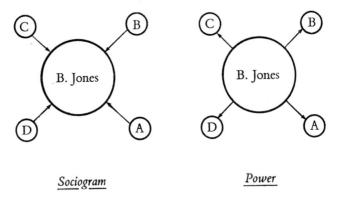

Sociogram                    Power

This simple device indicates one person's influence. I also try to
detect indirect influence. We can have chains of influence in which
pupil A strongly influences pupil C, not directly but through the
mediation of pupil B who transmits the message or tendency to C.
B can sometimes operate to amplify the impact of the message because
of his relationship with C, or he triggers off an imitative response in C
for other reasons. The group counsellor will find it valuable to build
up a set of simple diagrams about group mechanisms of this sort for
they reveal things we may miss in the actual group.

Whilst the literature on group psychotherapy offers much material of interest to the group counsellor, it would be abortive to try to force counselling groups in the secondary school into the pattern of these groups. For one thing, we are concerned with the normal developmental tasks of adolescence, for another, we lack a full therapeutic training for this. Certainly phases exist, just as in therapeutic groups, but I think it best to take the two-phase model presented, sub-dividing it into four stages as follows:

## GROUP COUNSELLING

| Basic phases | Sub-stages |
|---|---|
| A. UNDERSTANDING ONESELF | 1. Creating a relationship of trust. |
| | 2. Exposures of problems and attitudes. |
| B. ACTION AND ACQUISITION OF SKILLS | 3. The work phase. |
| | 4. Ending the group. |

### 1. CREATING A TRUSTING RELATIONSHIP

Although pupils may prefer group counselling it is often harder to create a relationship of trust in the group situation because group counselling brings fears of vulnerability, exposure, shame and ridicule into being at the very period in life when these are strong. Certainly the possibility is strong if the counsellor has unwittingly given the impression that the group experience is concerned with abnormalities rather than positive growth and the acquisition of social and intellectual competences. Undue difficulties are created in group counselling when the counsellor gives the impression that the pupils are required to talk about their home backgrounds or that the group is concerned with dramatic revelations. Far from this, the group counsellor is concerned with what the members *do* within the group, for he is concerned with their interpersonal relationships and the signals they send to others. Once pupils understand this, they co-operate very happily, for as practical creatures, they see the significance of this.

Trust must be built up, not only between the counsellor and each member, but also between the members: This again underlines the need for careful exploration of difficulties as part of selection. A lack of trust is evident when there is continuous carping criticism about the counsellor and when there are attempts to deny the utility of the group. The counsellor keeps a cool head in all this, seeing that it is a necessary aspect of testing him out, but he contains it quite firmly. The group is in fact checking on his integrity and competence, and they have every right to do this. In this stage the counsellor works to help each individual feel that he has a right to his own feelings, containing the aggressive and dealing carefully but firmly with the members who spend their time discussing other people negatively. One of the tricky jobs in this stage is that of creating a climate in which pupils can learn to accept constructive feedback. This means that members have to learn to receive and evaluate the reactions of the counsellor and members to their statements and behaviour. One of the strengths of group counselling is that freer expression than in the individual situation occurs, and more can be dealt with in context than in retrospect.

Adolescents who are tense and uncertain, however, are prone to treat feedback and the counsellor's interventions as criticism or attack. In this stage the aim is not only to build supportive relationships, but also to help each participant see that his fundamental concern is with his own developmental tasks. Our strategy is to focus attention upon a member's relationships with the others in the group and upon his feelings about a situation. When a pupil attacks another verbally we do not turn our attention to the victim: we turn to the attacker to try to help him discover why he does it. This we can only do slowly and with concern, yet we must do it, for if we turned our attention to the problems of the person who was being attacked, we are allowing the attacker to gain control of the situation. This is what I mean when I speak of the need for containment. In group counselling the counsellor works for trust and honesty of feelings in this stage of building relationships, helping a sense of purpose develop, but this only develops when he is firmly in control. The exact nature of this containment depends upon the reasons for the formation of the group, although the counsellor uses all his skills as a teacher in devising techniques similar to those in the first phase of counselling which facilitate development in the group. Even in this stage group counselling is not merely sitting in a circle talking about things; it is an occasion when real activities are devised.

## 2. HELPING PUPILS REVEAL THEIR PROBLEMS

The second stage is where the difficulties come into the open, and the counsellor's skill here is vital to the success of the group. He needs great sensitivity to what is being revealed, intervening to prevent pupils from saying things they would regret because they would be rejected by the group. Here we begin the task of looking at the motivation and meaning behind the behaviour (though once again there is a need to avoid easy pseudo-Freudian interpretations which no trained therapist would produce). We tend not to interpret; we try to see what it is that a pupil needs from the group in relationships and support. We do not exclude the hostile members, for they are bringing real feelings out into the open, although we still contain the expression of the hostility. The three basic personality qualities described in the first chapter are crucial because they allow the counsellor to provide good experience. Neutrality is useless, for the counsellor needs to present a model of honesty and openness. His aim is to keep all the members of the group, including himself, open to feedback whether this is positive or negative in nature. The group begins here to look at its problems, and the counsellor's skill at timing his interventions and confrontations is important. At this stage I find that some pupils try to disrupt me. They try to shock or push me into a "mimsy" attitude, or draw me into collusion, attempting to trap me into approving what I believe to be both personally and socially undesirable. This means that I cannot hide my personal values and hide behind a detached professional role. The book by Berne (1966) will give you some idea of the way in which this is done in other situations. Bates (1966) found such themes as the outwitting of adults, problem parents, the feeling of being unloved and the desire to change rules emerging in adolescent groups. It seems to me that these themes come out very strongly in this second phase of adolescent group counselling, but this may be due to the way in which I work. We must look for self-defeating strategies of behaviour such as that of "getting them before they get you" which in practice leads to the adolescent getting what he doesn't want. This seems to be a stage of stress for the counsellor, because he has to detect these patterns of behaviour, decide how necessary they are and what will happen if they are interrupted. Honest concern and the ability to learn from mistakes, honestly admitting them when they occur, carries him through. It is obvious that the group must accept him as trustworthy before he begins to confront and emphasize the meaning of feedback.

## 3. THE WORK STAGE

If we do our job reasonably well, pupils move into this phase fairly quickly and concentrate on solving their problems which are connected with difficulties in developmental tasks. We see that pupils who have goals related to school require us to act as mobilizers of resources for them. We have to give special attention to the transactions between the group situation and the school. Do not misunderstand this remark, for the counsellor has been concerned with it throughout. In the early stages, the task is that of seeing that the emotional expression and the tensions which are expressed do not flow into the larger environment in a destructive way. In the work phase we deliberately stimulate a flow of positive and realistic action over the boundaries of the group into classrooms, workshop, playground and peer groups.

## 4. ENDING THE GROUP

This causes tension in the counsellor just as much as in the pupils, for this is where one really begins to learn if one has achieved something permanent. Although the anxieties found in purely therapeutic groups composed of disturbed people are not present, some pupils will feel anxious. They express doubts about their ability to cope adequately, or even accuse one of rejecting them. We must bring these feelings out into the open, although usually the ending of the counselling group is fairly easy for one has built up a network of supportive relationships for the pupil with other teachers who should be the important people for him. Attention is given to helping each member formulate clearly his ambitions and intentions for the future, for counselling is always forward looking. We should emphasize the links with form master and teachers for it is more beneficial for a boy to work with these important people than to come back to the counsellor. If one has done the job properly, then pupils do not need one any more.

### Techniques in group counselling

Tyler (1960) produced the idea of counselling as a process of minimal change. The counsellor is not trying to undertake psychotherapy or change personality structures, but to help a pupil achieve his developmental tasks successfully. We have to use techniques which meet the problem underlying the group. Groups concerned with underfunctioning need to be treated differently from those based on problems of withdrawal and acute anxiety. We have a professional responsibility to protect the individual from others, and we must see that the group context leads to an emphasis of the problems of sibling relationships, peers and classmate interaction. Rather than the problems of dependency, those of relating to others, rivalry, sharing and competition may take precedence and provide the themes in which more personal difficulties are imbedded. Group counselling gives young people a chance to enter into a frank dialogue with an authority figure, which is how they see the counsellor despite all his attitudes of acceptance. In a situation of generational discontinuity, alienation and disenchantment with tradition, this may be one of the most valuable things we can offer.

It is as well to hold in mind the warning of Thompson and Kahn (1970) that "reliance upon the untrammelled operation of group forces" and "confidence in the group's capacity to solve its own problems" can be a rationalization for incompetent leadership and an abdication of responsibility. We need to provide the means for self-exploration and give the skills. In the first stage, we may need to stimulate activity quite strongly. Members can be asked to write down their feelings about joining the group: the best thing that could happen to them and the worst thing. This is respected as private material which they should keep, revealing it only if they wish, for each person has an inner core of privacy. This the counsellor respects, for he has no desire to indulge in psychological rape. We should utilize the ideas on self-exploration given earlier. In these activities, we should ensure that we focus on the positive aspects of personality at least as much as on the negative side of things. Blackboard exercises are useful where a list of adjectives describing personal qualities could be presented, and the members select those which they feel describe themselves. Then one can ask them to relate these to a fourteen-year-old, and develop discussion about this. Role-playing is also important in the second stage for providing a vocabulary and the experience of talking about behaviour and personality. Using the material of earlier chapters we would allow activities to evolve with the group. We should always use individual reactions to stimulate learning in other members. My response often is, "Well, this is what Jim did, I wonder what we would do?". Each member must apply to himself what he learns from others. I find it useful to set a group one of the tasks described above or some other which seems relevant. The group, however, is divided into two. One half performs the task, whilst the other half act as observers. Each pupil in the observation group is charged, not only with observation, but with the task of helping a partner in the task group improve his performance. The session is interrupted at intervals to allow consultation between coach and partner. When this has happened on two or three occasions (using different partners and coaches each time), a network of co-operative relationships is partially established which can be fostered to lead to an excellent working climate in the group.

To me the work phase is the most exciting, perhaps because it allows the skills of the teacher to be fully utilized. By this time, most pupils have seen that they need to learn new skills and to change their behaviour outside the group. There is no reason why group counselling should mean the whole group works as one unit all the time. The counsellor may split the group into small groups of three or four or even partners who work on prepared assignments and work sheets. These help the pupil to specify his targets in simple terms of behaviour, breaking them down into small steps and providing suggestions for implementing them, together with some scheme of assessment. The group functions as a source of ideas, provides a place where skills can be tried out, indirectly through role-playing or simulation or directly by bringing the activity inside it. It becomes a base from which they venture to make adventures in new styles of living, returning to discuss the results and develop the next steps. Together pupils formulate strategies, work on analysing failures and successes and learning to rectify errors of judgement. The role of the counsellor also changes, for it becomes diffused among a number of individuals, not only teachers, but sometimes also among the boy's peers. This is not haphazard, for the counsellor retains general oversight and devotes considerable energy to planning, checking, communicating and co-ordinating the efforts. Other teachers may enter into the group, making their contribution sometimes to the group as a whole, some-times to the pupils whom they feel especially able to help, or who have sought out their help. I have found it useful to develop some sort of record of this process. Critics could claim that this is not what they would call counselling, yet surely this is what we mean when we ask that counselling should be part of the everyday life of the school. Each pastoral care or form teacher contributes as he can; the effort is focused on the point in time where the pupil can use it and when he has been prepared for it.

At this stage, individual interviews can be quite short and are used to the full because they occur on demand and the pupil really needs them. The counsellor is warned that these interviews are very exhaust-ing; he is stretched to the limit intellectually and emotionally. It is very helpful to charge two or three boys with the task of helping another find a solution to some practical situation, putting them into the position of the recovering alcoholic who helps himself by helping another who is less advanced.

Disadvantaged children can be helped in this way when other methods fail to provide them with the activity needed. One of my ex-students recently counselled a boy very successfully through getting him to organize an exhibition of work for a group of leavers who felt they lacked status and ambition. At each point the counsellor used the practical consultations to build up a positive attack on the lad's own negative self-image and reinforce his enthusiasms. We have to provide competencies and skills which give a legitimate feeling of success. We tend to forget that frustration and anger mean that at some level they still desire success. Counselling becomes a series of encounters with a practical problem. Self-exploration is parallel to all this, because carefully planned activities provide a looking-glass self, totally different from the one reflected before. All this links well with team teaching, interdisciplinary enquiry and other modern methods of teaching. The group counsellor has to develop high powers of organization and co-ordination. He has to build up individual programmes which are used in a group situation; to use resource trolleys where materials are kept in good order and to use aids such as tape-recorders. Some of the groups are very deficient in the use of language, but this does not mean they are unable to think. The possibility of many creative approaches lie hidden in my simple description. These preserve the integrity of the individual and yet open up new horizons for him. We neither wish to impose middle-class values on him, nor do we want to romanticize the negative and restrictive side of working-class life. We cannot be hamstrung by rigidity or tied to traditional casework approaches which are not relevant to the situation, although we embody many thera-peutic skills in this active model of counselling.

## Variations

It is now clear that a lively mind and the ability to see possibilities apply to group work just as much as to individual counselling. Groups can be used in many ways. They can function as an extension of individual counselling, for once the pupil has worked through his most difficult and intimate problems, he can be transferred to a group. This provides him with the stimulus for consolidation of what he has already achieved in counselling, giving him the opportunity for learning necessary interpersonal skills. This use of the group makes it a "half-way house" which bridges the gap between individual counselling and real life, helping with the problem of transfer of attitudes. The kind of group which has continuous existence has a real place in counselling, for it allows pupils to be transferred when ready to a supportive group in which norms and values have been established. The opportunity to interact with pupils who are at a more advanced stage in counselling gives real incentive for growth without posing too great a sense of challenge. This is a very productive area for research and innovation, because there is no reason why other people should not run these groups. The members of the pastoral care team are obviously the right people for this task, for there are many advantages in having the form master or year tutor as the group leader.

The counsellor may find it more useful himself to run those groups which for several reasons are intended to prepare pupils for individual counselling. First, he can build up the essential relationship; next, he gathers useful information and stimulates developments which reduce the need for lengthy individual counselling; finally, he may in fact even eliminate the need for individual counselling altogether because he is successful in the group situation. It seems that such groups may demand a higher level of skill than the supportive ones because the individuals in them are are likely to be more than usually anxious, inarticulate or withdrawn. The counsellor must never lose sight of his responsibility to know his limitations and to refer pupils to specialist agencies without delay as soon as the need becomes clear. Although the counsellor role contains therapeutic elements, this does not mean he is capable of dealing with very disturbed pupils. This kind of group offers the chance of assessing problems more clearly and filtering off gravely disturbed pupils for psychological help.

### A note on "resistances"

The counsellor has to be prepared to deal with resistance to change by the pupil, although he appears to desire change in himself. The label "resistance" has a technical meaning in psychoanalysis which is very meaningful for the trained therapist, but is dangerous for us as school counsellors. From the outside resistance seems to mean that some parts of the pupil's personality are trying to prevent change. We could get trapped into behaving as if there were some little pupil within the big pupil who has a separate existence, and who, by devious means, manages to stifle the changes. This seems to be built into our thinking at times. It seems better to realize that, even when a pupil has honestly expressed a desire to behave differently, this is more laborious and costly than he had realized. We then get a situation in which he simultaneously possesses the desire for change and the desire to continue as he is. Resistance to desired changes takes many forms. Compulsive talking in the group, tempers, tears, withdrawal from active participation in the group and starting the scapegoating of another pupil can all hide resistance. The counsellor has to assess carefully whether or not such ambivalence is present. The best tactic is to discuss this openly, but non-judgementally. Resistance can mean that the counsellor is attempting to push the pupil too fast or that he has been insensitive to earlier signals of stress and doubt. If this is the case, then he must work to restore communication and the reasoned statement of feelings and difficulties. Such checks and hazards are part of counselling, a condition of life with which the counsellor has to learn to cope.

## Group guidance

A definition of group guidance has been given at the beginning of the chapter. This does not indicate the most efficient ways of using group guidance. During his secondary school period, each pupil experiences a number of crises, some of which are personal, whilst others are created by the system. The word "crisis" has negative association, but the work of Erikson (1965) shows that these crises hold the possibility of positive growth. Out of the tension comes growth if the situation is handled intelligently. We can make those system-created crises, which cannot be avoided, situations leading to growth and increased social competence. The final chapter will make some suggestions for the involvement of the whole pastoral care team in group guidance, whilst the vocational side of this will be discussed in the next chapter. The discussion here will highlight the need for group guidance in the first year, trying to show the benefits which follow from it. Entry to the secondary school is a major crisis in the life of all pupils. Foremost is the requirement that he should adapt to new relationships with his teachers. In the primary school most of his feelings and interaction were focused on one teacher who taught him most subjects for at least one year. In the secondary school he has imposed on him the need to adjust to a number of teachers who make varied demands and have very different styles of communication and teaching. This is a source of tension, if not fear, in some pupils, who can then begin to experience anxiety and a sense of confusion. This is accentuated by the increased size of the school in which pupils often get lost and do not know where to go. In a set of confidential essays, first-year pupils reported surprisingly frequently fears of getting pushed down the stairs, and anxieties about not knowing where to go when they felt ill or hurt themselves. It also seems that there are grave fears about bullying and of bigger boys. This does not mean that bullying is rife in the schools where this is reported, but fears are created in many ways. Older brothers, other boys talking at the primary school, and casual remarks of primary school teachers and parents are interpreted in a threatening way. All this means that pupils can enter the secondary school in an apprehensive state, and that it is all too easy for their anxieties to be confirmed. Some first-year pupils are unable to understand or plan homework assignments, especially quite able boys who come from un-supportive home backgrounds. These anxieties are inevitable, and they have to be recognized and constructively dealt with. It is true that there is another side to the coin. Many pupils enter the secondary school with very positive expectations which are dissipated by unplanned entry and the negative impact of events.

The aim of the first-year guidance programme is to aid successful adaptation to the secondary school. The counsellor will be very involved in this, probably planning the programme of intervention in consultation with other senior members of the staff. The specific objectives of the guidance programme will be those of:—

1. Eliminating unnecessary anxieties.
2. Teaching coping strategies.
3. Ensuring that pupils receive appropriate supports.
4. Giving them experience of success and satisfaction as quickly as possible.

It could be argued that a special programme is unnecessary because it is the function of the form master to help pupils adjust to the new school situation, but in practice it is often the case that the meagre amount of time allowed to him for his pastoral work is absorbed by registration and the passing on of administrative instructions. I would argue for an intensive programme by the pastoral care team during the first four weeks of the first year, followed by a weekly session taken by the counsellor. In such an intensive programme, careful practical steps would be taken to ensure that pupils know where to go and that they are given real instruction in safety in laboratories and craft workshops. Frank discussions on the fears of bullying are necessary, showing why other boys have created these fears, giving instructions about what is to be done if bullying does occur and suggestions for coping with it. It is useful if senior boys can be put into a helping position with new boys, keeping an eye on their well-being. The breaks are the source of some of the major anxieties, and the school can work out strategies for preventing the new entrants being overwhelmed in the crush that occurs in the limited playground space of many urban schools. Homework assignments can be discussed in some detail and the techniques of dealing with them should be systematically taught. The provision of a map is useful, but it is even more effective if they are taken from classroom to classroom on the first few occasions by a senior boy. Teaching method should be more consistently related to what has been done in the primary school and the introduction of simple projects which provide a feeling of success yields very good returns. These can then lead into the more usual types of teaching.

It could be argued that this represents unnecessary coddling at a period when independence is essential, but the "sink or swim" approach seems unlikely to aid many pupils to achieve constructive independence, and the costs may be higher than we care to see. We are concerned with the difficulties caused by the raising of the school leaving age at the moment, yet my feeling is that much of the negative behaviour that now taxes our ingenuity and resources has its roots in the period of induction to the secondary school. Perhaps we can learn from industry, where a growing need is found to develop good induction courses for young workers. If we can establish the fact that the secondary school is a caring community from the moment the pupil enters, then much of the truancy and bad behaviour will become unnecessary. We who teach have to see that not only do we care, but that it is clear to the pupil that we care. Even at this frankly pragmatic level the argument is strong, but it becomes stronger when we see that the investment of resources is actually very small. It merely requires that selected members of the pastoral care team shall be released from the normal teaching duties for only part of their time for the short space of four weeks to undertake a systematically planned programme of adjustment. They are still dealing with forms. Systematic analyses of the deployment of resources in the secondary school are still rare, and it is only occasionally that we undertake the equivalent of a job analysis. Such techniques, which go hand in hand with curriculum development, would probably reveal unsuspected possibilities for allowing the pastoral care team to do its work in a way which helps everyone in the school.

The counsellor can extend this intensive form of group guidance by regular weekly sessions for as long as is necessary. This allows him to detect pupils who seem to be especially vulnerable to stress or who are in need of support and treatment. Boys who constantly report the loss of property, who resort to sickness on certain days of the week, or who break down into tantrums or tears are all indicating their need for help. It is only too easy to miss the significance of these symptoms, expressing our surprise when they break down, start truanting or begin to underfunction very badly. Student counsellors are sometimes asked to see pupils urgently in the third year. The remark is often made that "They were no trouble in the first year". Yet there is often evidence that the child did in fact need some support at that time. I have learned to respect the remarks of teachers that a boy seems "different", even though sometimes they have not been able to specify this difference in any exact terms. Often something is very wrong with the child and his home, although he is containing the stress with some success. The counsellor can arrange unobtrusive support and surveillance for the first-year pupils, but he is also ready to make an approach to an outside agency should the need become obvious. This turns guidance and counselling from a first-aid measure into a preventative activity. The counsellor will be particularly interested in those pupils who, feeling a need for security and belonging, begin to attach themselves to groups, or form groups which are against the values and objectives of the school. We can see that they are being forced into the position of gaining essential satisfactions for status and support through activities which are not in their best interests. The counsellor links such boys with the pastoral care system, building up supports for him.

One important aspect is the recognition of ill-health and sometimes physical defects which are not noted on the record cards. Signs of ill-health are noted, and the counsellor tries to assess the impact of this upon the future school performance and adjustment of the pupil. Any information of this type is fed to the year tutor or form master, and the counsellor discusses further action with him. This is collaboration in a team situation in which teachers try to ensure that the pupil is able to use what the school has to offer. With some children from disadvantaged homes additional guidance and help will have to be offered. Not only do we have to convey to them the rules and objectives of a system which is at odds with their backgrounds, but as Ford (1970) points out, working-class children need not equal but better education, if they are to compete with those of equal ability from more privileged backgrounds.

Group guidance programmes are useful with those statutory age leavers who are finding school increasingly irrelevant and distasteful, as long as they are linked to the pupils' interests and ambitions and they are interested in the working world. It is fatal to try to use them as a soporific to ease a strained situation. These programmes will help them anticipate the transition from school to work constructively. Although they long to escape from school, they are often anxious about starting working, despite a superficial air of bravado. Many working-class fathers discuss their jobs at home in negative terms, often only when things have gone badly wrong. A negative perception of work is built up in some pupils, causing them to enter their first job feeling that they have to outwit and out-manoeuvre the "bosses" if they are not to be exploited. Others have to be prepared for the fact that the enthusiasm and energy which they take to their first job will earn them the resentment or amusement of their workmates. It is tricky dealing with this without destroying the desire to do well in work. Authority relationships change and group guidance can prepare pupils for this. The way in which orders are given, together with the terseness and inadequacy of the instructions by foremen, can be discussed. The shift in relationships with parents and the problems of budgeting are important; the content should include exploration of the new types of compulsions and sanctions faced by the young worker, such as clocking in and the penalties for lateness. The evidence from Hayes and Hough (1970) is that we fail to give pupils what they really need. Once they enter work they are concerned with relationships with their workmates and supervisors, the physical conditions of the job and the social facilities. They feel that they needed more help at school in preparing for the psychological and social changes of the transition from school to work.

## A general note

Steady emphasis has been placed on the need to avoid violating the expectations of pupils and colleagues, and nowhere is this more necessary than in group guidance. We cannot transfer the freer techniques of group counselling into the group guidance situation where the form is the unit of organization without running the risk of chaos. Pupils can manipulate the well-intentioned counsellor quite ruthlessly. Control is central, and it is necessary to plan the progression from more routine matters to the discussions of feelings and emotions so that it happens gradually. The counsellor maintains a firm control, whilst steadily involving pupils in the planning of the content of sessions and reducing his own contribution. The more formal the educational method of the school, the more essential it is that the counsellor should use this slow approach to guidance. He must always present an image of competence and control as well as one of caring and concern, for failure to do this in some classes will spark off both disruptive anxieties and a great deal of testing of the limits of the guidance situation. In every case the counsellor makes sure that he has reduced any tensions that have been produced or aired before completing a guidance or counselling session. The final activities should be such that they leave the group in a positive frame of mind. It is both incompetent and discourteous to leave a group in a state of emotional arousal, putting a colleague into the position of having to suppress this. It is almost unforgivable for the trained counsellor to do this, for he should be deeply aware of the impact of his actions on others.

### Summary discussion

This chapter makes a distinction between group guidance and group counselling, showing the former to be a structured informational process which reinforces the aims of the school. The form is the usual unit of organization. Group counselling is concerned with the solution of developmental and personal problems. A number of strategies of group counselling are possible. Groups may be the sole means of counselling, or they can prepare pupils for individual counselling, but sometimes they can be used to complete the counselling which began with individual counselling.

Many considerations have to be taken into account in forming a group for counselling. We have to decide whether similarity of age, problem and sex make a good basis for counselling or whether more heterogeneous groups will better suit our purpose. The counsellor has to learn to state his objectives and then carefully decide upon those which suit him. Group counselling falls into four stages, making a relationship of trust, revealing the problem, the major work phase, and the ending of the group. All the techniques which have been described in earlier chapters can be employed, although role-playing and simulation are especially suitable.

Group counselling forms a bridge between individual counselling and the work of the classroom or workshop. Some attention is given to the way enthusiastic counsellors can link counselling with creative approaches to education.

Group guidance can be helpful in enabling pupils to deal with the crises of transition in the secondary school. The discussion concentrates on entry to the secondary school and the transition from school to work, showing that guidance has a preventative aspect. Discussion of the transition from school to work is dealt with briefly, because much of the chapter on vocational counselling is relevant to this topic.

## REFERENCES

Bales, R.F. and Strodtbeck, F.L. (1951) "Phases in Group Problem Solving", *Journal of Abnormal and Social Psychl.* 46. 485–495.

Bales, R.F. (1968) "Interaction Process Analysis", In *Encyclopedia of Social Sciences*, New York: Macmillan.

Bates, M. (1966) "Themes in Group Counseling with Adolescents", *Personnel and Guidance Journal.* 44. 568–575.

Berne, E. (1966) *Games People Play*, London: Deutsch. (Also Penguin 1968.)

Bion, W.R. (1961) *Experiences in Groups*, London: Tavistock Publications.

Bruner, J.S. (1966) *Toward a Theory of Instruction*, Mass.: Harvard University Press.

Erikson, E.H. (1965) *Childhood and Society*, London: Penguin.

Ford, J. (1969) *Social Class and the Comprehensive School*, London: Routledge & Kegan Paul.

Hayes, J. and Hough, P. (1970) *Occupational Perceptions and Occupational Information*, Dept. of Psychology, University of Leeds.

Hollander, E.P. (1964) *Leaders, Groups and Influences*, New York: Oxford University Press.

Mahler, C.A. (1969) *Group Counseling in the Schools*, New York: Houghton Mifflin.

Sherif, M. (1948) *Outline of Social Psychology*, New York: Harper.

Thompson, S. and Kahn, J. (1970) *The Group Process as a Helping Technique*, Oxford: Pergamon Press.

Tyler, L. (1960) "Minimum Change Therapy", *Pers. Guid. J.* 38. 475–479.

# CHAPTER SEVEN

# VOCATIONAL AND EDUCATIONAL COUNSELLING

## The purpose of this chapter

We now begin to explore the relationship between personal and vocational counselling. We shall find that these fields are intimately linked. The main ideas behind this chapter are (i) that vocational choice is a developmental process, and (ii) that the self-image of the pupil is of fundamental importance in vocational guidance and counselling. We shall see the need to consider the life style belonging to an occupation and its relationship to the picture of himself possessed by a pupil. We shall have to consider the implications of the idea that vocational choice is itself not only associated with development, but is a developmental process. We will also explore briefly educational guidance, looking at the counselling of underfunctioning pupils.

## The questions asked

We try to answer these questions:

(i) What is the meaning of retarded and impaired vocational choice?

(ii) What do we mean by the concepts of *field* and *level* in vocational counselling?

(iii) What is the relationship between the counsellor and the careers team? How can the specialist skills of the counsellor be used when this is necessary?

(iv) What programmes can be developed to help the pupil achieve satisfying decisions in the vocational field?

(v) What can the counsellor do which helps the total team in the field of educational guidance?

*A point*

If you have not had much first-hand acquaintance with the topics, you may find it useful to read the summary discussion at the end of the chapter.

*Life styles and the self-concept*

A pupil asks himself two basic questions which he answers more or less adequately during his secondary school career. These are "Who am I?" and "What am I to be?". They indicate the two lines of self-exploration which not only occupy the counsellor's attention but are essential for healthy development in adolescence. They also illustrate the link between the acquisition of identity and the choice of a career or job. Unless the pupil knows himself, he will be handicapped in his choice of a job. This still applies, even when his abilities and opportunities are sharply limited. The experienced counsellor or teacher will appreciate the significance of the wording of the second question. "What am I to *be?*" is a very different question from "What am I to *do?*". "What am I to *do?*" emphasizes the task rather than the personality needs and the life style which is part of a job. The life styles of the long-distance lorry driver, the milk-roundsman or the unskilled or semi-skilled worker on the assembly line of a car plant are very different, although the level of ability is very similar in general terms. Noble (1970) has suggested that occupational life styles influence the family roles of workers in a very powerful way and that there is an intimate association between the job and particular styles of family life. The foregoing is perhaps enough to suggest that counselling and vocational guidance are closely linked. This very link has been a source of difficulty. Some teachers and local authority administrators have assumed without bothering to investigate that counselling is merely another name for careers guidance, whilst many careers masters have incorrectly assumed that the advent of the counsellor threatens their existence. We can answer this confusion briefly. Counselling has been shown to be a particular kind of approach to the developmental problems and stresses of pupils. It embodies certain techniques which are sometimes necessary to help a pupil and sometimes quite irrelevant. The efficient careers teacher will find it helpful to learn some of these techniques and approaches, and to develop the ability to see when they are necessary.

It seems to me that some of the arguments about counselling and careers work come from the confusion of a *method* of approach with a specific *area of application of that method*. The method is applied, at the correct level of specialization wherever it is needed, by someone who has acquired the necessary skills, and the name given to the person doing this is of superficial interest only. Perhaps it is a mistake to separate vocational counselling from personal counselling. It may be more useful in exposition and teaching than in real life. The important thing is that help at the appropriate level of skill should be available to the pupil who needs it. Any attempt to see either personal counselling or vocational guidance as a separate entity is delusory. Both are equally concerned with choice process; both emphasize developmental factors, stressing the need for the pupil to make decisions. Each school will have to work out the relationships between these areas of developmental work in the light of the general objectives of its guidance system and the pastoral care scheme. Sometimes the role of the school counsellor and careers master may be combined in the same person, although this may be an unrealistic demand to make of anyone in all but the smallest secondary school and may result in poor work in both areas. When the positions are separated, it is possible to work out the relationships between careers master and the counsellor in a way which allows them to co-operate and give each other mutual support, rather than to create an uneasy situation of competition. In any case, they are both only individual members of the larger team concerned with guidance and pastoral care, and it is crucial that the headmaster should work out with the whole team, areas of specialization of function, areas of overlap and the methods of collaboration. Careers work cannot be satisfactorily carried out by one person even when it is restricted to the grossly inadequate function of supplying information.

We continuously talk about careers guidance, but is this realistic in our secondary schools? The word *career* carries connotations of steady advancement and long-term planning which are unrelated to what actually happens to at least half of the secondary school population. These pupils will not have planned careers, but will occupy jobs as and when they can get them. They will reach their maximal earning capacity early in life, although other satisfactions than the monetary rewards may be very important for them. We must see that the intrinsic satisfactions of the job may be less important than the people with whom they work, whilst the fringe benefits may assume surprising importance. One must be careful not to overstate this argument, for many manual workers get a sense of satisfaction and have a pride in competently performing what to many of us would be intolerably dull repetitive jobs. When we think about vocational counselling in schools we must remind ourselves that many manual jobs will disappear with the growth of automation, whilst new techniques and machines will eliminate many traditional skills. This is where we have to face the fact that the accelerating pace of social and technological change makes the future increasingly unpredictable and the past less useful as a guide to action. On the one hand it becomes even more desirable that every school should have a well-designed programme of vocational choice, whilst on the other it seems less clear as to what can be usefully incorporated in it. The solution seems to me to be one of bringing into the centre of vocational guidance the need to establish a sense of stable identity, which keeps a pupil socially and emotionally a whole person in the midst of uncertainty and change. In group counselling we stressed the need to be aware of the connection between identity and social competence; this is equally important in vocational guidance. It means, I think, that schools will benefit from the earlier introduction of vocational guidance based on methods which lead to increased self-awareness and success in the constructive task of building identity. We have to raise the level of general education of all pupils, and for this it is crucial that the pastoral care team are aware of the influences which help or retard attainment. A whole group of teachers has to be aware of the way in which such factors as home regime and the parental styles of thinking interact with the school influences to aid or cause difficulties for a particular pupil. I stress this because broad statements about social class can operate to cause a new kind of determinism in which teachers feel hopeless.

### The nature of vocational choice

The most productive way of looking at vocational choice from the teacher's viewpoint is to see it as a developmental process in which a series of choices have to be made. These choices are the product of the chooser's picture of himself. This fits in with the approach to counselling outlined in this book which states that self-awareness is the basis for adequate decision making. It is a little intimidating for us to see vocational guidance in these terms, for we cannot hold to the comfortable idea that vocational guidance is simply concerned with making a simple decision at one point in time. Nor does it allow us to push the responsibility outside the school on to the Careers Advisory Officer, although he has a large part to play in the process. It is easy to say that vocational choice is a long-term process rather than a single event in time, but it is difficult to understand the process, for a wealth of theories about vocational choice exist. This can cause confusion, but it is proper that a number of theories should exist; for one theoretical formulation, however complex, is unlikely to be a satisfying guide to vocational choice. We should remember, however, that theory forms the groundwork for a guide to intelligent action. I must acknowledge that the discussion which follows is a very unsatisfactory picture of very refined theories which ought to be read by the seriously interested; I hope it provides at least a map to a complex field.

It is salutary to begin by admitting the possibility that the most relevant theory of vocational choice for many pupils is the *accident theory*, despite the investment in vocational guidance in recent years. This may be due to the reluctance of schools to admit the Careers Officers to full partnership, but is even more frequently due to the fact that the careers master and counsellor have insufficient, if any, time for their work. Vocational choice is still a largely unplanned and haphazard process for more pupils than one cares to concede. The practical situation of lack of jobs means that many non-academic pupils finally get a first job through trial and error procedures in which the luck element is the main factor.

*Cultural and sociological* theories of vocational choice are based on the premise that a pupil will be influenced by his family, peer group, social class, religious affiliation and racial background. Which of these actually influences choice? It seems, from the evidence currently available, that the critical factor in the job choice of the statutory age leaver is still parental choice, despite the care lavished on this group by the careers service and school. This reminds us to look at some of the extreme statements about the adolescent's alienation from parents with a degree of scepticism: Reading some of the literature, one would never guess that adolescents mourn their parents if they die or plan to live near them when they marry or recognize their indebtedness to parents. The point for the vocational counsellor is that we can go sadly astray if we omit the influence of the *parents* in our work. *Family background* produces a characteristic pattern of accumulated advantages and disadvantages which we know affect motivation to work in school, but sometimes we do not see the way it influences work ambitions.

We must also allow for the way in which *the educational system* itself shapes the choice of career through allocation to a particular stream or band, the offering or absence of certain subjects and the facilities for non-examination work. Let us also be clear that subject choice can be vocational choice. A girl who omits mathematics or physics from her O Level subjects may find that her later choices are sharply restricted by this, whether she is going into a job or proceeding to further education. Staying on at school may automatically exclude pupils from occupations requiring lengthy on-the-job training such as traditional apprenticeships. This must be borne in mind with the new sixth form which includes boys taking C.S.E. and O Levels. Such boys are often giving undue importance to minimal educational qualifications and have grossly unrealistic aspirations and ideas about what they can do. I have recently counselled several such groups, finding that they also tend to feel devalued by school staff and the more academic sixth. Their negative self-image has been a source of tension for them and they have been in a highly ambivalent state resulting in some very odd behaviour and tensions. Perhaps we should become more alert to the way in which the school sends signals of success and failure to pupils which indicate what is educationally appropriate to them. The middle streams of the comprehensive school may well be in need of special study and concern on this account. We must also be prepared to look at the way in which working-class boys of good ability fail to invest in themselves, although gaining access to the six form. Swift (1973) provides some evidence about this. Within the last month I met a group of fifteen-year-olds about to leave school at Easter whose learning at school was summed up in the statement, "We don't feel that we are any good at anything". This may be exceptional, yet in my visits to a number of schools I get hints that this attitude is more widespread than is comfortable to accept.

Roe (1956) has produced a theory of occupational choice which has been neither satisfactorily confirmed nor disproved. She suggests that family regime influences a pupil's occupational choice by making him desire to work primarily with either people or things. The causal element is said to be the level of familial warmth. If this is low, or parental rejection exists, then her thesis is that the adolescent moves towards occupations concerned with things rather than people, whilst those who have good relationships with their parents choose work connected with people. The theory is interesting, although complex: it may link with Hudson's (1966) work on creativity. Roe says little about compensatory drives which might cause a person to move towards work with people as a result of deprivation within the family, or about what happens when one parent is rejecting and the other accepting. In such cases the sex of both the child and the rejecting parent may be the critical variables. This work is reported to highlight the way in which researchers have felt impelled to look at rather remote and less obvious factors to explain vocational choices. The school counsellor may well find himself doing this in difficult cases.

The most widely known and probably the most useful theory of vocational choice is that of Super (1957). This is based upon his belief that choosing an occupation is the major way in which a boy translates his self-picture into reality. His is a psychological theory of vocational choice which requires the job chooser to say more or less explicitly, "I am that sort of person". The greatest difficulty in using *self-theory* is this question of explicitness. If, in its earlier stages, adolescence is a period of identity crisis, marked by uncertainty and difficulties in establishing a firm sense of self-awareness, then it is sensible to ask how relevant this approach is to the statutory age leaver. At least some of those who are disadvantaged will leave school before any firm sense of positive identity has been established. Whilst this emphasizes the post-school work of the careers service, it also indicates the need for vocational guidance to include activities which stimulate self-awareness and realistic self-assessment. It certainly is a big assumption that a boy selects and goes into an occupation which mirrors his picture of himself. I think we must remain critical of the validity of this approach for individual pupils, although a great deal of supportive evidence exists. Sometimes I feel it is more accurate to say that a boy chooses an occupation in terms of what he is not, rather than in terms of what he is. Negative choices are at least as important as positive choices, and careers teachers are often aware that many pupils can only begin by making negative choices, that is, saying what they would not do. Perhaps all of us are clearer about the negative factors than the positive ones. Many of us would not be bookmakers, butchers, clerks or accountants because we do not see ourselves as that kind of person. Pupils tend to make the best of what is available after some fields have been rejected because they are impossible or because they cause distaste. Certainly the vocational counsellor must know how a pupil sees an occupational group. He may be attributing to these workers characteristics which are very unreal. This can be seen in some of the conceptions about the armed services. The effective careers worker will (although he often has insufficient time) explore the significance of the distorted stereotype of a group for a pupil, for until this has been modified, satisfying vocational choice is unlikely to occur. Although we emphasize the self-concept in choices, let us be clear that the self is never fully crystallized when a pupil leaves school, but continues to develop during his working life. Perhaps the most useful thing to underline is that a discrepancy of large proportions between the pupil's self-image and the life style imposed by the occupation is a danger signal.

Daws (1968) in a valuable study discusses the fact that the precision of the "talent matching" approach to vocational guidance was an illusion, mainly because it failed to include as basic data motivational and other personality factors which were indirectly related to the job. "Talent matching" is the process of identifying the skills and aptitudes needed for performance of the task. Some means of assessing these qualities in individuals was then devised. Applicants for the job were assessed on these measures, and were either rejected or accepted on their test results. It was a necessary attempt to fit a round peg into a round hole and a square peg into a square one. Unfortunately, the full nature of roundness and squareness is difficult to identify because it seems to depend on many variables other than the task. Tyler (1962) makes the point that if a person has the necessary minimal quantity of the requisite skills, including intelligence, then actual satisfaction and success may depend upon the personality qualities he possesses. In some cases these will increase the likelihood of success and in others make it less likely to occur. She also suggests that it may be more profitable to examine the nature of an individual's decision very closely. I would accept this, arguing that the vocational counselling team will be very concerned with decision making, including defining the situations in which a pupil appears to be able to co-operate with enthusiasm and where he appears to be threatened.

So far the trend of the argument has been that vocational choice is a long-term process. I have said nothing yet about the precise nature of this process. Ginzberg (1951) argues that it represents a compromise between social and environmental influences and personal needs and drives, whilst Super goes against this, saying that it is a creative kind of synthesis in which a pupil becomes truly fulfilled. If we think back to the three basic models of personality, then it seems that Super's work rests upon the model of "man in the process of becoming". Ginzberg seems to see the ability to compromise as a hallmark of sound development, whereas Super seems to regard compromise as somewhat regrettable. These are not abstract speculations; we have to decide where we stand on these issues, for our position determines the way in which we work with pupils. Ginzberg has qualified some of his original statements in recent years, but the argument is still relevant.

The most important thing which emerges from these theories is the fact that vocational choice is a developmental process. For those of us who teach and counsel this has enormous implications which need to be spelt out clearly if we are to do our work with integrity and benefit the pupil. If it is a developmental process, then we must be prepared to accept that individual boys or girls will develop at different rates in their capacity to make vocational choices. The fact that they are of the same chronological age gives us no necessary guide to the realistic and self-satisfying nature of the choices they will make. Let me illustrate by a brief reference to remedial education. In this field, we are at last able to see that it is possible for a pupil to be retarded in a specific subject such as reading or mathematics for social and emotional reasons, without necessarily lacking a fair measure of general ability. This does, of course, have consequences for the level of functioning in other ways. I argue that something of the same sort is often present, but not recognized, in the developmental process of vocational choice. This idea of the *impairment and retardation* of vocational choice seems to be a crucial step for the development of really effective vocational counselling and careers work in secondary schools, although as yet we have little precise evidence about the extent of this problem.

Examination of the work that is available together with my own experience in this field strongly suggests that, if we were to examine the vocational choices made by a large group of pupils as they moved from the age of ten to eighteen, we would be able to fit them into definite stages similar to those detected by the eminent theorists quoted above. Phantasy would almost certainly be a major element in the earlier stages, followed by a more realistic period in which preferences emerge based on a sense of definite interests and growing contact with, and awareness of, the adult world. They are often very definite, but seem to be based on limited conceptions of the self and the occupational world, and they reflect very important personality needs of early adolescence. This then seems to be followed by a period of doubt, out of which comes a *probable choice* based on more accurate self-knowledge, greater awareness of interests and aptitudes and of the qualifications needed for an occupation and the demands it makes. In my own counselling and the counselling of my students, it has seemed to us that certain pupils remain in the stage where phantasy is the major element behind their choice, or that personality factors retard them from reaching the stage where preferences begin to reveal themselves. In any school it seems there are pupils who have insufficient self-knowledge, lack the confidence to choose or are prevented from making a choice by environmental pressures and personality factors. These children possess only impaired or retarded capacity for making vocational choice and need carefully planned individual or group help. Often a great deal of personal counselling has to be done before the vocational problems can be tackled. When it seems that the pupil is ready, then specific vocational counselling can be introduced; more often it is inextricably mingled with the personal counselling.

How then can we deal with this? It seems that we need to look at the problem in terms of *field* and *level*. Field refers to the general characteristics of an occupation such as scientific, outdoor, computational, mechanical or persuasive. The field is related to aptitudes, but also reflects interests, and the counsellor may find it useful to apply tests of interests standardized upon a British population to learn about the pupil's ideas of attractive fields and those he would reject. In using these interests tests we have to be aware that interests in such pupils will probably change during counselling and that the results of any single test must be taken with caution. Interests are important as Nelson (1968) has shown, because they are related to the amount of satisfaction obtained from a job, as measured both by intention to stay in that job, and the actual length of stay in it. Satisfaction and competence in a job are only partially dependent upon interests, for the worker must possess the necessary aptitude and ability. The identification of fields of interest gives us a starting point for developmental counselling, but it is only one way of breaking into the problem.

The second major structuring factor is the concept of level, which brings in many considerations, especially the pupil's level of aspiration for himself. The level of occupation to which a pupil aspires may be either unrealistically high or low for many reasons. Different occupational levels imply very different life styles, drawing our attention to social class and home background. Many difficulties are created when the proposed choice differs from that of his parents or from the level they desire for him. I am reminded of an eighteen-year-old of low average ability and marked practical bent who was prevented from doing what he wanted. When he left school he got great pleasure from ostentatiously parking the lorry he drove in front of his executive parents' house in a status-conscious suburb! As you can see he eventually accepted a realistic level of occupation. If he had been allowed to become a motor mechanic he would have been more satisfied, but the parents could not accept this whilst he was at school. Parents often need parallel counselling in this matter of level, for they may be working out their own aspirations through their child, often putting such pressures on him that the development of vocational preferences is frozen, or else the boy makes widely vacillating choices as a reaction. Some working-class parents have to be aided to see that not only is their child's choice legitimate, but possible of attainment. Middle-class parents may have to reach acceptance of the fact that choices within the fields of technology, applied science and the practical or mechanical fields are socially acceptable these days. Such parents often have limited and rigid conception of very traditional routes to advancement and occupational success. Trying to impose these ideas on pupils causes emotional distress and retards their development.

Tyler (1958) has pointed out a third structuring factor for the vocational counsellor which is related to the impairment of choice processes, particularly in very able and sensitive pupils. Such pupils may not see that although they possess many potentialities, they cannot become everything that it is possible for them to be. Such adolescents often feel the need to explore and express every aspect of their personality, resisting what they feel are attempts to make them give up any of these. They react by talking about "moulding" by the system, and it is sometimes difficult to deny the truth of this, yet healthy development does require them to exclude some alternatives, deny some ambitions or else reduce them to the position of hobbies. This can only be done by them; we cannot do it for them, but they do need support. This is, I think, what Ginzberg is talking about when he calls vocational choice a process of compromise, although he also means much more than this.

### Some ways of helping the choice process

Our techniques must aim at aiding the consideration of alternatives and narrowing down the possibilities, whilst simultaneously building up the pupil's ability to make decisions. One way is to give the pupil a set of cards, each of which bears the name of an occupation. These are then sorted into two groups, those which he sees as suitable for himself and those which appear to be unsuitable. A third group of doubtfuls is sometimes included. The results are then discussed thoroughly. I find it useful with a number of boys to begin with the exclusions, not only because this is easier for those lagging behind in the vocational choice process, but this makes them less inclined to feel that they are being pushed in any one direction. It seems best to keep the numbers of cards small in each set. Then the counsellor can compile a new set based on what he has learned from the preceding set. A duplicated form can be used to record the results in an easy way. The next step is probably that of introducing sorts on the basis of *level*. We begin by looking at field, which is related to interests, but we need to explore choice processes according to his ideas of qualifications, abilities required and the social level of the job. I vary between two strategies at this point. Sometimes I repeat the whole series which has been used, or I confine myself to the ones he has chosen as suited to himself. This depends upon time, but when the pupil seems very retarded and unable to make decisions, then the more practice he has the better it is. Is this technique futile if the pupil has insufficient knowledge of the occupations? Far from it. The objective of this approach is to help the boy see the way in which he evaluates occupations, the ones he sees as appropriate for himself and to bring gross inaccuracies to his attention, for the counsellor participates by giving information. In any case, his occupational stereotypes are important, even if inaccurate, and we have to get these out into the open. We are also beginning to train him in the techniques of making a choice.

The counsellor can aid the decision making process and link it with the self-concept in several other ways. Pictures of people wearing dress which indicates the occupational activity and the social status attached to it can be presented to a boy. These pictures might include people wearing donkey jackets, overalls, lounge suits, white coats or jeans. He then begins by selecting the ones which show the type of clothes he thinks he would like to wear if he were working. Important facts about body image and the self will often emerge in the subsequent discussion. We can also give him sets of pictures illustrating people at work, such as operating a machine or answering the telephone, asking him to sort these into those he finds attractive and those he dislikes. These can be used as modified construct tests as suggested in Chapter Four. Such simple stimuli bring out important responses which would not emerge in an interview based on verbal exchanges alone. The counsellor looks for inconsistencies and discrepancies, drawing the pupil's attention to them.

What constitutes adequate information for vocational counselling? It seems best to utilize all the information which is available in the school, rather than attempt heavy testing programmes. If we gather information in this way, we are again involving other members of the staff. Rodger's (1968) Seven Point Plan provides a good framework for information, although the suggestions made here do depart from this. Sometimes quite obvious factors get overlooked, simply because they are so obvious, and vocational counselling can go awry because of this. The emphasis upon perceptions, attitudes and feelings can lead one to ignore the physical conditions of a pupil. The record card should be checked, not only for details of any defects of hearing or vision, but for evidence of past illnesses such as rheumatic fever, which may act as limiting influences on vocational choice. We don't assume that it is going to be important, but merely recognize the possibility that it *may* be so. It is useful to ask the physical education department to provide an assessment of physical co-ordination and motor skills, obtaining evidence on this score from the craft teachers as well. Comparison of different types of physical behaviours in different contexts can be very illuminating. Such reports are subjective and coloured by teacher-pupil relationships, yet they provide valuable information. We need to check for any tendency to become unusually fatigued, or for signs that prolonged physical activity is likely to be a source of strain. Certain occupations may have to be eliminated because they are too demanding physically. I have had to bring this to the notice of a pupil quite firmly, sometimes because he was unaware of the demands of the job, or more seriously with a few boys, because they could not accept the limits of their physical strength.

Next one looks at the special abilities needed for a job, the entry requirements and the relationship between the life style of the job and the values of the pupil. The source for this is rarely to be found in the record cards and report forms, because these usually give examination marks which are often difficult to interpret meaningfully and say very little about personality qualities. Disillusioned, I have come to the conclusion that not only are they inaccurate, which is bad enough, but that they seem to be instruments for creating self-fulfilling prophecies about pupils. Entries are often only made after the teacher has scanned the previous entries which can influence him, for most of us do not like to be at variance with other teachers about our reports. This danger is reduced with the growing tendency to supply pads of report forms, the entry being made on the master card by the year- or house-tutor. The record card can supply evidence of such trends as constant deterioration of work, but the counsellor always needs to check carefully. He does this by talking in an informal way with the pupil's teachers, who often possess valuable knowledge which has not been recorded; sometimes, indeed, they may not realize the significance of the information they hold. Information which has little meaning in isolation may be extremely helpful when it is related to other details, therefore the counsellor collects and collates it in the way described. This seems clumsy and slow, but my discussion is concerned with those who are in difficulties about vocational choice. It is, however, surprisingly easy to get the information if one knows whom to ask, and not much time is required. We do not try to get all the information before we begin counselling, we gather it as we begin to see what is wanted.

We must make an attempt to assess any changes in attitude which have occurred fairly recently, especially if the pupil has begun to work. Some pupils do develop late or only realize the relevance of school in their last year, and it may be that they will do extremely well if encouraged to stay on at school. This is a healthy reminder that we are concerned with the positive rather than the negative. We look at general ability, but do not place much reliance upon a single intelligence test score which happens to be entered on the record card. This may be the result of a test given in the primary school, or at the period of transfer, when the child had not settled down; the type of test and the conditions of administration may make it a very poor guide to current capacity.

As counselling begins to move into a constructive phase, we begin to centre the sessions on important topics. The extent to which a boy is prepared to invest in his future training and job is an obvious one. We look at the tensions between immediate costs and later gains, and at the acceptable and unacceptable costs involved in taking up an apprenticeship. We have a responsibility for outlining the compensations attached to such investments as full-time further education, part-time study or the delay in leaving school, showing the pupil that these are a form of self-investment. The willingness to train is linked with the self-concept and a sense of worthwhileness, and I have often pointed out that as a responsible person I do not advise anyone to invest in bankrupt concerns or those with grossly uncertain prospects. This really makes a boy see that he is not being viewed as useless. At this stage, pupils often begin to produce their cherished ambitions which often contain strong phantasy elements. These will, if treated with respect, modify, and the infantile elements disappear almost unnoticed. I confess to a feeling of irritation and almost helplessness when a fifteen-year-old tells me he intends to be a professional footballer and I have evidence that he could scarcely be persuaded to put his football boots on during the whole of his secondary school career. I accept this and then work on the positive aspect of what comes out, for to attack his phantasy ambition would be to make him cling to it more desperately.

At this stage we begin to narrow down possibilities; this does not mean a grim experience of the elimination of ambitions, but a positive and cheerful experience of planning ahead. We look at the work environments which attract or repel a lad, for pupils react very divergently to noise levels, working in isolation or in a team, the size of the firm and the sort of responsibility that has to be taken. Some pupils are very frightened of being trusted with money, as on a milk round. The counsellor very quickly learns that naive sounding questions such as "Would you like to be able to sit down most of the time or always be on the move?" have real point.

Testing can waste both time and money and a discussion of its snares is included in the next chapter. Tests certainly only have real use when the pupil understands their relevance for him and is prepared to co-operate. I was once an avid tester, but I now tend to argue that any uniform plan of testing will ignore individual needs. When necessary we can assess the pupil's general ability through Raven's matrices or a sound test taken from the N.F.E.R. list. Useful attainment tests could include the English Progress Tests, the Neale Analysis of Reading Ability, the Secondary Mathematics Series and the Luning PRAK Mathematical and Technical Test. Jackson and Juniper (1971) provide a good guide to testing for the counsellor, but the counsellor is recommended to discuss testing with his educational psychologist who will advise him about the professional implications and also know the local conditions which may affect testing. Tests of aptitude, such as those concerned with clerical aptitude, should be used with care because the norms may not be drawn from comparable populations. The careers service will usually be glad to advise and help in this area and any co-operation between the Careers Advisory Officer and the counsellor is to be welcomed. Without this there can be overlap of effort and waste of time by the counsellor. One of the most useful tests is the Morrisby Differential Test Battery which consists of twelve tests covering general ability and special aptitudes. Three excellent interest tests exist which have norms drawn from British secondary school populations, the Rothwell-Miller Interests blank, the Connolly Interests Test and the A.P.U. Occupational Blank. Training is available and should be obtained if these tests are to be administered and interpreted with beneficial results. The Bristol Social Adjustment Guide can be very useful, but this means making demands on the time of fellow teachers. Perhaps it is best to restrict the use of this to the cases where there seems to be a need for a more precise definition of specific patterns of behaviour in school, and also where referral to a child guidance clinic is under consideration.

### The counsellor and the careers team

Perhaps this sub-heading is too hopeful for many Heads give little attention to careers work, appointing anyone who volunteers for the job and giving them the minimal reward for what, if it is done properly, is extremely demanding and time-consuming work. Some Heads still see careers work as an intrusion or as an activity confined to handing out a pamphlet, not seeing the great benefits for the school when it is properly done. This is not a discussion on careers guidance; the book by Hayes and Hopson (1971) provides an excellent guide to this topic.

Let us ask now how the counsellor functions if there is a separate and well-developed careers team. In this situation, counselling need not involve standard careers work. The role of the counsellor is complementary, and he uses his skills where they are appropriate. His techniques are based upon an integration of the findings of sociology and psychology (although trainers of course realize that these are separate disciplines involving different levels of analysis) whilst they are backed by an ethic springing from casework. This makes the counsellor very useful in helping pupils where emotional and irrational factors are distorting a pupil's level of aspiration from what is optimal for him; where gross external pressures, particularly those stemming from parental ambitions for their child, force him to make choices conflicting with his conception of himself; and where serious deficiencies in decision-making skill prevent him from making a choice. This is close to, but not identical with the earlier statements about retarded and impaired development of vocational choice. It gives us a basis for the amicable and mutually helpful separation of the activities of the careers master and the school counsellor if we need it.

There are some pupils for whom a fairly prolonged period of group or individual counselling is necessary as a pre-requisite for sensible vocational choice. These are a minority, but some will be of high ability, and faulty choice may mean life-long frustration for them. They include the highly sensitive and deeply moral, who have tried to find salvation in rejection of the system, repudiating materialistic standards and industrial society and stressing the validity of inner experience. This does not mean counsellors attempt to adjust them blindly to the system, but accepting the fact that access to a creative career now seems to require greater investment and earlier choice. It is sometimes essential for them to drop out of school for a year, in order to have some experience of work or to sort out their feelings and attitudes, and then return to take A Levels or other courses. The increased facilities for further education and the growth of A Level courses outside schools makes this a growing possibility. Yet it is often still difficult for these people to opt back into the system after their period of self-definition and exploration is completed. None of this means that the counsellor advises such pupils to opt out; indeed, we are only too conscious that these valuable individuals can be absorbed into drug-taking groups without seeing the dangers they run. Caution is necessary; one urges the pupil to think of all the dimensions of the problem, and offers concern and a lifeline by letting them know that one is available whatever they do. I certainly fail. In the last year I have been very concerned about a boy I saw who felt, like several others in his group, that the only honest people were the workers. By this he meant manual workers. His ideals were admirable, but his concept of the relationships between manual workers was completely out of touch with reality. This boy who was full of romanticism and possessed a very slight physique took up a manual job, found the strain too great and is now drifting aimlessly. Such situations are part of the counsellor's life: we have to live with them and with the inevitable question, "Was it my fault?" When I can no longer ask the questions then I think my capacity to be of service has gone. But it is extremely uncomfortable living with the associated feeling.

In this discussion of the specialist role of the trained counsellor in relation to the vocational guidance team, I shall return to my original remarks about the importance of retarded and impaired vocational choice. The skilled counsellor is needed to cope with cases of deviant vocational choice which are based upon one factor alone, such as interest and aptitude. These considerations have become so predominant in the boy's choice that other important aspects never get considered. Sometimes choice is distorted by the presence of factors which are still prime at a much later stage than usual. Recently a student saw a boy who wanted to teach and stubbornly insisted that he wanted to teach, whilst giving many signals that he was also doubtful about this. After some counselling, he saw that he was still deeply identified with a primary school teacher who had been extremely important to him after the death of his father. Until he discovered this, it was impossible for him to move towards what he really wanted to do, which was accountancy. There was a sense of debt and gratitude which somehow tied him to this man. May I again caution that these simple statements about the counselling hide the real nature of the process; they are given to illustrate the point. Quite often we find that an interest that is not backed by ability or aptitude is taken as the only possible basis for deciding on a job by fifteen- and sixteen-year-olds. It is often impossible to find a job in that field at the level they need, and very carefully planned counselling has to occur.

Experience suggests that the most difficult condition is where the pupil is unable to make a choice of any kind. This may be symptomatic of deep personality maladjustment, and this means referral to the psychologist. Even if this is not so, such pupils require a great deal of help. We can see that in all these cases, attempts at reasoning and the provision of information would fail, unless they were incorporated into counselling. Such boys can absorb a great deal of time of the careers staff which could be given to other pupils, yet they never benefit from the usual approach to careers work. When they begin to implement their choices they experience panic, conflict and dissatisfaction, and they can only cope by projecting the blame for the situation on to the careers master and the school.

Those pupils who have unrealistic levels of aspiration present a very special problem because we can easily damage them. I often find that they seem to be motivated by a fear of failure rather than a desire for real success. This leads them to set impossibly high targets, avoiding reality, but also occasionally revealing that their strategy is that of avoiding blame, for nobody will blame them for failing in such difficult tasks. Others seek safety in setting themselves very low targets, building up a false picture of themselves as incapable. This may sound fanciful, yet such feelings are brought out by the adolescent. We find that these are purposeful strategies which function to defend their users against threats to a very fragile sense of self-esteem, helping them avoid some of the stresses of competition and the threat of failure. They gradually see this, and can only be helped through this. If they are left alone and unhelped, they shift their target from day to day in some cases, letting their occupational ambitions vary with every chance stimulus that comes their way. I have met cases where they were a great burden to the careers teacher because they accepted advice with gratitude one week, only to turn up the next to request information totally unrelated to that provided previously. Often they leave school without firm plans, although this does not mean they then benefit from the aid of the Careers Advisory Service any more than they did at school. Indeed they are likely to display a compulsive pattern of entering and leaving jobs, scarcely knowing why they do so, until finally they get some intensive help or are labelled as work-shy and unemployable.

The main theme behind this discussion is incorporated in the word "team". The concept of a team carries with it the idea of specialization of function and a profitable division of labour, and this should apply to the careers and pastoral care team. Although each member sees to different things, this does not mean that any individual is superior, but that an attempt is being made to establish an efficient division of function. If the counsellor who is trained operates with the type of pupils I have been describing, not only does he work at the level which utilizes his specialist skills, but he allows the others to perform their functions more adequately. Underlying the argument has been the basic theme of levels of counselling and guidance and of using available resources efficiently.

## Vocational guidance

When we discussed group guidance it was suggested that it is profitable to intervene at transition points in the school life of pupils, trying to ensure that these are used constructively. As we saw in the first chapter, adolescence itself is a marginal period in society, when not only is a major transition from childhood to adulthood accomplished, but a crisis of identity occurs. Vocational identity is part of the identity which is acquired during adolescence, although the process is never completed, and the secondary school is vital in aiding this development. A longitudinal study by Gesell, Ilg and Ames (1956) covered adolescents for a period of seven years. They found some evidence that periods of crystallization of choice occur at the ages of thirteen and sixteen. In between came a period of doubt and uncertainty about vocational aspirations. Results like this are time and culture bound, but they fit our experience of what happens in the secondary school. Many statutory age leavers experience this uncertainty in the middle of the secondary school life. This uncertainty is partially resolved for them by their allocation to certain streams or courses of study, and sometimes by their resolute disassociation of themselves from the goals and objectives of the school. The exact form in which, and the age at which, these stages appear, is a product of the system, especially a product of the clarity of the signals of success and failure sent to the pupil, his intended age of leaving school and the system of guidance and choices existing in the school. If a boy experiences success then he is less likely to reject the role of the "ideal pupil" as it is defined by the school. Many a statutory age leaver is pushed towards allegiance to roles lying outside the school long before he leaves, making his school work seem irrelevant and boring, causing him to categorize it as childish.

This idea of initial clarity and a sense of purpose, followed by doubt, offers the possibility of developmental forms of vocational guidance. The aim is to aid the development of self-awareness and the capacity to make decisions. It is tempting to leap in with the assumption that the best thing is to shorten the period of uncertainty and make firm decisions which allow the school to provide supportive learning experiences. This has the danger of causing pupils to make premature choices which may then be hard to change. It may be more useful to adopt methods which prolong the uncertainty, allowing growth and providing experiences which aid the capacity to make sound decisions.

It seems sensible to begin group guidance in the vocational sense at the age of thirteen, because if the pastoral care team has done its work and the programme of orientation was successful, the pupil is beginning to use the resources of the school. Sometimes the process of alienation has begun in some pupils, but it has not gone too far. The counsellor or careers master can devise programmes which use questionnaire type instruments, role-playing and simulation situations which stimulate the development of critical thinking and self-knowledge. This is preparation for the important choices which have to be made about courses, and options around this time. Schools differ in the timing of choice points, but the principle behind this book is that we should anticipate these periods of decision, deliberately teaching pupils to prepare for them by concentrating resources on guidance programmes. In this the careers team and the pastoral care team as a whole will play a large part, although the involvement can be even wider. In one school the drama department plays a large part in the role-playing and simulation, allowing groups to enact what may happen in a bank, in a department at a nearby factory or on a building site. The stimulation provided by this is then followed up in the guidance sessions where boys begin to see that the occupational world is concerned with personality, interests, physical qualities and qualifications of many kinds. The simple questionnaire type instruments suggested earlier can be modified to produce their occupational stereotypes, to make the pupils more aware of themselves and to help them gain practice in seeing the way in which a job matches the picture of themselves. They are beginning to discover if they seem to be the kind of person who is going to be satisfied doing a certain kind of job. Let me make it clear that this is not asking them to choose an occupation, but provides them with fairly intensive practice in self-assessment and relating the results of this to the outside world. Again this can be linked with the pupil's own projects and library work for he would build the simulations up himself. The type of thinking which is developed in this guidance programme can be utilized in the teaching of many subjects.

Group guidance has a place also when the pupil reaches the stage of making a definite choice. Hayes and Hough (1971) have shown that the careers guidance we supply is felt to be deficient by young workers. Part of the guidance programme will be pre-choice, and part post-choice. We tend to assume that the job is finished once a choice has been made. We need to train pupils to look very critically at the brochures and handouts about employment, for many of these are biased unless they come from official sources. They should be trained to look at such documents as examples of persuasive communication, being alerted to omissions, distortion and selectivity. This training in critical thinking is a valuable asset which the school should consciously utilize in other areas.

Visits are indicated at this stage, although I suspect that they often occur too late and in a haphazard way. We need to think carefully about visits, because industry is becoming resistant to the increasing demands, especially when they realize that schools are not prepared to allow them to be used for recruiting purposes. This is a proper attitude for the school, but these visits are costly for the firm because they tie workers up for several hours. I am sceptical about the value of visits. It is often more productive to bring back boys who have recently left school and allow them to discuss their first-hand experiences. This should include those who are finding life difficult as well as the obvious successes. Counsellors engaged in vocational guidance report that the interaction and amount of learning is far greater in such circumstances than when talks are given by personnel managers or other representatives of management.

Once the choice has been made, a great deal of important work can be done through group guidance. The post-decisional phenomenon called cognitive dissonance operates with pupils who have chosen a job. In most cases, choice means that certain alternatives have been rejected which held certain attractions. This causes a kind of tension which is reduced by concentrating on the attractive and positive elements in the chosen job, whilst the snags are ignored. We can fall into the trap of reinforcing this, hoping that the pupil will go into his first job with positive attitudes. This is unrealistic and many pupils fail to adjust to the work situation because they did not anticipate the difficulties and the snags. Programmes which prepare pupils for this are not to be considered as negative, but rather as real preparation for a situation which is far from easy. Young workers are still sent for rubber hammers, sky hooks and striped paint; they still find it difficult to cope with this and the other forms of initiation into a work role.

This post-decisional area of vocational counselling and guidance may be at least as valuable as the pre-decisional stage. Our strategy to the difficulties raised above could be that of giving pupils an innocula-tion against the stresses and strains found on entry to work. This is very close to the way in which a behavioural therapist works when he gets a patient to mentally rehearse an anxiety-provoking situation. We shall not rely on discussion alone, but discussion after experience pro-vided by role-playing and simulation. It can be argued that simulation of conditions of battle never stopped one from being frightened, but many of us coped better because of it. We will prepare pupils systema-tically for the negative experiences of meeting terse instructions, getting the most unpleasant jobs and having to adjust to the pace of a machine. More important than this, we must help them deal with anxiety-producing situations such as dealing with complaints from customers whilst another member of staff is being obstructive; answering the telephone and taking messages; or adding up in front of an audience or under very noisy conditions. Perhaps the most crucial thing we can do is teach the future worker how to cope with his mistakes. Does he take a chance, cover it up, tell someone and get advice or give up the job? Young workers do report these things as causes of stress and reasons why they leave jobs even when they risk unemployment. It is curious that much of education is concerned with errors, yet we never consciously and constructively teach pupils how to deal with mistakes without feeling guilty, embarrassed or ashamed. Why?

My contacts with a number of firms show a big gap between the expectations of the firm and the objectives of the school. There is no reason of course why the school should passively adjust to the very limited expectations of some firms. Yet it is disturbing to still hear from personnel workers that pupils have little idea of how to behave in an interview, or how to put a coherent point of view. Sometimes they apply for jobs having no idea what the firm does, or any understanding of the nature of the training involved in an apprenticeship. Such complaints may reflect the lack of contact between certain schools and local industry; for this reason, too, one is suspicious of the personnel manager who says he places no credence upon the school report. It would be more profitable to spend more time in systematically analysing with pupils the ways in which judgements are made in interviews, and in providing them with a basic training in putting themselves across to other people. Occasionally this situation reflects a lack of use by the schools of the very real contribution that the Careers Advisory Officer can make to the content of the guidance programme, for he is the essential link between school and industry. He knows what the firm wants, and he is in a unique position to put the viewpoint of the school. He should be involved in the guidance programme from the moment it begins, although the activities may be carried out entirely by the teaching staff. If we realize that employers often do not know the difference between the C.S.E. and G.C.E. examinations and often undervalue the former, we can see his importance in this field. Not only should the school involve the careers officer more fully, but it must ask if it is proper for the school to take over his placement function even when the opportunity arises. He alone knows why pupils should be discouraged from going to a certain employer. A case came to my notice some time ago where a fairly large garage had built up a link with a school at some distance away, and the careers master was sending boys for apprenticeships to this place. It was found that there was no apprenticeship scheme, and that these boys were being kept as cheap labour, either being discharged when they got too old or discharging themselves when they realized the truth of the circumstances. Unfortunately, they then found it almost impossible to get an apprenticeship because of their age. Contact with the careers officer in the area would have prevented this.

### Educational guidance and the counsellor

The heading indicates the limits to the discussion on educational guidance at this point. Educational guidance is closely woven into every counselling interview, but this does not mean that the counsellor sees it as providing direct advice and giving information about options and subject choices. There are other teachers better qualified to do this, and it not only is inefficient but it can lead to conflict between the counsellor and his colleagues. Heads of department, form masters, year- and house-tutors often regard this advice-giving as an inalienable part of their own role and react sharply to trespass by the counsellor. It seems that the major factor is that of efficiency, for such guidance requires a specialist knowledge of the subtleties of each subject area. It is unlikely that any counsellor possesses the necessary competencies, therefore it may be more realistic for the counsellor to function as a link between the pupil and the teacher who possesses the information, once a pupil has looked at the emotions and the nature of the attitudes which are making his choice difficult. This is the same kind of demarcation of role as that suggested when the counsellor and careers master were being discussed.

From the viewpoint of the counsellor, the primary aim of educational guidance is that of helping a pupil function more adequately in the school by helping him build up his decision-making ability and understand himself better. Once this is achieved, we initiate the next steps through our colleagues, feeding them with information which allows them to adjust their actions to the needs of the pupil. If the counsellor is doing his job, then he is helping to create conditions in which his fellow teachers can provide educational guidance more easily and efficiently. Again we see that our object is to help a pupil perceive himself and the school more positively, seeing that worthwhile satisfactions are available for him and that school activities are relevant to his ambitions and future life. This is not stifling the just criticisms of a pupil, it enables him to make the best possible use of the school as it is.

Educational guidance for the counsellor often seems to centre around children who are thought to be underfunctioning, perhaps because such pupils provoke anxiety in their teachers. Certainly waste of talent is to be deprecated, although the counsellor appreciates the possibility that so-called underfunctioning may reflect deep-seated attitudes and a malaise which permeates many areas of the pupil's life. Change may be extremely difficult and slow. Counselling may nevertheless yield results, as Shouksmith and Taylor (1964) demonstrate, although we may be uncertain why this happens. We begin by asking ourselves questions which, when answered, allow us to formulate strategies. Is it all round underfunctioning? Is it restricted to a certain broad area or a specific subject? Why is he considered underfunctioning? Is it on the basis of the results of standardized tests which are appropriate and which have been properly applied? If so, is there still the possibility that the results have been misinterpreted? More often, one finds that the judgement has been made unsystematically and impressionistically. We then find that some of these pupils actually lack the degree of ability which they are thought to possess, but are extremely positive towards the school and teachers. They often fit very closely the implicit model of the "good pupil" which is extant in the school. The idea that they are underfunctioning is an example of the "halo" effect found in interpersonal judgements. Unrealistic expectations of good performance academically can be created by pleasant manners, good appearance, smart dress and a precise manner of speech, especially when these are rare qualities in a school or form.

We then proceed to look at ill-health, parental attitudes towards learning, absences at a critical period in the teaching of a skill and indifferent teaching. Some of these may well contribute, but often we have to look at less obvious factors. The standards he sets for himself and the type of peers whom the pupil wishes to emulate are two of these. We have discussed both these, but it should be pointed out that in the second case, the counsellor may once again find himself in the difficult position of trying to help a pupil adopt the values of a group which has very unattractive characteristics. I find that some able boys associate academic attainment with snobbery and femininity, whilst they want to emphasize their toughness and virility.

Some of the arguments regarding the lack of attainment in pupils from poor backgrounds seem to stress their inability to forgo immediate rewards and work for long-term goals. This suggests that the pupil who works to capacity in school is one who was trained early in life to plan ahead and work for more distant goals. Perhaps this argument contains a version of the old conflict between the pleasure and reality principles, although we must be careful how we interpret this. If we stop to look at a successful boy who is working for a long-term goal such as entry to a profession or success in an examination, we begin to see that he is not deprived of immediate gratifications. He is bombarded by rewards which compensate him for the efforts he makes and for some of the pleasures he has to forgo. The rewards provided by parents and teachers are meaningful to him, whereas those supplied by age-mates and figures outside the school and home may be more meaningful to the boy who is failing. It is a question of *different* gratifications, rather than their presence or absence. The counsellor's task may be that of making the verbal and symbolic rewards offered by the school meaningful to a pupil, whilst he will also look at the ability to approach a learning task methodically and see if pupils can plan ahead. If these skills are deficient, then he tries to supply them through educational guidance.

Group methods of the type outlined in the previous chapter would be employed for this. The exercise is one of specification of the objectives and behavioural changes that will be needed if the pupils are to succeed in school. In dealing with underfunctioning pupils, we need to face the fact that we may have to change attitudes which are basic to the pupil's way of life. Let me illustrate. Some very able working-class boys I have met have a great belief in "luck" as a factor in success. This, of course, goes against the life style necessary for success in the school where effort, hard work and acceptance of responsibility for one's success or failure is stressed. Such boys also seem to be marked by the desire to "get by" rather than excel, the avoidance of obvious trouble and a resolute determination never to do more than the minimum that is possible. This view of life makes the demands of teachers irrelevant to them. In a good-humoured way they have a contempt for intellectual activities which reduces learning in school to boring triviality for them.

Once we see this, it becomes clear that counselling such pupils calls for the full skills of the trained counsellor because we are often intervening to modify a total life style. Not only is skill necessary, but we also have to look at the morality of this. Do we suggest that there is something wrong with the basic view of life when we begin counselling such pupils? Although the school is built on middle-class attitudes, have we the right to suggest that this is a better life style than that found in working-class pupils of the type we are discussing? The problem seems to be that counselling is necessary for these pupils if they are to use their ability in the school and work systems. We can avoid saying that the middle-class life style has any intrinsic superiority, but as the world exists and seems to be developing, it does have *instrumental superiority*. In other words, it is a more effective life style leading to greater success and satisfaction. These remarks do not mean that the life style is not modifiable; indeed, we can all see the way in which the middle-class life style has changed in the last twenty years. All I am saying is that if pupils want to be successful then they have to learn how to do this. As things are, they are most likely to get what they want through the life style adopted by the middle class.

Educational guidance, as we conceive it in this discussion, will be concerned with attitude change and the modification of the perceptions of school and of teachers which are held by a pupil. We then proceed to the development of successful coping strategies in the way described in the work phase of the counselling group. The crucial element in the first step is to understand the type of relationship which pupils see as existing between themselves and the school. In practice, this means the type of relationship which pupils think exists between them and those who teach them. Every under-achieving pupil seems to have (i) an ideal for himself, (ii) a view of himself in the everyday life of the school, (iii) his own idea of what teachers demand from an ideal pupil. It is this third facet which has often seemed most important to me when I have been counselling a pupil of ability who has wasted his time in school, but who now has decided to work. For all sorts of reasons, they see the demands made on an "ideal pupil" to be frustrating, unreasonable, infantile or impossible to meet. They sometimes feel it means a choice between independence and maturity and the acceptance of a position of gross tutelage. Unless we deal with these feelings and show pupils that it is possible to avail themselves of the facilities provided by the school, becoming more individual rather than having identity diminished, the counselling will not get very far. Sometimes I find the conflict comes because a boy's ideal for himself and the ideal which he *thinks* his teachers demand are sharply discrepant. Both are modifiable and it is always likely that he is misinterpreting the demands of his teachers. His view of the ideal pupil can be distorted and infantile. If the gap between the way he sees himself as succeeding in school and the demands he attributes to his teachers is too great, then again he will opt out. There is still the possibility that he is not seeing things as they are. What I am saying is that achievement in school seems to be related very closely to the way in which a pupil experiences himself in school, but these perceptions may not be accurate or represent the truth of the situation.

Group guidance and counselling provides a good atmosphere for constructive change. It gives the pupil a chance to compare himself with others and explore other views about the school. We have been looking at the educational situation as a complex system of interaction and feedback which builds up sets of expectations and predictions which sometimes have to be modified. In this case, the most vulnerable point of modification lies in the pupil's perceptions of the demands and needs of the school and their relationship to his own development and aspirations. This is then followed by analysis and teaching of necessary skills. The new perceptions are reinforced and developed by bringing in colleagues as participants in the counselling process. Again we see the need for the two-phase model, for we cannot provide reinforcements until we have understood his view of the school and helped him modify this. Until this has been achieved, any attempts at help by colleagues would be wasted, simply because the pupil would not see their relevance or would misinterpret them.

The discussion has been kept brief, because the last chapter is concerned with the wider implications of counselling and guidance in the school. Parents and other teachers will have to be involved in educational guidance if it is to be useful.

You may find it interesting to consider the following notes on group guidance and the choice of subject options. They have proved to be valuable in stimulating discussion and structuring the planning of choice of subject options in a number of schools. The counsellor or guidance team would find it useful to produce their own statements for consideration by colleagues.

## GROUP GUIDANCE AND THE SELECTION OF SUBJECT OPTIONS

The aim of this brief discussion is to examine the reasons for guidance in subject options; the objectives we should hold in mind; the nature of this type of guidance; and the strategies which should be employed. It will isolate the considerations essential for effective action, not only linking these with the individual pupil, but the long-term well-being of the school as a community.

### Why should we focus on guidance at this point?

1. To make school meaningful at the point where many pupils begin to opt out.

2. To prevent them making choices which may lead to under-functioning or making decisions which will have negative long-term consequences.

3. To help them become active partners in their own education and avoid creating situations in which they begin to feel that they are being moulded by the system or have to conform to the edicts of an uncaring organization. In other words, guidance at this point is essential for gaining and retaining pupil co-operation.

### What are our broad objectives?

1. To produce the greatest possible satisfaction for the individuals making the choice.

2. To ensure that maximal use is made of the facilities present in the school.

3. To eliminate situations where subject choices are made on immature, inaccurate or irrelevant factors.

*Can we justify these objectives?*

These objectives do not represent an abdication of responsibility by the teachers, but truly professional behaviour based on *realistic adaptation* to the following:

1. If pupils do not feel that their subject choices are both meaningful and their own, they will begin to disaffiliate from the school. Some will begin to express their dissatisfaction in negative behaviours and hostile attitudes. This may be particularly true of pupils in the middle streams or ability range of the comprehensive school. Little is needed to push these pupils into subscribing to the aims of the school or into alienation from the school.

2. It is essential that we should be able to forecast and anticipate demands for the future. We need to avoid situations in which two or three pupils are taking A level in a subject at an uneconomic use of teacher resources. Group guidance at an earlier point in the school may alert the head to the desirability of a joint course with another school or lead him to ask pertinent questions about the reasons for pupils' rejection of certain subjects.

3. To make pupils aware of the long term consequences of choices, e.g. the girl who tries to avoid taking mathematics and physics at O Level because of disinterest, or the feeling that these are subjects for boys, is sharply restricting her career possibilities when she needs higher education. Subject guidance is a second point in the school where it is possible to gain the active co-operation of parents. The value of this allegiance cannot be discounted in the secondary education process.

4. We need to be aware that many pupils and parents need help with subject options and decisions, but resent the impression that they are being forced or told what to do. Guidance programmes help in this.

*What are the basic principles in this guidance?*

1. Intelligent anticipation which means that preparation should begin during and throughout the preceding twelve months to the time at which the decision is made. This allows consolidation of the information by pupils and means that the guidance can be fitted into the timetable.

2. All the parties concerned should be involved in a planned way. Pupils, parents and teachers need to be consulted, and all of them have standpoints which are relevant.

*What form should our strategies take?*

1. The basic form is best seen as a three phase strategy. The first two phases are a preliminary to the third which finalizes the decision.

2. *Phase one:*

    (a) This is concerned with a systematic programme of group guidance within the form. Note that the form is the unit, therefore no teacher is required to do extra work for the purposes of guidance.

    (b) Pupils will need to have information about courses. Departments might well produce simple brochures which explain the nature, the demands, difficulties, and rewards of the subject. This might include the career prospects attached to certain subject areas and it is useful to be aware of market demands, e.g. the market for social scientists, biologists and chemists may have reached the point of saturation. The careers staff could administer tests of interest which create greater self awareness in pupils as well as deal with the points mentioned above. It is necessary to remind ourselves of the fact that subject choices are also potentially vocational choices.

    (c) From the viewpoint of the individual pupil the guidance programme would focus on exploration of these questions:

(i) *What am I good at?* This would be followed by the crucial question, '*Why am I good at it?*' This leads to an examination of aptitudes, the contribution of past experience, support and held received from parents.

(ii) *What do I like doing?* This leads to consideration of such factors as a good relationship with the teacher, the possibility that the liked subjects are easy for the pupil, although not of great utility and many other questions of a similar type.

(iii) *How does this subject fit in with my purposes and aims?* It can be seen that this will make many pupils recognize that they are not clear about their long-term goals.

(iv) *What are the costs of not doing this subject?*

(d) Teachers would also give a description of the courses. Note that this should not be confined to the heads of department for sometimes departmental heads do not teach less able pupils.

3. *Phase 2.*

(a) This will consist of discussions with parents in groups during the evening. These will be staggered so that they can be kept small, possibly the parents of pupils in one form coming for two or three discussion groups. Again the investment of time is relatively small, particularly when the potential 'pay-off' in co-operation is taken into account. It is suggested that this is the second stage because many parents will discuss this with their children and it is therefore desirable that pupils have accurate information to share with parents.

(b) The load would be shared amongst counsellors, careers staff, heads of departments and others.

(c) Why is it important? Parents often hold unrealistic views of the child's ability or have inflated or inadequate aspirations for them. They want pupils to follow courses for which they are not suited and sometimes are working out frustrated ambitions through the child. We can alert them to the issues; can reinforce the positive attitudes; and prepare them for the stresses which come with increased homework assignments and subject difficulties. We lay the ground for further co-operation.

*Phase 3.*

(a) This is the stage of an informed interview between form master, year tutor or year head and the pupil and parent. In this difficulties are resolved.

(b) The final phase should clearly demonstrate to the parent and pupil that the comprehensive school is able to tailor educational programmes to fit the need of the individual pupil.

(c) The form master will record final choices on some simple form and ensure that this information is immediately fed to the appropriate person.

### Final note

This approach to subject choice guidance is quite economical in time if it is carefully planned and phased over a period. It is an essential if pupils are to receive full satisfaction from their schoolwork and is a way of preventing the increasing disassociation of pupils from school. It is a skeleton, to which the flesh has to be added by the pastoral care and guidance team of a specific school. It can be modified to suit each school and the choice of A Level.

### Summary discussion

In this chapter vocational counselling and guidance is described as a process which extends over much of the pupil's secondary school career. In this process phantasies are gradually replaced by interests, and these are in turn superseded by probable choices, until at last a realistic decision is made. There is little place for the conception of vocational choice as a single event restricted to a limited amount of time. The choice of an occupation is most likely to lead to real work satisfaction when it has a close relationship to the self-picture of the chooser. Every job has a more or less definite life style attached to it, and it is the match between this and the pupil's self-conception which aids adjustment to work. This means that not only should we encourage pupils actively to understand themselves and the life styles attached to a job, but that the theories of vocational counselling which have most relevance for the school are those which are based on the development of the sense of self in adolescence.

All this means that anything the counsellor can do to stimulate self-awareness can be used in vocational guidance programmes. Without the development of self-awareness the essential element in vocational choice is lacking. If we take this view of vocational guidance then it can begin quite early in the secondary school without meaning that a pupil is pressured towards a definite choice of a job. It is a process which stimulates the emergence of interests; the realistic evaluation of aptitudes and abilities; and gradual acquisition of knowledge of work conditions and the replacing of crude occupational stereotypes by more realistic evaluations. The evaluatory and decision-making processes involved add to the pupil's capacity to work in any lesson, whilst the whole activity adds to the feeling of relevance of school for the pupil.

The counsellor uses the two concepts of field and level in his work. The former is the broad area to which the pupil is attracted and the latter indicates the difficulty, responsibility and expertise involved in the job. These divisions provide the basis for the strategies outlined in the chapter. The fact that vocational choice has developmental connotations leads us to consider the possibility that vocational choice processes can, like all other developmental processes, be retarded or impaired. If this is the case, then the services of the highly trained counsellor may be necessary to supplement the efforts of the careers team. Although such developmental difficulties cannot be described as abnormal, there is a need for special help from the counsellor when irrational factors or personality inadequacies make choice of an occupation difficult.

The discussion of educational guidance recognizes that this should be a team effort and that the counsellor is only one of a number of people involved in this. Group counselling may help underfunctioning pupils, and the counsellor is necessary when the usual measures of preparation for educational choices have failed. When subject options or courses have to be chosen there will be a small proportion of pupils who will require special help in making a choice. It is with these pupils that the counsellor may intervene in his specialist function.

## REFERENCES

Daws. P. (1968) *A Good Start in Life,* Cambridge: CRAC.

Gesell, A., Ilg, F. and Ames, L. (1956) *Youth: The Years from Ten to Sixteen,* New York: Harper and Row.

Ginzberg, E., Ginzberg, S., Axelrad, S. and Herma, J. (1951) *Occupational Choice,* New York: Columbia University Press.

Ginzberg, E. (1971) *Career Guidance,* New York: Mcgraw-Hill.

Hayes, J. and Hopson, B. (1971) *Careers Guidance,* London: Heinemann.

Hayes, J. and Hough, P. (1971) *Occupational Perceptions and Occupational Information,* Bromsgrove: Institute of Careers Officers.

Hudson, L. (1966) *Contrary Imaginations,* London: Methuen.

Jackson, R. and Juniper, D. (1971) *A Manual of Educational Guidance,* London: Holt, Rinehart and Winston.

Noble, T. (1970) 'Family breakdown and social networks', *Br. J. Sociol.*

Nelson, D. (1968) 'Predictive vale of the Rothwell-Miller Interest Blank', *Occup. Psychol.* 42. 123–131.

Rodger, A. (1968) 'The Seven Point Plan', Hopson, B. and Hayes, J. (Eds.) *The Theory and Practice of Vocational Guidance,* Oxford: Pergamon.

Roe, A. (1956) *The Psychology of Occupations,* New York: Wiley.

Swift, B. (1973) 'Job Orientations and the Transition from School to Work', *Br. J. Guid. and Couns.* 1.1.

Shouksmith, G. and Taylor, J. (1964) 'The effect of counselling on the achievement of high ability pupils', Br. J. Educ. Psychol. Vol. XXXIV. Part 1. 51–57.

Super, D. E. (1957) *The Psychology of Careers,* New York: Harper and Row.

Tyler, L. E. (1958) 'Theoretical principles underlying the counseling process', *J. Couns. Psychol.* 5. 3–10.

Tyler, L. E. (1962) 'Research on instruments used by counselors in vocational guidance', *J. Couns. Psychol.* 7. 99–105.

# CHAPTER EIGHT

# PROBLEMS OF
# SCHOOL COUNSELLING

## *The purpose of this chapter*

We look at three major areas of counselling which cause many problems for the school counsellor. They are those of confidentiality, parental contact and testing. It is hoped that this chapter shows how crucial it is to think carefully about these areas and to take a flexible approach to the associated problems.

## *The questions asked*

(i) What do we mean by confidentiality in the school counselling situation?

(ii) Can we misuse the principle of confidentiality?

(iii) What are the costs, dangers and consequences of working closely with parents?

(iv) What positive strategies can we use in involving parents in the counselling process?

(v) How can we use testing effectively in counselling?

## Confidentiality

The heading of this chapter is quite intentional. It shows that our attention is shifting from the problems of the individual counsellor to those which are general to the process of counselling. One major problem—that of confidentiality—arises from the attempt to perform the role competently. In common with other therapeutic activities, school counselling is based on the idea of confidentiality of *certain information* which is given to the counsellor by the pupils. It seems that it may be difficult for a headmaster to accept that there are certain things that he will not be told about, especially when it is a fact that the school counsellor works with his delegated authority. Colleagues may feel resentful and assume that they are the subject of discussion in the counselling session, and this can work against the need to involve them as active participants in the counselling process. It seems imperative that we should try to understand the nature of confidentiality in counselling. Unless we do this, we are in danger of using the idea of confidentiality in a provocative way which alienates the trained counsellor from his colleagues in the pastoral care team. Even worse, we may be trying in a naive way to be more therapeutic than the therapists in our attitudes about confidentiality, unintentionally doing a great deal of harm to the pupil on occasions.

Confidentiality is necessary for the establishment of the basic trusting relationship which is at the heart of counselling. Unless it is there, a boy or girl will not disclose facts that produce anxiety, guilt and shame. The welfare of the pupil is the over-riding consideration of the counsellor (although he is far from alone in this) and this means that on occasions he cannot pass on information to other people. He may have to maintain this position, despite expectations or even direct demands that this information will be given. He may be submitted to heavy pressures to break confidentiality, therefore he must have given some careful thought to this. A whole group of factors make the issue of confidentiality an emotional one, and clumsy action on the part of the counsellor can turn co-operation into resentment. Many teachers assume that the idea of keeping confidence means that they will be given no information at all, which is untrue. The competent counsellor does give information, and when he refuses to do this, he will do so without producing a confrontation. The fact that he is usually willing to give some information makes it possible for his refusal to be accepted as necessary. Teachers have well-developed social consciences, concern for law and order and a sense of justice, all of which can be threatened by the emphasis on confidentiality.

Real conflict can occur in a teacher, if a pupil reveals to him that he is engaging in delinquent activity outside the school. Perhaps during the interviews a pupil reveals that he is stealing, and that another friend, who is also a pupil, is involved. Everyone has to make up his own mind about this, but I would urge caution before we rush into action. First, we would want to consider our own motives for revealing the information. It could be that we are frightened of the responsibility, or, that for some odd reason we want him to be punished. We have to ask whether restitution or reparation is possible, and whether this would be a more truly moral approach than getting the boy punished. We would almost certainly stop and ask ourselves if what the boy has described is in fact true, for if it were merely phantasy it would be stupid to report it. Therefore we need to check indirectly, but carefully. Then we must ask ourselves what we are going to do about the friend. Can we call him in? Can we ask the first boy to bring his friend along? What of the parents? Circumstances vary so much that I can provide no easy answer, but I would argue that the first thing to do is to discuss this with someone outside the school such as the educational psychologist or a probation officer without revealing the name of the pupil. This kind of situation brings out clearly the fact that it is unrealistic to begin counselling by telling a pupil that "*everything* you say here is confidential and will never be repeated to anyone". Indeed in the active model of counselling, it is untrue. We might well substitute for this statement, "usually we do not tell anyone what you say without asking your permission, but sometimes we will have to disclose certain things". This seems to be a more mature approach and if we think it necessary we can tell a pupil to think this over and come back and discuss it. I have found that this adds to counselling rather than diminishes it, leading to really purposeful counselling, for most pupils have sufficient *nous* to see that total confidentiality is impossible.

Let us be clear that we have loyalties and responsibilities to the school as well as to the pupil. We must decide the occasions on which responsibility to the school and other people within the educational system takes precedence over the maintenance of *strict* confidentiality. Equally important, it makes us look at the *way* in which we pass on information. If we are not prepared to see that the headmaster has the ultimate responsibility for his pupils and that concern is not confined to the counsellor, then we should not attempt to counsel within the school setting. We have to ask ourselves if we are misusing confidentiality to reinforce our own importance and power. If we do this we are in danger of damaging pupils whilst deluding ourselves that we are behaving properly.

None of this denies the importance of confidentiality, but it does suggest that we need to avoid seeing things rigidly in terms of black and white and adopt a more flexible standpoint. The authoritarianism behind such a viewpoint can prevent us from doing what is in the best interests of a pupil. I think the whole problem gets distorted by the illicit assumption that counselling is concerned with delinquency or dramatic revelations about the home circumstances of the pupil. Most counselling is in fact concerned with feelings, perceptions and interpersonal relationships which are personal without being deviant or delinquent. Hence confidentiality is preserved in these areas and the material is kept inviolate, for a pupil has trusted the counsellor with his inner feelings of loneliness, inadequacy and shame, and to reveal this is unforgivable. The information we pass on belongs to the second, action-directed phase of counselling.

We work with delegated authority and often with legal minors and we must never forget this. Hence in certain severe and rare situations we have a professional duty to pass information on in an ethical way. The conditions for this seem to be that the pupil has revealed, and the counsellor verified, as far as humanly possible, that conditions exist which are likely to harm others for whom the school is responsible. This should be reported directly to the Head and nobody else in the school should be informed without his permission. We should try to ensure that the pupil is protected in every possible way. One thing which occupies us is the question of drug taking. My discussions with the police have shown that in most cases an enlightened and responsible attitude exists. The police are not concerned with hounding pupils down, and in my own area they regard drug taking in school children as a medical problem which should be reported to the school medical service. They are interested in the sources of drugs, but only if we have firm information. They appreciate that hysteria, publicity and impulsive action exacerbates rather than reduces the problem. It is important that the Head and counsellor have knowledge of where to go and what to do in such situations, for it is fatal to ring up the sergeant on the desk at the local police station about this. The specialist officers of the drug squad are the people who should be contacted if it is necessary.

On occasions we get evidence that a girl is in urgent need of a pregnancy test, and we cannot evade the responsibility to do something about this. Medical advice has to be obtained, and this is not an attempt to push the responsibility elsewhere. Many girls still have strange phantasies about what is implied in having such a test. They may not see the counsellor as a credible source of information in this field, and the doctor can give reassurance, sound advice and provide understanding in the accepted context of the doctor/patient relationship. Certainly a male counsellor may lack the necessary sensitivities to the subtle *nuances* of the problem.

We can see that confidentiality may be broken constructively when the pupil is in grave physical danger or when serious consequences are likely if the counsellor fails to act. If we begin to look at moral danger as a reason for breaching confidentiality then we need to be aware of our own prejudices and aversions. We must always try to obtain the consent of the pupil, and in most cases this is freely given. The boy or girl usually wants the counsellor to do something rather than just keep quiet. Occasionally we get the serious situation of incest. We have then to remain calmly professional, weighing up the situation from the viewpoint of what is best for the pupil. This is a situation in which it is possible to panic. First, we must remember that it is remarkably hard to get any clear evidence, for confirmation of the fact that physical intercourse has taken place does not mean confirmation that incest has occurred. This is a medical and psychological problem and one beyond the school counsellor. It seems to me that the school counsellor cannot report this to the police; indeed, my experience shows me that this would be harmful. If a charge is made, then the girl is likely to be submitted to questioning and if the case were taken to court, she could be the object of quite devastating cross-examination. All this would compound the psychological damage and introduce new guilt and anxieties. It is better for this to be dealt with by the psychological services and the social service department, without the trauma of court appearances to complicate the situation. The experienced counsellor always recognizes the possibility that the father or older brother may not have seduced the daughter or sister, but that they themselves may have been seduced by her. As with cases of adolescent homosexuality, clumsy action can turn what was a situation capable of repair, into one which permanently damages the pupils causing them to label themselves as deviant and bad. The counsellor, however, learns his limits and does not deny pupils the aid of highly trained specialists.

These extreme situations should not be the focus of our attention. They would give the impression that school counselling is concerned with the pathological, which is not the case. Other aspects of confidentiality may be more important, although less dramatic. It is the right of a pupil to gain access to the counsellor without having to ask for permission. Confidentiality of access must be possible: without it some shy or anxious pupils would not refer themselves. This means that the counsellor has to make himself available at lunch-times and after school, allowing a pupil to consult him without missing a class. Perhaps it is important too that we learn to prevent pupils telling us things before they have thought about the implications of their revelations, and before they are certain that they want to reveal them. The premature sharing of confidences and intimate problems can have detrimental consequences for the counsellor and can cause trouble. A student of great concern and integrity had a girl sent to him and it was found that she thought she was pregnant. In fact she was not: it was merely an irregularity in her period, which occurred the next day, possibly because of the reduction of tension. She was furious that she had revealed herself to a man and reacted by accusing him of asking her improper questions about sexual intercourse. It was all sorted out, but quite a lot of energy had to be invested in this tricky situation.

We must also be aware that the records kept by school counsellors have no privilege in law. Extreme caution is necessary in making entries on records. They are intended to aid the counsellor's conduct of the sessions, rather than to be a repository of confidential information. The records also act as a basis for providing facts about the number of pupils seen by the counsellor, the broad types of problem, and any action which is taken by him. Copies of letters and the dates of home visits should be carefully recorded together with details of counselling conferences and contacts with outside agencies. All records should be kept under lock and key, being accessible only to the counsellor. He has a responsibility to plan what happens to the records if he is ill or changes his post. If a person has a legitimate right to information, even then he should never be given *free* access to the records. Individual records can be misunderstood easily, just as someone's lecture notes read by another person who was not at the lecture can give a wrong impression. It seems that confidentiality does not really pose an intolerable threat to teachers and counsellor, and in most cases it can be preserved. It only becomes a major problem when the counsellor has created a climate in which his colleagues feel shut out or threatened by his activities. If a counsellor who wanted to pass on certain facts in a proper way found himself frequently unable to do this, then he needs to ask himself whether or not he should continue working in that school.

A partial solution to some of the grosser problems of preservation of confidentiality in record keeping is for the school to adapt some variant of non-verbal recording. A summary card or strip index can be produced which contains small boxes which are numbered. Each box refers to a relevant category such as family, health or delinquency. A mark in that box indicates that the pupil falls into this category in a particular way. A number of strategies are available for the school. It is possible to devise a positional code, using the four corners and the centre of the box to convey information. A mark in the upper left hand corner might indicate that there was no father at home, whilst one in the upper right hand corner would indicate that the mother was absent or dead. The other three points could be used to indicate other forms of a broken family. This could be combined with colour coding.

A great deal of information can be stored in minimal space in this way, although one has to ensure accuracy in recording and interpretation. One intrinsic advantage of such a system is that it is specific to the school and only those who have been taught the code can interpret the significance of the positional mark and colour code. These cards can be arranged in folders so that the name of the pupil and the main coding is visible at a glance. This means that the boxes are printed on strips or come at the bottom of a record form. It is then possible to see the problems of a specific form or year group at a glance, whilst relevant sub-populations such as the physically handicapped or the delinquent can be identified quickly. This is very useful in the resources analysis which is discussed in the final chapter.

This brief discussion of confidentiality hides one important thing. I recently met a girl who had gone to a party where she became very drunk. Sexual intercourse occurred without her permission and possibly without her awareness. I also have seen a girl who was raped more violently. Her father brought her to the counsellor, but he had not informed the police. Both these girls when seen were emotionally and intellectually numbed. The need for specialist help for these girls seemed to me to be greater than the need to preserve confidentiality. My referrals were to clinics who worked on a basis of confidentiality. This made it very clear to me that the rigid imposition of the principle of confidentiality could be destructive in depriving pupils of urgently needed help.

### Parental contact and counselling

Quite a lot of social work has been based upon the dictum that the most effective way to deal with a client is within the total context of his family life. Most social workers would be concerned with the brothers and sisters of a pupil and would work with the family in depth. It is an open question whether or not the school counsellor should try to work with parents in the same way as these social workers. Once we have looked at the nature of the problem, two considerations seem to guide our decisions: what will be the impact on the pupil if we contact his parents? What will be the effect upon our own efficiency? In doing this we have to take up some of the points made in the simple systems approach to counselling. We often quite rightly see parents as responsible for many of the difficulties of pupils, but in some schools we do not accept that contact with parents is either necessary or desirable. Parents can then be seen as the source of all difficulties and an impediment to the smooth running of the school. They perform a scapegoat function for us. In such a climate it is difficult for the counsellor to do much in the field of parental counselling. If the counsellor has poor links with the outside agencies he may find himself intervening in homes where a social worker is visiting, and he can impinge upon the therapeutic relationships which are being built up by the social worker with unintended, but destructive consequences.

Before dealing with some of the aspects of home visits it is necessary to point out that parental counselling does not necessarily mean home visiting. Most teachers point out that the parents they most want to see can never be got at because they refuse to come to the school. Perhaps this is because they have a shrewd idea that they will be "got at" if they come. But the counsellor may be able to get them there without creating this feeling. In any case the counsellor must see that there is no single best method of parental contact. He must evaluate various strategies, and select what fits the school, the pupil and himself. The first question is whether we should always inform parents that counselling is about to take place and get their permission. If counselling is seen as normal and part of the everyday life of the school this is not so essential as when it seems to be restricted to the "very difficult section" of the school population. At the same time, it is useful to invite the parents' co-operation, and most of them respond warmly to the fact that "somebody is taking an interest in my child". Against this is the fact that a stereotyped request for permission produces an automatic rejection in some parents who have no idea what is meant by counselling and may see it as part of a move to send their child to the "silly school" or "put him away" or as yet another example of the way "teachers pick on him". We have to take these attitudes into account and anticipate reactions, for if we have something to offer it is a pity if those who need it are deprived of the benefit because of our poor attempts at explanation. We can use the P.T.A. to explain, but we also need to invite parents to come to discuss this in a friendly way, writing a personal note rather than sending a duplicated slip. Many short-term cases of vocational counselling and minor problems could be undertaken without informing parents, but it seems best to inform parents of personal counselling as soon as two things emerge. Firstly, that an unanticipated and unexpectedly severe personal problem is present. Secondly, that counselling is likely to last for more than four or five sessions. Needless to say, the counsellor must tell the pupil that this has to be done, giving him the chance to think about it, even if this means that the counselling has to be discontinued. Most of us would be concerned if we had children and found that they had received lengthy counselling without any reference to us. Certainly a counsellor could find himself in difficulties if referral to another agency was necessary and the parents had been unaware of the counselling. Trust between school and parents is likely to be diminished by this. Parents will have phantasies about the meaning of counselling which can cause unnecessary fears and friction which rebound on a pupil and make the counsellor's job harder than it need be. The rule of thumb approach which seems to work is that the younger the pupil who is counselled, the more essential it is to obtain parental permission. It is possible to inform parents of counselling without revealing personal feelings and other confidences given to the counsellor by the pupil. Parents do feel threatened and guilty when their child is counselled, and they often need some reassurance that they themselves are not the cause for the counselling.

We must distinguish clearly between parental knowledge of counselling and active association with them. Pupils can have legitimate objections to counsellor contact with parents beyond the initial step of explaining what is happening, especially when the difficulties lie in the boy's relationships with his parents. Active contact between counsellor and parents can distort counselling unless the pupil wants it, for the pupil may fear a breach of confidentiality, or he may suspect that his parents will try to use the counsellor against him. This risk cannot be denied, for intelligent parents will try to utilize the counsellor to bring about changes of behaviour and attitude in their child which they have failed to achieve. Such changes may not be possible or desirable. I find that work with parents may be impossible in the early stages of counselling, but in the later stages of the process the pupil asks for and co-operates in it. This is the equivalent of the stage in the active model, where other teachers also become involved in the counselling.

We have a number of strategies available to us. It is often better to ask a parent to visit us at school in the evening, rather than for us to visit the home. This protects the parents from the inquisitiveness of neighbours, and it uses the counsellor's time less wastefully. Let us also remember that visits to homes reveal inadequacies which parents wish to hide, creating resentment and a further loss of self-esteem. We can run parent discussion groups in the evening, providing a form of group counselling. We should be clear that our fundamental responsibility is to the pupil, for we only deal with parents to the degree that this is helpful to a pupil. When we attempt to do more with parents than is strictly necessary to achieve the targets of the counselling we are inefficient. Home visiting needs therefore to be looked at with caution. It is only too easy to get involved in situations which require long-term skilled casework of a type for which we are not trained, and harm can be done if we attempt to cope. Parents who are disturbed or resentful are sometimes highly manipulative and prepared to play off one person against another with disastrous results. The counsellor who visits without first checking if other agencies are concerned in a home should not be surprised when an angry caseworker rings up with a highly coloured account of the counsellor's visit, which the parent has provided.

It may be more profitable for the counsellor to work with a pupil in school whilst a caseworker visits the home. Counsellor and social worker then share information, collaborating and reinforcing one another's efforts. Information may be obtained through the educational welfare officer who often has detailed and accurate knowledge of home circumstances, but we must not forget that once we have established a good relationship with a pupil, relevant information will emerge without our probing. The future of parent contact may well lie in the development of groups run by counsellors which involve them in helping school activities. Once parents begin to do something useful for the school it is possible to work with them informally.

I would like to illustrate more fully the difficulties of home visiting. We know that parents and pupils have very different views about the amount of autonomy and independence that is proper. This can be a central issue, but at least two possibilities exist. Both sides can see the counsellor as a potential ally to be used to gain their ends. Machiavellian parents tend to produce machiavellian children, so the counsellor expends energy in dealing with this situation, which perhaps cannot be resolved at all. On the other hand, both sides may see the counsellor as a representative of the other's point of view, thereby leading to misinterpretation of almost everything he says or does. If we had the time and skill we could then counsel pupil and parents together, but this is difficult until one is really experienced. A pupil may see the home visit as a form of desertion or rejection if we unwisely time it during the first phase of counselling, when he is beginning to trust us and reveal his picture of himself and his hidden anxieties. Perfectly normal adolescents can then feel that they have been trapped into self-revelations, and the home visit means that they are about to be exposed, or that adults are leagued together against them. Even when we have the pupil's consent for the visit there is no guarantee that the kind of feelings I am describing will not be aroused in him.

More subtle effects exist. A parent may concentrate upon giving the school counsellor a good impression, almost splitting himself into good and bad parts to do so. Such a parent, who is almost certainly disturbed, may, if counsellor and caseworker are not collaborating, present the "good" side to the counsellor (as he feels he ought to do to a teacher), whilst the caseworker is left with the "bad" side of the parent. In other words, the caseworker is left with all the negative aspects of the problem and his relationship with the parent is almost destroyed, whilst the counsellor happily operates in cloud cuckoo land. If there is no caseworker, then the counsellor may run even greater dangers without realizing it. He can create expectations of help and support which cannot be met in reality. He may precipitate the focusing of irrational feelings upon himself, finding that he cannot cope with them. I became aware of this some years ago when I visited a mother who was

very unstable underneath a pleasant and responsive façade. Her perceptions of the school and of her child's teachers were very negative, but
after a talk or two with me, she seemed to have almost completely
reversed them. She then began to interpret her son's complaints as
evidence of his badness and proceeded to pressure him. This made the
boy increasingly negative to school and to her, and I had to intervene.
This intervention was enough to reverse her expectations and perceptions and I was seen, probably not unfairly, as the distillation of
everything bad, and the situation ended worse than it was when I
began. I still blush with shame at my stupidity, but it does show what
the dangers can be. Parental contact can be very important, but in some
cases we get enmeshed in very puzzling and negative interaction and
this is helpful to nobody. I learned to look at the risks involved and the
likelihood of gains which outweigh the risks. I would not get involved
in a family where the prognosis is poor, especially when other agencies
have failed to achieve anything; I would rather concentrate on providing the pupil with success and compensations in the school in
areas and ways which are meaningful to him.

The age of the pupil is important. If he is sixteen or older, then it is
quite likely that he will shortly separate himself from the home and
our best strategy is to help him equip himself for this.

This has been a negative discussion, and the negative is foreign to the
counsellor's approach. So it seems best to give some idea of the special
part the counsellor can play in building up relationships between school
and home. Rather than overstress the importance of visiting a few
atypical parents, it is better to look at ways of fostering real co-operation
between parents and teachers. In any case, we need positive activities
in which parents can be involved. Educational methods are developing
fairly rapidly, hence many parents cannot grasp the nature or purpose
of new teaching methods. They resist them, often devaluing them to the
pupil by their attitudes of amusement or scorn. Teachers and parents
tend to hold stereotypes of each other which are not only mutually
unflattering but foster negative attitudes. Contact is necessary if these
are to dissolve. Evidence exists, e.g. Cave (1970), McGeeney (1969) that
the usual methods of contact with parents such as the Open Day or
Open Evening or the P.T.A. fail to meet the needs of parents for real

contact with those who teach their children. The opportunity to talk is too brief, and in some cases the parent is confused and inarticulate, so that these meetings can breed frustration and further resentment rather than the desired co-operation. The picture of the teacher presented by these formal occasions is very unrealistic, creating further feelings of inadequacy in working-class parents. The well-dressed woman teacher talking to the poorly dressed mother and the strangely respectful and obedient pupils who are on show create a false picture of school life. When counselling is part of the everyday life of the school then counselling means involvement of parents at choice points and as helpers. This is no mean task, for the Newsom Report (1963) showed that the lower the occupational status of the father, the less likelihood there is of the parents establishing positive contact with the school. As the failure of the child is made evident, so does parental interest in the school decline. If we are not careful, the middle-class parents monopolize contact with the school. This is unhealthy for such parents tend to produce "mark hungry" children and block educational developments if they do not seem to lead to increased examination successes. The withdrawal of the working-class parent is regrettable, and is something we should strive to prevent.

The counsellor will have to play a part in the initiation and development of activities which lead to wider contacts with parents. Different things will have to be done with different sections of the school population to involve them. The ideas given here have been tried out in a number of schools. One first step is the need for the counsellor in conjunction with the pastoral care team to begin a systematic examination of the nature and impact of communication between school and home. Letters and reports often create an adverse and hostile reaction in the recipients. Often our letters and circulars are not only drab and uninviting, but also they are couched in terms reminiscent of a Dickensian civil servant. The school report can create misunderstandings, for many parents do not understand the meaning of being third in Form Y, which is almost at the bottom of the streaming or banding system. Their child could tell them, but doesn't, and suddenly the parent learns of this in an unhelpful way. The school report could be designed so that it is a meaningful and personal communication between home and teachers, inviting feedback and co-operation by showing the parent in positive terms what he can do to help. This, to me, is constructive counselling of parents. Parents need to be given direct experience of the use of new apparatus and of teaching methods, for it is only by handling materials and directly trying to do the things their children do that they begin to see the purpose of new methods of teaching. To tell them about it will not work; like their children, they need to be active. The teacher has nothing to lose by this and everything to gain, because parents begin to see things from the teacher's standpoint. The counsellor and pastoral care team will provide working-class parents with activities which puts them into a helping role where they can be successful. They are glad to come to school to use their hands and this is the surest way of achieving attitude change. Even "rough" parents will do an enormous amount to help, working directly for the school in a way which many middle-class parents avoid. When such parents come to school to "help rather than holler" they are amenable to teacher influence in a way not previously possible.

The teacher needs to apply his skills in counselling, for the interviewing of parents is tricky. Many of them are slow at putting their meaning into words, and yet they also resent it when the teacher imposes his meaning on their questions. They know that what he is saying was not what they meant, although they cannot put it into precise words. Lack of skill and patience in allowing parents to formulate their own questions can spoil much of the good work we are doing. The point where most parents are willing to be involved and actively to co-operate with staff is when their child enters the secondary school. This is particularly true when it is the first child in the family to enter the school. The counsellor and pastoral care team will be working efficiently if they make a special effort with parents when this is the case, for it is easy to build up a fund of goodwill which can be utilized later on. The team can devise a programme of activities for parents which reinforces those occurring in the orientation programme for pupils. Parents can be taught how to provide support for the pupil when he is under stress; how to create the conditions for good homework; how to use the form master; and above all, how to help in the activities of the school and become a partner in the educational process.

## Testing and counselling

Considerable emphasis is usually given to the function of tests in counselling, but they bring into counselling elements of evaluation and grading which can be threatening to a pupil. More than this, testing, or more properly, an unjustified reliance on and interpretation of the test results can obscure a pupil's real problem just as a flow of words by the counsellor can distort. Yet we do not give up using words because of such difficulties, nor should we give up testing. Rather we must strive to use both more effectively and creatively. Tests should only be applied when the counsellor has a good idea what the problem may be. This suggests that testing is often inappropriate at the commencement of counselling, for the problem for which the pupil was referred may not be the real one. Super and Crites (1962), discussing vocational counselling, point out that an effective counsellor knows when to use tests, when to avoid them and when to rely upon other approaches than testing. The question as to which are good tests for counselling is in one sense almost meaningless, for as the previous discussion has indicated, unless we know the needs of the pupil, his aims and purposes and the way in which testing can contribute to these, tests are irrelevant. Purposeless testing has been condemned by Hopson (1968) who points out that the Americans appear to have an obsession for the completely filled record card, but that only a small proportion of the information which is accumulated and stored is used. Perhaps the best discussion on testing in counselling is that of Goldman (1961) who concluded that many of the tests currently used in counselling in America may be either wasted, or, more alarmingly, used in such a way that they misinform and mislead.

How does this happen? First, it seems possible that testing may be related to the insecurity of the counsellor in such cases. It seems that if the counsellor feels he lacks adequate techniques or if lack of role definition makes him insecure, then he can resort to the application of tests because they give the impression of technical competence, if not actual superiority. It is unnecessary to tease out the likely reactions of the counsellor's colleagues to this, although perhaps the most dangerous situation exists if they accept these signals of separation and superiority.

Trained school counsellors use tests with caution, ensuring that they are well standardized upon a population comparable to the pupils with whom they are to be used and interpreting them very carefully. Perhaps, as a number of writers suggest, the biggest danger in the use of tests in counselling is due to the fact that they create anxiety in the pupil, stimulating in some pupils very harsh self-judgements which may be quite unrealistic and encouraging them to push the responsibility for decision making on to the tests and tester. This is scarcely useful when one is claiming to be engaged in a process intended to develop autonomy and decision-making ability in the pupil. This heavy emphasis upon the misuse of tests is at least as important as is discussion of the positive uses of tests, and this is illustrated in Lister and McKenzie's interesting discussion of the way in which errors enter into the using of tests by counsellors. They suggest that premature interpretation and use often occurs. The test was given before the pupil's needs were clear or he was ready to use the results. This could occur when the counsellor is unable to take appropriate action and uses the test as a last resort. A test may also be given which yields information which is not useful or comprehended by the pupil, usually because he assumes the test has a different purpose than it actually has. A pupil could easily assume that a test of interests is a test of aptitude and ability unless the counsellor anticipates this confusion by clear preliminary explanation. Another major source of confusion lies in the use of tests not intended for a British secondary school population, but perhaps the biggest single source of distortion is the pupil's attitude. Often the test situation arouses only one question in his mind, "How did I do?" for this is what many factors and forces converge to convince him tests are about, and even the concerned and competent school counsellor can do little to modify this attitude. If he uses a test, then the counsellor must be clear (a) that it is necessary, (b) that the pupil is positively motivated towards taking it and (c) that he himself has a moral responsibility to explain the function and purpose of the test, making its limitations quite explicit.

Goldman's principle that an economical counsellor tries to clarify a pupil's real needs without having to resort to tests seems very sound in the British secondary school. Much of the information needed is already present in the school and a counsellor taking an active role can quickly locate it. Just as teaching may be more productive than testing, so, unless there is a clear reason for employing a particular test, the counsellor may be well advised to spend his time in counselling. This does not deny the utility of testing, but warns against a retreat to it away from the dynamic process. Relevant tests will be interest tests, on occasion social competence scales, behavioural rating scales such as those of Stott (1966), attainment tests, verbal and non-verbal tests of general ability. No comment will be made about the value of certain tests, but the counsellor and teacher will be well advised to seek the advice and guidance of the educational psychologist. It is, of course, taken for granted that the counsellor or teacher will always seek out appropriate training before administering any test. Testing in counselling should be minimal, but when it does take place it should be in a way which engages counsellor and pupil in a search for understanding of something which has puzzled both of them. It should not be a process of passive reception of information by a pupil who has been kept in a dependent position. Participation seems to remove much of the threat and mystery from testing, but more positively it seems to allow maximal information to be obtained by the boy or girl.

Goldman makes some interesting suggestions about the areas which should be explored by the counsellor. Obviously it is crucial to look at the basic meaning of the test, and this must be done even if the counsellor has already talked about it to the pupil, for his experience while taking the test may have erased some of this discussion. Goldman's next point is not so easy, because he suggests that one might explore the reasons why the pupil became whatever it is that the test suggests. This could be both time-consuming and very inaccurate and should be undertaken with caution. One will then need to look at the predictive aspects of the test, making some assessment of what the relevance of this result is for the pupil's future life or occupation. Again caution is necessary for, as Tyler (1962, 1963) points out, research in this field has shown tests to be rather inadequate. Lastly, Goldman suggests that we need to look at the evaluative question of the meaning of this for the pupil's choice of job or further education. This does seem important as a use for testing in counselling.

The trouble is that it is easy to state the principle that testing should always be used to stimulate the developmental process, but surprisingly hard to put this into practice. Some simple suggestions may stimulate further thought in the reader. The counsellor can begin interpretation by exploring the pupil's expectations about the test. He can be asked first what results he has anticipated. When this is known, it can be compared with the actual results and the discrepancies examined. The test result can then be compared with the self-picture of the pupil which has emerged during counselling. Then this can be followed by a comparison of the results with his interests out of school, the areas of school which are relevant to the test results and with parental expectations if necessary. The somewhat hoary platitude stating that learning is an activity of the pupil rather than of the teacher can be recast profitably to read, "learning is an activity both of the pupil and counsellor". This is given behavioural form by such devices as getting the pupil to draw up a simple bar profile showing his position in each area of the Rothwell-Miller Interest Blank. This simple visual presentation, when drawn up by the individual who completed the test, stimulates meaningful discussion and a great deal of learning occurs for both pupil and counsellor. Attention might be given with profit to the development of similar techniques both for individual tests or comparing a number of tests taken by an individual. Note, however, that this does not influence the scoring and administration of the test, which should always be in strict accord with the instructions.

The approach to test interpretation should always fit the ethos of developmental counselling, which means that the counsellor's function is restricted to clarification and the provision of increased information about himself for the pupil as a result of taking the test. It must always be the pupil's decision whether or not he utilizes the results of the tests. In the recent discussion on problem-solving techniques, the old naturalistic fallacy found in philosophical discussion was behind the statement that the counsellor might not be able to subscribe to a goal set by the pupil. This statement that what is desired is not necessarily desirable is now matched by a distinction between probability and desirability. Tests say something, albeit always in conditional and propositional terms, about the probability of an outcome, but this does not necessarily mean that this outcome is desirable. We should be clear that because a test indicates the probability of an outcome, it does not mean the counsellor has the right to impose this outcome upon the pupil. A pupil may go against the test results, and it is possible that he will either fail or succeed, but the risk is his and not the counsellor's. Imposition and the creation of a prophecy which fulfils itself is no part of the counsellor's task; in interpreting tests he concentrates upon helping the pupil to understand the results and to relate these to his actual and ideal self-concepts, and also to compare his performance with that of others who belong to a relevant group through the norms of the test.

The counsellor and teacher engaged in pastoral care who use tests should study carefully the reasoning that lies behind them. They must, for example, avoid the naive assumption that the better is a pupil's performance in a certain test of aptitude which appears to be related to some occupation, the more suited will he be for that job. This may be the case, but questions should be asked about the relationship between the test score and success on the job. Often clear evidence is lacking or the relationship may be found to be disappointingly low. It may be important to ask if there is an optimal level for this quality in a particular occupation, excess being just as negative as a deficiency, because it leads to boredom and dissatisfaction. A little thought suggests that there may be certain personality qualities, not measured by the test, which are more important for long-term success than this specific aptitude, even when the test accurately measures the aptitude. Certain combinations of personality qualities may impede a pupil's progress in some occupations, whilst many experienced careers teachers know that with some pupils greater attention has to be given to the general environment of work than to the content of the job. These considerations, vital when a test is being used to help a pupil make a choice of occupation, show the need for integrity and intellectual alertness in the user of tests. It is important to note that the good counsellor who has administered a test makes careful account of the findings. This does not mean that he is rigidly bound to the results, but rather that he begins to see whether appropriate corrective experiences can be provided, and he attempts to help create conditions within the school in which compensatory strengths are built up, if this is possible. Tests are far from meaningless when used in this way, but the counsellor is refusing to allow them to become self-fulfilling prophecies because he is conscious of the limitations of tests.

Counsellors and teachers undertaking pastoral care should be clear about the three categories of tests specified in the N.F.E.R. catalogue. The first category is comprised of tests which require minimal knowledge for their administration and can be used by teachers generally. The second group is made up of tests which may be given by people who have gained some qualification through a course of training acceptable to the N.F.E.R., or who are able to produce satisfactory evidence that they have been taught to use the test by some qualified person. A last category is composed of tests which should only be used by qualified psychologists. School counsellors will respect these limitations upon the use of tests because they are intended to protect, not only those to whom they are given, but those who administer them. Caution is certainly necessary in applying tests in counselling, but this caution should extend to the availability of tests within the school. A trained counsellor may quite properly order certain tests; he then leaves the school for another post and one is left wondering what happens to some of these tests. The discussion of testing as an aid to the interview has been brief, and interested readers would do well to consult the scholarly work of Goldman (1961), Hayes (1968), Hayes and Hopson (1971) and Tyler (1962, 1963) for more thorough analysis of the problems of testing in counselling. A very practical discussion can be found in Jackson and Juniper (1971).

*Summary discussion*

The need to respect confidentiality is stressed but the responsibility of the counsellor to other pupils and the school is also demonstrated. The counsellor has a duty to protect the pupil when he is in grave physical or moral danger, or when other pupils are in such danger. This means that the principle of confidentiality cannot be blindly applied to the school counselling situation, and all those involved need to think out the issues clearly. It is possible for the idea of confidentiality to be misused by the inept counsellor, thereby alienating colleagues and depriving the pupil of valuable supports. More seriously, it can prevent him from referring a pupil who is in urgent need of specialist pyschological or medical help.

The practice of home visiting is shown to be fraught with many dangers. The counsellor must evaluate the costs and risks involved in visiting a home. He must see that this can have a very negative impact upon the pupil and parents in come cases, and he may destroy the work being done by other caseworkers. Many possibilities for alternatives exist, such as holding discussion groups with parents, or interviewing parents at school. In the developmental counselling with which the school is largely concerned it is more useful for the counsellor in conjunction with the pastoral care team to try to involve parents as helpers with the ongoing activities of the school. This may be the only way of constructively working with many parents whose own educational background is limited. It is sensible to concentrate much of this effort on the parents of first-year pupils.

Testing can occupy an important place in the counselling process. Many difficulties have to be overcome if we are to use tests in a way which provides the maximum benefits for pupils. A full explanation has to be given to the pupil about our reasons for using a test. If we fail to do this we may be threatening him because he sees tests in a negative way. We have a responsibility to explain the limitations of the test and the meaning of the results. The interpretation of the test is the key part of testing and this makes considerable demands on the counsellor. We must ensure that a boy is not attributing too much to the result and that he has really understood the significance of the score. The timing of the test is crucial, and it has been argued that premature and irrelevant testing is not only inefficient, but sometimes can be harmful. We should always know why we are resorting to testing and take pains to involve the pupil in the interpretation of the results. Although this is time-consuming, it is necessary if the test is to facilitate counselling rather than hinder it. Tests should never be the central factor of counselling for this would deny the real nature of counselling. We have an ethical obligation to adhere to the restrictions on the use of certain tests.

## REFERENCES

Cave, R. (1970) *Partnership For Change,* London: Ward Lock, Educational.

Hayes, J. and Hopson, B. (1971) *Careers Guidance,* London: Ward Lock, Educational.

Hopson, B. (1968) "Key Concepts In The Use of Psychological Tests in Vocational Guidance", In Hopson B. and Hayes J. *The Theory and Practice of Vocational Guidance,* Oxford: Pergamon Press.

Goldman, L. (1961) *Using Tests In Counseling,* New York: Appleton-Century-Crofts.

Jackson, R. and Juniper, D. (1971) *A Manual of Educational Guidance,* London: Holt, Rinehart & Winston.

McGeeney, P. (1969) *Parents are Welcome,* London: Longman.

Newsom Report (1963) *Half Our Future,* London: H.M.S.O.

Super, D. and Crites, J. (1962) *Appraising Vocational Fitness,* Rev. Edn. New York: Harper & Row.

Tyler, L. (1962) "Research on Instruments Used By Counselors In Vocational Guidance", *Jn. Counsel. Psychol.* 7. 99–105.

—— (1963) *Tests and Measurements,* Englewood Cliffs, New Jersey: Prentice Hall.

# CHAPTER NINE

# COUNSELLING AND THE DAILY LIFE OF THE SCHOOL

## *The purpose of this chapter*

This chapter tackles the problem of making counselling a real part of the school. Basic tools for analysing the processes which decide whether or not the aims of the school are achieved are offered to the reader. These are then linked with a discussion of the three levels of counselling, pastoral care systems and the new development of peer counselling.

## *The questions which are asked*

(i) What simple tools can we use to find out where we need to focus our efforts and to see that counselling is effective?

(ii) What do we mean by levels of counselling?

(iii) What are some of the major considerations in developing a pastoral care system?

(iv) Can peer counselling be of any use? If so, what do we mean by this term?

(v) Perhaps the most basic question underlying this chapter is about the nature of the changes in our roles as teachers and the kinds of adaptations that we need to make ourselves if our approach is going to be creative.

### Other points

You will find it very useful to return to the critical incident analysis and draw up one for your own school or some section of the pupils. It will be very enlightening to produce the necessary content which relates the socialization model to your own school. These exercises will provide you with substantial understanding of your own school situation.

---

### Resources in the secondary school

A philosophy of education similar to that presented by Whitehead (1959) underlies the concept of school counselling which has been presented to you. Whitehead argues that one of the major aims of education is to produce young people who not only know something well, but who are capable of doing something well. The two-phase model of counselling incorporates this view, for it is concerned with the emergence of a sense of purpose and direction. Once this is found, it is given realistic behavioural shape by the combined efforts of pupil, counsellor and other teachers. This insistence on the need for direction and purpose reflects crucial features of the psychology of the adolescent: the sense of urgency; the need for potency and identity in social interactions; the desire for achievement and recognition in some field of activity; the constant evaluation of school activities as meaningful or purposeless. From the perspective of secondary education, school counselling can be seen as being concerned with the processes by which pupils affiliate themselves with the school or by which they disassociate themselves from the values and purposes of the school. The active model represents an attempt to respond to this constructively. It is emphasized that the counsellor must not separate himself from the daily life of the school, and that colleagues should have a recognized and legitimate place in the counselling process. Theirs is an active and participant role. This was also a product of my firm belief that teachers are truly professionals. The feature which distinguishes the professional from the non-professional is not just the possession of expert and specialist knowledge, but a constant concern for the well-being and the best interests of his clients.

If the counsellor is concerned with the understanding and prevention of alienation and the production of attitudes which allow pupils to avail themselves of the resources of the school, then he cannot afford to separate himself from the ongoing life of the school. I think most trained counsellors are now aware of the danger of seeing counselling as a "sacred activity"—sacred in the Durkheimian sense of being in the category of "things set apart" and having no connection with the profane everyday life of the school. Such a viewpoint would be useless, when profound and rapid changes are occurring within the secondary school. Amongst examples which come to mind at once are the size of schools (although we must be cautious: Monks (1968) shows that we tend to exaggerate this), the additional year of statutory schooling, the development of a new type of sixth form in which non-academic pupils are becoming increasingly important, and curricular innovations. Some form of *management by objectives* is needed from the effective secondary school head. His function as educational leader and co-ordinator becomes crucial. We can see that on the one hand the day-to-day running of the school has to be delegated, whilst on the other the Head is developing skills in:

1. The specification of objectives and the analysis of the conditions in which teachers can provide appropriate learning experiences for the pupils.

2. Clearly defining the means by which these objectives will be obtained.

3. Co-ordinating and establishing policy-making machinery which involves as many of the staff as possible.

4. Effectively deploying and using the resources within the school.

Many social forces outside the school exert pressure on it, and many sections of the population have definite views about its purposes and the way in which these should be achieved. However, this section is concerned with the way the school functions as a complete system of itself, without implying that the secondary school should be insulated from society. Within a school, the expectations of the teachers, the nature of the pupils and the viewpoints of all the participants in the educative process interact with teaching methods and the general regime in a very complicated way. Inevitably some pupils will be in conflict with aspects of the school system, possibly through no fault of their own. We know that methods of organization such as streaming have unintended consequences which are detrimental to certain pupils. We have scarcely begun as yet to look at the self-defeating strategies we use in our daily work in the school. Our tendency to label individuals and build up sets of expectations about certain groups or pupils provides one example. In any case, the school may be only partially successful in meeting the needs of many pupils. Much of this will be elaborated later in relation to counselling, but we can see that the factors of social class background, familial regime and personality may cause discrepancies between the goals of the school and the needs of the pupil. Either the school has to adapt, or the pupil has to adjust. In practice it always goes both ways, for teachers have worked hard to provide sufficient elasticity in their method and procedures. The need to modify the impact of the school system on individuals has always been recognized. Yet, despite this undoubted fact, the increasing complexity of the demands made upon the adolescent, when coupled with the growing size of schools, requires us consciously to assess the degree of elasticity in the secondary school and to create the capacity for adaptation to pupil needs in the systems we build up. Note that this is not necessarily an argument for smaller schools; indeed it could be an argument for larger ones, for these may, if properly devised, have greater inherent possibilities for variations in the treatment of pupils.

The basis of this elasticity seems to lie in the efficient use of the pastoral care team, the guidance team and the trained counsellor. The fully trained school counsellor may have a very special contribution to make to working parties which are intended to increase the flexibility of the system, making realistic adaptations of method at periods of discontinuity, crisis and choice during the school career of pupils. The headmaster has to maintain a delicate balance between rigidity and flexibility, trying to avoid a situation of drift. In his managerial role, he has to make decisions about the deployment of resources, and this is his ultimate responsibility, although the decisions are made on a basis of consultation with fellow professionals. Our question then becomes that of methods of analysis which avoid both chaos and inflexible crystallization. It seems that the first logical step to take is methodically to detect the crisis points for pupils, the times when difficult decisions have to be made by pupils and staff and the points at which critical incidents seem to occur. For our purposes a critical incident can be described as an event which decides whether or not the goals of the individual and the organization will be reached. To illustrate the approach I have drawn up a hypothetical analysis of the progress of a typical pupil through an all-through 11—18 comprehensive school. He is of good ability. The school has a common course for the first two years, pupils choosing their options at the end of the second year.

This very crude analysis shows the choice points and the potential discontinuities which will influence pupils on the left-hand side of the path, whilst resources and a general indication of the strategies the school will use are shown on the right hand of the diagram. The first and most obvious discontinuity is that of entry to the secondary school. In general, it is a sound principle that coping strategies should be devised which prepare the pupil for the situation before he enters it, thereby giving him maximal chances of coping successfully. Visits by staff from the secondary school to the primary school and by pupils to the secondary school during their last term in the primary school do help to overcome the problems of this transition to some degree. Once they enter, the methods advocated in the section on group guidance can be employed. We should also look at pupils' reactions to having to travel long distances, if it is necessary, and to the enlargement of social relationships thrust on them when they enter a large school.

The next point which merits attention is the allocation to options and bands which occurs in the third year in this school. This is anticipated by the provision of group guidance sessions which help to explain the nature and the consequences of the choices which have to be made. If alienation of pupils is to be avoided careful thought and preparation

## CRITICAL INCIDENT ANALYSIS FOR A PUPIL OF
## GOOD ABILITY IN A SENIOR SCHOOL

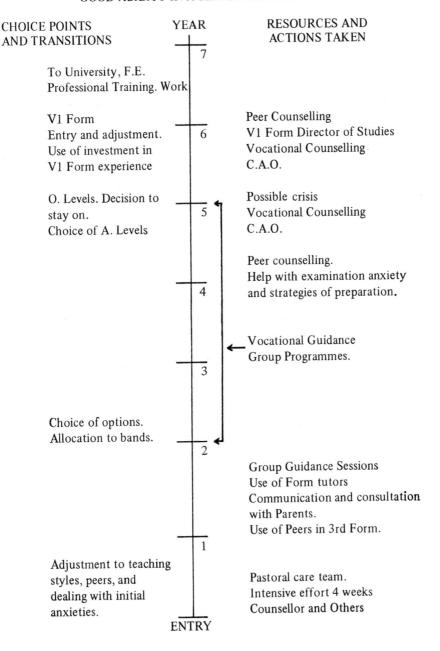

| CHOICE POINTS AND TRANSITIONS | YEAR | RESOURCES AND ACTIONS TAKEN |
|---|---|---|
| | 7 | |
| To University, F.E. Professional Training. Work | | |
| VI Form Entry and adjustment. Use of investment in VI Form experience | 6 | Peer Counselling VI Form Director of Studies Vocational Counselling C.A.O. |
| O. Levels. Decision to stay on. Choice of A. Levels | 5 | Possible crisis Vocational Counselling C.A.O. |
| | 4 | Peer counselling. Help with examination anxiety and strategies of preparation. |
| | 3 | Vocational Guidance Group Programmes. |
| Choice of options. Allocation to bands. | 2 | |
| | 1 | Group Guidance Sessions Use of Form tutors Communication and consultation with Parents. Use of Peers in 3rd Form. |
| Adjustment to teaching styles, peers, and dealing with initial anxieties. | ENTRY | Pastoral care team. Intensive effort 4 weeks Counsellor and Others |

is necessary. It is not sufficient to provide a few superficial guidelines or a duplicated sheet, for this will confuse many pupils as much as it helps others. A number of carefully spaced group guidance sessions should be incorporated into the timetable, whilst form masters, year tutors or house masters should be allocated time when they can deal with individuals. Parental consultation is necessary at this period, not only through meetings, but through individual interviews. This again highlights the need to make the preparation a fairly lengthy process. A potent source of help is that of the pupils' near peers. Indeed if we really want to ensure affiliation to the values of the school and change the quality of interpersonal relationships within the school, it is essential that we use pupils themselves. We can take pupils during their last term in the third year. They are still close enough to the choice point to recall it, and they have had enough time to assess the quality of their decisions. They can then be used in group guidance sessions or small group discussions as very effective supports. This would also apply to second-year pupils helping first-year pupils adjust to the new conditions.

In this school, vocational guidance is seen as a process and not an event. It is therefore spread out over three years. The process is seen as one linked to the development of self-awareness; but from the head-master's viewpoint it is seen as an essential instrument in helping to make the academic work of the school relevant to the pupils. This area is covered by the earlier discussion on vocational guidance, although the work by Hayes and Hopson (1971) also provides an excellent guide. A major point comes at the fifth year, when C.S.E. and O Levels are taken and pupils make the decision to stay on or leave school. This is anticipated by group guidance sessions concerned with examination anxieties, study habits and planning strategies for successful study. The subject matter of counselling is the learner himself, but it is curious that we so often concentrate solely upon subject content and fail to analyse the learning process in a methodical way. This needs to be done at intervals, and it seems important to do this during the fifth year, so that pupils approach examinations constructively. Not only should group guidance be provided, but it is also useful to give the lower sixth a chance to undertake peer counselling. They have recently gone through the experience and can make a very positive contribution.

Participation should not be restricted to those who did very well; we should also use those who experienced difficulties and who overcame them. Their determination to succeed and willingness to stay on at school to try again can encourage those who wish to opt out to think again. To discover that their anxieties are not unique and to have the opportunity to benefit from the experiences of those who have overcome anxieties and worked through the situation will help many pupils raise their level of performance and competence. Discussion of choice of A Levels at this point is not a luxury or a waste of time, but a source of motivation and an incentive to raise one's level of aspiration. At this stage, the diagram indicates the need to provide some crisis vocational counselling or educational guidance when a pupil unexpectedly fails or does much better than he and others thought likely. We have a responsibility to point out to pupils the costs of staying on at school, and we should not automatically assume that it is better to stay on than leave school.

Entry to the sixth form produces the need for another set of resources. This can take the form of providing a sixth-form director of studies as overt recognition of the fact that the traditional "special relationship" between the headmaster and the sixth form is no longer possible, nor entirely desirable. We see that this Head has given thought to the special needs of the sixth form for counselling and guidance by providing a director of studies who also has a counselling function. Many pupils still go to university scarcely knowing why they are going. They are often uncertain of the real nature of the courses they will take and the demands which will be made upon them.

We must also be alert to the fact that the polytechnic is in danger of becoming a safety net for those who fail to get into university, perhaps being seen as an alternative to the other strategy of reluctant recruitment to teaching through entry to a college of education. This means that, if left unchecked, pupils do not see the innovatory nature of many polytechnic courses, especially the new degrees in such subjects as environmental sciences, and the imaginative combinations of subjects. This does not imply that we take an uncritical view of the polytechnic for, like other institutions in higher education, it has its peculiar collection of advantages and disadvantages.

Considerable adjustments have to be made by pupils if the experiences provided for them in the sixth form are to be productive, and there is no automatic guarantee that boys and girls will make these without help. This is particularly true of bright pupils from poor backgrounds who have relied very heavily on the signals of success provided by streaming and the approval of teachers. They may be very dependent upon these reinforcements and may not adjust to the new demands. Many such pupils who are successful in the sixth form do not use this investment of time and energy to proceed to higher education, and this may be the beginning of life-long frustration for them. Those sixth formers who take O Levels and C.S.E. seem to be in need of counselling supports because they are vulnerable on several scores. They do feel inferior; comparing themselves with more able peers. They reduce their own performance and deny their worthwhileness. Often this process is being unwittingly reinforced by teachers and academic peers. It would be a pity if a healthy development in the school were to be marred by problems akin to those of a rigid streaming system. I have just seen several groups of this kind who are beginning to compensate in ways which are unhelpful to themselves and the school. I had cause to ponder on the fact that this group actually had the greatest amount of free time, yet were unable to use it constructively. A number of negative attitudes towards school and work were being generated during this free time, despite their desire for educational qualifications of some type. Their over-valuation of minimal educational qualifications seemed to be making them develop unrealistic vocational aspirations, and they experienced considerable anxiety. One pointed out that he had reached the stage when he was almost afraid to leave school and was looking for another group to which he could attach himself and from which he could gain security. We need develop programmes which see these pupils as valuable assets to the school, giving them opportunities for real responsibility through involvement in peer counselling schemes. We should work to increase their sense of competence.

I have made no attempt to discuss these crisis points in the critical incident analysis in any detail because such discussions would be meaningless outside the context of a specific school. I have simply attempted to suggest one way in which the analysis could be begun, showing the way in which we can attempt to allocate resources effectively and reach our objectives. Such an analysis could be done with each band or definable subsection of the school population, and the needs revealed and the resources required could be then assessed and compared. It has seemed to me in visiting a large number of comprehensive schools that such an analysis may well be crucial in the middle forms of the comprehensive school, for these are the ones in which pupils are submitted to conflicting expectations by teachers, and where they are confused about their role as pupils. Very little is needed to push pupils in these forms towards affiliation with the school or into alienation from it. In passing, it is relevant to remark that such a critical incident analysis can be very helpful to the individual pupil in helping him see where he is going and the hazards and barriers which have to be surmounted if he is to be successful. This analysis is just a first step. To integrate counselling and guidance into the daily life of the school it seems that we need to break down the steps by which the secondary school socializes its pupils. To this we now turn.

### The secondary school as a socializing agency

For my purposes I will define socialization as the process by which an individual acquires the standards, values and behaviours which mark him out as belonging to a particular group. Our objectives reflect the standards and behaviours which we hope to develop in pupils as a result of their exposure to the educative process in the secondary school. This does not imply the production of a uniform product; we hope, rather, to produce individuals with a clear sense of identity who are able to use their unique combination of abilities and personality qualities in a satisfying way. It is this view of socialization which lies behind the developmental concept of counselling. We will also have in mind the idea of maturation and change, which is crucial to socialization and development. This will mean that we adjust our demands; we recognize different rates of development, and we also recognize that what a pupil cannot do this year may well be within his capacity next year, providing that our methods do not stifle his potential for growth.

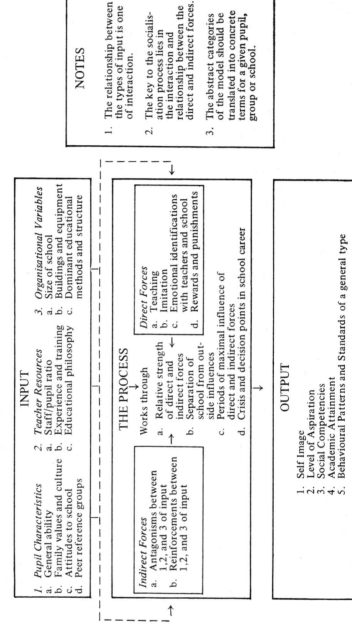

A BASIC PROCESS MODEL

**INPUT**

*1. Pupil Characteristics*
a. General ability
b. Family values and culture
c. Attitudes to school
d. Peer reference groups

*2. Teacher Resources*
a. Staff/pupil ratio
b. Experience and training
c. Educational philosophy

*3. Organisational Variables*
a. Size of school
b. Buildings and equipment
c. Dominant educational methods and structure

**THE PROCESS**

Works through

*Indirect Forces*
a. Antagonisms between 1, 2, and 3 of input
b. Reinforcements between 1, 2, and 3 of input

a. Relative strength of direct and indirect forces
b. Separation of school from outside influences
c. Periods of maximal influence of direct and indirect forces
d. Crisis and decision points in school career

*Direct Forces*
a. Teaching
b. Imitation
c. Emotional identifications with teachers and school
d. Rewards and punishments

**OUTPUT**

1. Self Image
2. Level of Aspiration
3. Social Competencies
4. Academic Attainment
5. Behavioural Patterns and Standards of a general type

**NOTES**

1. The relationship between the types of input is one of interaction.

2. The key to the socialisation process lies in the interaction and relationship between the direct and indirect forces.

3. The abstract categories of the model should be translated into concrete terms for a given pupil, group or school.

## A MODEL OF THE SOCIALISATION PROCESS IN
## THE SECONDARY SCHOOL

BASIC POINTS

1. Socialisation is the process by which an individual acquires standards, values and behaviours of a particular kind.

2. A socialisation model for the secondary school should look at:
   a. *the process* by which a pupil affiliates with or alienates himself from the school.
   b. *the objectives* of the school and the actual *outcomes.*
   c. *the outcomes* which should be analysed with the following in mind:
   
   (i)   Intended versus unintended.
   (ii)  The costs of these outcomes to pupils and staff.
   (iii) The strategies which have to be employed to shape behaviours in the desired ways.
   (iv)  The detection of critical events which determine whether or not the outcomes occur.

As soon as we begin to think about socialization and define our objectives, key questions emerge which are relevant to the integration of counselling and guidance into the daily life of the school. The most important ones seem to be these:

1. Do the behaviours and values of the pupils actually alter in the way we hope they will?

2. If they do not, are we using self-defeating strategies which produce results which are contrary to those we desire?

3. What are the costs of our actions and methods? Are they costs which we have not recognized?

4. What strengths and deficits seem to be important in the school's intake? This then leads to the further question: what adaptations are called for by the school?

5. What changes must occur in the pupils if our objectives are to be reached?

The simple model which has been presented is again a guide to action. To have meaning, the abstract categories have to be given content derived from the actual school situation. In filling it in we need to look especially carefully at the system of rewards and punishments, especially the former, for it is this that is crucial in achieving the objectives. Not only shall we try to provide answers to the questions specified above, but we find additional ones arise. We must define areas of conflict; this definition has already been dealt with in the critical incident analysis in a superficial way. Here we look at the possibility of conflict in a more complex way, assessing the interaction between the characteristics of the pupil and the methods and aims of the school. In individual cases, as well as with groups of pupils, we need to ask penetrating questions about the relationships which exist between the pupil's past school experiences, his personal history and the standards of his family. Unless we spell these out in detail we are unlikely to provide appropriate learning experiences and a school regime which allows us to achieve our objectives. The principles of compensatory education need to be incorporated into the secondary school in a carefully planned way for whole groups of pupils. The importance of the self-image in producing constructive behaviour has been stressed throughout this book, but we still need to ask ourselves about the impact that our organization and teaching methods have on the pupil's image of himself. Unless we try to create a climate in which a positive image of self is built up, we are socializing pupils in a way which does not integrate them into the school but alienates them from it.

The *basic level of input* merits close attention. A little thought shows that the relationships between the basic categories of input is one of interaction and mutual influence rather than isolation. Some schools have intakes where a larger than expected proportion of pupils possess family backgrounds which are apathetic to the aims of the school, if not actually antagonistic. This has an effect upon the teaching resources. These schools are often those where the teacher—pupil ratio is higher than desirable, not simply because it is hard to fill posts, but because in practice the rate of absenteeism among teachers is high. This is due to exhaustion and the frustrations experienced by teachers in dealing with certain forms. It is a salutary exercise for a headmaster to analyse the absenteeism figures amongst his teachers and find out the nature and pattern of absenteeism. Sometimes these schools have to accept a higher than desirable proportion of teachers who are in their probationary year or still relatively inexperienced. A great deal of energy is then spent in the maintenance of control and order, diverting attention from creative innovations. Another interactive influence can be found in the buildings. If these are inadequate and out-of-date, this not only influences teaching method, but creates further difficulties. If the school is housed in buildings which are at a considerable distance from one another, not only is there fragmentation and insulation leading to discontinuity, but other effects occur. Some schools have to house the sexes in separate buildings, bringing them together for the last year or two. Nor surprisingly, a great deal of energy is often invested in dealing with pupils' reactions to this novel situation. Even more serious than this is the fact that sometimes some pupils never reach the upper school because they opt out at the earliest age of leaving. The upper school is therefore composed of the academic and largely middle class and many pupils possessing ability never reach it. We know that pupils can covertly modify the aims of the school as Hargreaves (1967) shows. An intake in which the negative elements predominate not only calls for massive adaptations by the school, but for an emphasis on constructive intervention during the early part of pupils' school careers. In planning, it is desirable to focus a great number of resources in the first and second years and the counsellor and pastoral care team will be most effective if they concentrate their efforts with the younger forms when negative features appear to be a marked characteristic of the intake. Much of the behaviour which caused alarm in discussions on ROSLA is a product of the negative socialization which we provide quite unintentionally during the first two years of secondary education. Once we try to incorporate counselling and guidance into the daily life of the school, then it seems to be clear that we need to re-evaluate the rewards offered to teachers. The hardest and most skilled work has to be done, not only with the less able pupils, but with those in the middle range. The first and second years are critical, for they provide the foundations for later work. This requires considerable adaptations to ensure satisfactions of a meaningful sort for these pupils if they are to be affiliated with the aims and values of the school. Unless we do this, we cannot achieve our objectives. Not only is there a need to focus pastoral care very specifically towards these pupils, but we need financial rewards to encourage teachers to move towards those sections of the school where professional skills are crucial and in which creative innovation is all-important.

The central or process section of the model enlightens us a little more. Here we begin to see the existence of indirect forces which have an impact upon our aims. Direct forces such as teaching, rewards and punishment are obvious. Less obvious direct forces are those of imitation and identification. We have long said that religion "is caught and not taught". The same thing applies to acceptance of school values. We have to look at the models we provide, for Bandura and Walters (1963) point out that children follow and imitate powerful and competent models. This again underlines that we are not concerned with a loose purposeless process, but we must also see that imitation and identification usually occur under certain conditions. They are dependent upon the meaning of the model for the child. Warmth, concern and positive interpersonal relationships are the essential conditions. This makes the form master and pastoral care team crucial in helping children assimilate and accept the basic values of the school. This is especially true of pupils who are "at risk" because of home background and other reasons, and supportive conditions have to be created rather than punitive ones. For many reasons it is easier to look at the punishments than the rewards of a school, yet we have to ask ourselves about the potency of the rewards we offer. How meaningful are they to the pupils? Do we emphasize them as much as we emphasize the negative sanctions we sometimes feel forced to use? A related question is whether we use as an incentive something which rather than being seen as desirable is in fact seen as actually punishing for many pupils. This is, of course, the comparison process in which we compare individuals with other individuals or forms with other forms, causing the less favoured and able to reject everything associated with the approved models. We can ask whether or not we build up an optimistic view of pupils' abilities or whether we unknowingly convince many pupils that it is no use trying. You will recall how important the pupil's self-image and his set of predictions was found to be in the first phase of the counselling process.

The indirect forces consist of the antagonisms and mutual reinforcements which exist between the three parts of the input. If school and home values go together, and the bulk of teacher attitudes contribute to the declared aims of the school, then it will be much easier to reach them. The process is concerned with the balance between direct and indirect processes. Many of the indirect processes can be negative in nature. It is not until we isolate them that we begin to detect their influence and are able to take steps to modify them. One technique used by the grammar school was the insulation of school activities and values from those of the home. This was possible because of the prestige of the grammar school and because it was able to give strong confirmation of success and offer very tangible rewards to its pupils. In the comprehensive system it is far from easy to insulate the school from outside influences, neither is it desirable even if it could be done. We have to develop new ways of gaining the co-operation of parents rather than exluding them. We need to link up with the community, for the relevance of school activities to life is one of the major questions in the minds of many pupils. Boocock (1972), in a discussion of the sociology of learning, points out that the relationship between the structure of the school and the local community must always be considered. The external environment always has an impact on the school, which means that it has an indirect one on the pupil. The school makes various adaptations to the locality, sometimes almost unwittingly, and it is through the mediation of these that the environment influences the pupil within the school. We cannot assume that a simple direct relationship exists between the school and the local community. Prior to comprehensive education it was not uncommon in densely populated areas to find two secondary modern schools almost touching and drawing from the same population. Yet on investigation one would find vast differences in the characteristics of the pupils, teaching methods and level of attainment.

We should consciously develop procedures which counterbalance unfavourable peer or home influences without suggesting that these families and groups are undesirable. Rather we need to assess the positive things they offer and then extend them in our own activities. Often we can quite quickly devise ways of providing satisfactions which are previously denied to certain groups of pupils, and this is sufficient to tip the balance in favour of affiliation to school. Ask yourself how often the less able boys in your school are given the chance to represent the school at sports or in any other way. It is very sensible to work out the times at which each factor has the maximal influence. The statutory age leavers will be strongly pulled towards outside influences during their last year of school if they are not taking examinations. Counter steps which link the outside with school in a constructive manner are therefore indicated. Pupils taking examinations are very susceptible to teacher influences in the two terms prior to the examination and we could use this more profitably. Guidance would consist of structured teaching about learning to set their own targets and goals, which increases their sense of autonomy and personal efficiency, and also strongly reinforces the educational objectives of the school. With forms composed of less able children, or when pupils are partially disassociating themselves from the school, the skill and training of the teacher becomes the variable which is of greatest importance. Appropriate teaching methods and the ability to reinforce a sense of achievement would then be the factors needing emphasis in the socialization process.

Perhaps this has given some idea of the interaction between the input. It may become clearer if we examine the relationship between teaching methods and other factors. If team teaching is to be the major method of instruction then we would need more flexible spacing and the provision of a number of different sized rooms. We should also need new facilities for team planning and the preparation of material. If mixed ability grouping were to be the method of organization then not only would we have to supply more equipment, but ideally we need different classroom furniture which allows pupils to work in small groups. Truly individualized programmes of instruction in which every pupil has his own programme would require, amongst other things, individual study rooms, more library and laboratory spaces and increased secretarial help. Programmed learning holds possibilities, but this means thought about storage spaces, the provision of booths and adequate systems of recording and assessing progress. If the school is seen as a community centre then extra facilities and space are necessary. If we return to the concept of education for leisure then we require expanded facilities in obvious areas of the school. This catalogue demonstrates some of the relationships between method and facilities. In using the model one needs to spell these out in relation to the actual situation. The model has isolated some of the variables which appear to be important, but it is only a tool intended to make the relevant strategies in pastoral care, guidance and counselling visible to the staff of a school. It only becomes useful when the content is supplied, and this cannot be done apart from a real school.

This section on socialization has implicitly linked the activity of counselling and guidance to that of curriculum development showing that as soon as we treat them as an integral part of the school, we cannot evade the task of critically examining the relationship of teaching method and classroom regime to the attitudes and behaviour of pupils. The topic is too formidable to tackle in depth in this introductory book, but I would argue at this juncture that there is a very strong case for developing a resources centre for guidance and counselling within the school. The materials would be the joint product of the pastoral care team and the pupils. Workshops could be formed for the production of the materials. Without these aids, I find that many form teachers who are given time for their work by Heads complain that they cannot use the time efficiently. Again, I stress the need to involve pupils in the development and making of apparatus. There is no better way of discovering their needs and making school relevant than involving them in the teaching process in this way.

The resource centre would include the guidance carrels mentioned in Chapter Five supplemented by duplicated materials, tape recordings and video tapes when the facilities are present. The library of materials should be systematically arranged according to topic, activity and age range. Recent Schools Council projects have produced very useful ideas and activities which should be included. The material could include a library of personal problem situations which are written by pupils as dramatic excerpts and then acted and recorded by them. These could be supplemented by questionnaires which give a number of strategies and solutions from which one has to be selected and justified.

Pupils can be presented with open ended situations where small groups discuss and produce an ending which satisfies them. They may be asked to decide why a particular solution is unsatisfactory. Examples of such situations could be:

> Being accused of stealing when one is innocent.
> Discovering that someone is cheating in a game or during an examination.
> Fear of being asked a question in class.

Provided that care is taken to prevent identification it is possible to use Kelly's idea of character sketches to promote discussion of personal development in the more able pupils and the sixth form. The instructions to the pupil take the following form:

> I want you to write a character sketch of yourself just as if you were the principal character in a play. Write it as it might be written by a friend who knows you very closely and understands you, perhaps better than anyone ever could. Be sure to write it in the third person beginning, "John Smith...". The example which follows is one of a large number written for one of my students whilst undertaking group guidance with a sixth form. Although it demonstrates a striking capacity for self-awareness and sensitivity, it is far from exceptional. Sixth form pupils report that they find this a fascinating exercise and derive a great deal of benefit from discussing them with the counsellor.

*Character sketch technique. VI form pupil girl.*
*Comprehensive school (rural)*

"                " is seventeen years of age. Sometimes she could and, indeed, often has been mistaken for someone much older. This could be due to the way she dresses and appears, but I think it is more likely due to the fact that she has a gift for looking intelligent and interested when she is not. As far as this goes she is a downright hypocrite.

Somehow she manages to keep face with both the person who is boring her and with her fellow-sufferers—I bet she finds this a strain sometimes. She will rarely commit herself to one side of an argument. Sometimes she comes out best by doing this but other times it has the opposite effect and she finds herself left out completely because of her indecision. This indecision is a great failing of hers and subconsciously I think she worries about it. She'd like to be able to make up her own mind but always ends up adopting the safe, middle path or following the general trend. Of course, she never says anything about this to anyone. I am not even sure if she is consciously aware that this is a big fault of hers. She really makes this noticeable only through little things like her indecision about buying clothes. She will rarely act on impulse and head for what she wants, regardless of the consequences, but always stops to consider what other people are going to think. She loses a lot of fun by not acting on impulse. She cannot even be complimented on her stopping to think of others for her real motive in doing this is not considering other people's feeling but maintaining her own image in their eyes.

Few people would notice this indecisive nature of hers, for, to most people, she seems to be forceful and go-ahead. She gives the impression of being able to handle most situations and able to converse freely. Except with her friends, she finds conversation difficult, and her outward confidence hides inner shyness and insecurity. She is easily embarrassed and childishly sensitive. This is annoying, when she makes it obvious that she cannot accept an innocent joke about herself. She also has the horrible habit of relating any incident that may be talked about, to her own experiences. At times this becomes intensely annoying as she virtually monopolises the conversation on a subject that is of no interest to anyone except herself.

She is not, however, particularly selfish. Her desire to be on good terms with everybody ensures this. Yet her outward generosity is for her own ends really. She detests arguments and quarrels, simply because she cannot really hold her own, yet it annoys her to lose.

She is probably most at ease with her friends. She can be extremely funny without trying hard; she relates a story with full enactment and exaggerates beyond credibility in doing so, sometimes. Her own sense of humour is weird and macabre. Often, she forces laughter to jokes at which everyone else is really weak with laughter and then she will see the funny side to a serious situation, in which no-one else sees anything to laugh at.

She has intense enthusiasm for certain things but it is never long-lasting. While it does last though she can manage to put spirit into the most indifferent character, but it does not take more than one set-back for her to lose interest.

Earlier on, I said she is often mistaken for someone much older. This annoys me because, although she plays up to these people, I know that she can be extremely childish over petty things. Although she usually laughs off these annoyances, she can make her point only too clear by a cutting remark.

Her moods fluctuate from moment to moment and it is best to take them as they come, without paying any particular attention to her or to her moods. Yet her character seems to demand attention and can become miserable if she does not receive it. She is at her best when she is popular. I don't think she could ever manage without friends for it is these that she clings to, to destroy, or at least hide her loneliness. And inside she is lonely in the constant battle to find herself.

She is very inconsistent. When she talks about her parents she sometimes adopts an indifferent attitude to them, whereas, in fact, she has a very deep and loving respect for them though she will seldom admit this. Her boyfriend receives the same treatment. One moment she wants to do well in life, the next she sees no point in trying. It's extremely difficult being a friend to someone who changes as quickly as the wind.

I feel sorry for her when her seemingly confident nature gives way to reveal some of the insecure person underneath, for this latter state is often mistaken for snobbishness. It is strange that her abominable shyness can be mistaken for snobbishness.

She is also strange in that she can usually find sensible, comforting solutions to other people's problems, such as my own. Indeed, it is partly this which makes her a good friend. She can listen well, and one feels they can tell her everything. Yet, when it comes to her own problems she cannot easily confide because it seems that she's not quite sure what her own problems are.

She seems to be searching for her own character. She adopts so many roles that she has lost herself somewhere along the way, or, perhaps she has never really found herself. Life is one long act of playing the right character at the right time.

I am not sure that her continuous acting is just to hide her insecurity or if it is governed by a genuine desire to act. She is often more "natural" on the stage than she is off because her own lack of identity makes it easier for her to assume someone else's role.

Even I cannot make a character sketch of her, for I only see the side of her character that she shows me. If I was her teacher, I would write an entirely different character sketch of her, because she is so flexible in character.

Home-made material which supplements the professionally produced information is very useful in the vocational guidance lesson Slides produced from the pupils' own photographs can be coupled with commentaries recorded on tape by pupils or young workers in the occupation. This provides information coming from what is a credible and acceptable source to those who may reject adult messages. Yet another simple device is the life style sketch which can be written by pupils after interviewing workers in local occupations. Two examples below suggest the form these can take and the way in which the positive and negative aspects of a job are explored, although I must apologize for the fact that these were written by students taking the counselling course.

### Worker's life style sketch

I work as a student nurse in a big teaching hospital. The wards are light and pleasant with plenty of room to move about. There's a glorious view from the windows and it's always beautifully warm. When on duty we have to look very clean and tidy of course, but the uniforms we wear now are also very smart. Mine is a yellow nylon overall type of frock with a ducky little white cap.

It's a very busy life. We're on the go all the time. But it's very interesting. There's plenty of variety and there's certainly no time to get bored. In the ward our duties include waking up the patients in the morning or seeing that they're settled down for the night; washing those who can't wash themselves; bringing bowls of water for those who can wash; making beds and tidying lockers; taking round bed pans and emptying them (I didn't like this at first, especially when they were a bit smelly, but I'm getting used to it now); giving out medicines; changing dressings; taking temperatures and pulses; helping with treatments and going round with the doctors. We have to be very careful and accurate because a mistake could be fatal, but I like the feeling of responsibility I'm beginning to get.

The patients, of course, are a mixed lot. Some are very good and never grumble; some think you're at their beck and call all the time and are always shouting, "Nurse, I want that! Nurse, bring me a bed pan!" just when I'm especially busy. Most of them, however, are very nice. They chat to us when we're doing the beds, and we often tell them about our boy friends. They're sometimes very grateful for what we do for them and give us presents of sweets or chocolates from what their visitors have brought. Many of them give us little gifts when they go home as a way of saying "Thank you". At first I used to get very attached to some of the patients and it used to upset me when they were very ill but I'm trying to stop this because I think it will hinder me from being a good nurse. The first time I saw someone die I was really shaken. I don't know if I'll ever get used to that. But it's great to see people going home much better and it's nice to feel that you've helped a little bit to make that possible.

Sister is the "boss" of the ward and she keeps us on our toes, but the discipline isn't half as bad as I believe it used to be. The hours are a bit long, especially when we have to work on the "night" shift, and sometimes I get very tired, but we do have quite good time off. Once a week we get a day off to have lectures with Sister Tutor. They're very interesting but there's a lot to learn, and though swotting is a bit of a bind, as it was in school, I'm keen to get my SRN, so I know I must do it. We move around the wards so that we get experience of all types of cases and we are going to do a spell in the theatre. I'm hoping when I get my SRN to do my Midwifery Certificate and then become a Staff Nurse and perhaps one day a Sister. I live in a hostel with a lot of other

nurses, most of them my own age. I've made lots of friends and we have
good fun. Because it's a big hospital, the social life is quite good. We
have dances frequently, get invited out to parties quite a lot, and have
plenty of chances to meet some smashing Med. students. The .pay
isn't very good at the moment, but we do get our uniform and our
keep and the food isn't bad at all. Of course, when we're qualified,
we'll do very much better. Like all jobs, nursing has its ups and downs,
but I find it most satisfying and interesting, and I wouldn't change it.

### Workers life style sketch

I was bored in school, did not want to sit my C.S.E. in the Summer
Term, so when I read an advertisement for a trainee sales assistant I
answered the box number. It turned out to be "Burfords". This quite
pleased me because I liked to be well turned out and had often bought
clothes in the branch where I should have my interview.

My interview was timed for 10 o'clock but I arrived at 9.45. This
was one piece of advice I remembered from "Jinks" the Careers Master—
"Always be early for an interview!" I was asked to wait in a small room
which contained a door marked "Manager" and at 10 exactly a gentle-
man who introduced himself as Mr. Thompson invited me into his
room. He asked about my interests, my school performance (he explained he would ultimately need a testimonial from the school); he
gave me a couple of simple problems involving £. s. d. and asked me to
copy a paragraph from a book on the desk. Finally he thanked me for
attending and said he would inform me of the outcome of the interview within seven days. It seems as if all that took place yesterday
whereas it was actually February 1966.

What do I do?—make sure the customer is satisfied. He expects not
only new clothes but pleasantness, courtesy and interest and there are
times when it's difficult to give all these things to some silly old fussy
"bod" of 60.

I'm expected to arrive first in the shop in the morning so this means
I'm entrusted with the keys of the Branch. I think it was when I was
given this responsibility that I realized I was becoming successful in the

job. If the Manager hadn't trusted me, he would never have let me take the keys home. This causes me to sweat a bit at times but I've learned to live with it now.

I make a quick check to see that there has been no illegal entry during the night and then prepare for the day's work. I dust and tidy the selling area, perhaps alter the position of a few models and generally see that the shop presents the correct image—who wants to buy clothes in a scruffy shop? By this time the Manager has arrived so I am able to ask him for money from the safe to stock the tills. At the end of the day the Staff have to balance the record of sales with the money in the till. This sounds simple and obvious but there are days when they just don't match and no one leaves the shop until they do match and a good explanation is found.

I have a basic wage but I also earn commission so I'm keen to start selling as soon as possible. But I refuse to sell anything to anybody. I really believe that if you are honest with the customer he will return. Let me explain. If I can sell a £30 suit I get more commission than by selling a jacket worth £8. If I think that the style and colour of the suit does not do anything for the man I'll tell him if I'm asked. But I tell him politely and with reasons.

Every Wednesday I arrange goods for display in the shop window. I really love doing this because it enables me to appreciate balance, design and perspective. I first heard those words in school but they first had meaning for me on the National Retail Distribution Certificate Course in the College of Technology. I had been working in the shop for 18 months when Mr. Thompson suggested that I studied for the Certificate on Tuesday evenings. I found it a bit of a bind but I suddenly realized I was seeing the job from a new angle—I knew what worsted, nylon, terylene really were; I saw how a backcloth would accentuate the clothes, I discovered that a shirt and tie had a relationship with a suit. Not without importance, I had a rise and I had "arrived in Burfords". I've acted as assistant manager in smaller branches during sickness or holidays. I have no C.S.E. or "O" level but I have a qualification in the business which would enable me to apply for better positions in similar stores.

When I first started, I thought I would never exist without my game of soccer on a Saturday afternoon. Well, now I play on Thursday afternoon and Sunday morning so I've got over that hurdle. I've learned to deal with people and their peculiar ways—I've found there are big spenders and penny pinchers but they all get encouragement. For the first few weeks, my feet and legs ached terribly but now they are conditioned to the job although there are times when I'm one degree under during which I'd love to be able to sit in a soft chair, but in our game you must always be upright on your feet and ready for action i.e. the next customer.

What "perks" are there? A discount on clothes purchased in the shop, luncheon vouchers and free tea.

Every morning I put on a clean shirt and leave the house with a smart appearance. In work I use common sense and a business like manner. The other morning I was reading about the importance of "job satisfaction"—I know it's true because I have it!

Other departments, such as the English and drama departments or the religious education specialists can become involved in this. Projects such as the local radio station programme—or in the better equipped school television interviews of pupils, staff and local people—would link guidance with social education and the humanities. As this approach is developed, two things seem to happen. Firstly, we shed the last remnants of the idea that school counselling is only concerned with pathological conditions. It is concerned with the full education of emotions and feelings, helping young people to control, express and use constructively the tensions arising from the challenging developmental tasks of adolescence. Once we free ourselves from any tendency we have to confuse emotions and phantasy with deviancy and pathology we can introduce creative counselling which is a meaningful part of the everyday life of the pupil. We then stumble on a fundamental truth lying behind the educational approach to counselling contained in this book. It is that in school counselling we do not see pupils as determined by their pasts, but believe that our task is to help them understand that the present determines the future, and also that through creative forms of guidance in the school it can re-determine the past. Adolescents need not be and do not want to be the victims of their earlier childhood.

Counselling is one way in which the school can help them achieve their freedom.

The output is obvious, yet we still need to specify it clearly. The most obvious feature is that of academic skills, but this will need breaking down into sections. The academic skills of the statutory age leaver and the under-privileged pupil will be very different from those of the able sixth former, although they should not be regarded as less important or as inferior. An important part of the output is the self-concept of the pupils. We rightly claim that education is for life, and one of the most important things that a pupil carries from school into the larger society is his image of himself. We need to specify in detail what sort of self-image we hope to produce in pupils and then we must assess the impact of procedures on it. With this goes motivation to succeed. This means the desire to do something well and carry around some standard of excellence whatever job you may do. Those who work with their hands can have the same motivation to succeed in the sense I have just indicated as those who work with their minds. The discussion of vocational adjustment showed that many pupils fail in work because they lack social skills, but as yet we are slow to state in behavioural terms what social skills we hope pupils will have developed by the time they leave school. Adolescents often feel extremely inadequate in these areas of social skill and we need to help them deal with social anxieties. Some feel great difficulty in making an intimate relationship, and they avoid closeness with others, whilst some pupils feel unable to cope with situations in which they are asked to interact with a number of people. Some fear the limelight, some act in an exhibitionist manner, whilst others may fear a loss of control. Our guidance programmes must include this type of social education, but we should also state the behavioural norms and standards that we hope to develop. This becomes clear if we look at the confusions which surround a pupil's idea of his role as a pupil. He has one idea of his role as a pupil, but this is not necessarily the same as the way in which his peer group defines the role of pupil. Consider the middle-class boy who for some reason finds himself in a form composed of working-class boys who see school negatively. This is an extreme situation, yet I have met it on a number of occasions. Such a boy is under extreme pressure. The teacher's definition of the role of pupil may differ from that of the pupil and his peers, a fact which is very clear in the de-schooling movement's arguments. The pupil's parents may have an idea of the role of the pupil which may be out of date, limited and unrealistic. This again shows the urgency of methodically spelling out some of these factors which alienate pupils from schools, for without this we will be unable to understand their reactions and almost certainly be impotent in our attempts to be of service.

We now have some basis for understanding the underlying factors which have to be considered if we want to integrate counselling into the daily life of the school. The next step is that of specifying levels of counselling more exactly.

### Levels of counselling in the secondary school

The danger is that the presence of a counsellor may make the form teacher feel that his contribution is either inferior or unnecessary. The argument of this book has been against this view, pointing out that the counsellor is dependent upon his colleagues, and that different levels of contribution do not mean judgements about superiority and inferiority. A simple schema of levels of counselling would consist of a three-fold classification into immediate, intermediate and intensive.

#### I. THE IMMEDIATE LEVEL

This is the level of counselling with which the form master or class teacher is concerned. It is clear that this level of counselling should not conflict with the teacher's other professional responsibilities. It does not imply concern with compatibility of the teaching and counselling roles, for this has already been dealt with. Rather it means that the demands made upon him must be kept to a reasonable level and that he must not be asked to do things which mitigate against the achievement of competence as a teacher. There is a level of adaptation to the individual beyond which the class teacher cannot go without doing harm to other pupils. Excessive attention to one boy or girl means that others are being neglected, and in fact it is also harmful to the one pupil. I saw a boy yesterday who remarked, "I know Mr. Smith has been a great help to me, but I wish he would help the others, then I wouldn't stand out so much". This was a deficiency of the particular teacher who had been too ostentatious in his attempts to help and in doing it had created a difficult situation for this boy with his peers. The thing about the immediate level of counselling is that it occurs in context. Even in the school counselling situation we not only have to deal with much in retrospect, but also with much that is out of context to some degree. The immediate level provides reinforcements and supports for a pupil where they are effective—in the classroom situation. You will recall the brief section in Chapter Five which related this to behavioural and social learning theory. It is a very practical level because it involves concrete action such as the adjustment of demands, giving the small bit of extra help, the words of praise and the provision of signals of success. It sounds as though this is just what happens in the good classroom anyway, but here it is more consciously planned and an integral part of a concerted effort. If we think back to the opening remarks of this book, this is how we learn to speak the prose of counselling better. This immediate level is part of a planned campaign of remedial action in the situation most significant to the pupil in school—the classroom.

Several important functions form part of this immediate level. First there is the application of emotional first aid without which many awkward situations develop. We would not ignore a bleeding nose, but we often gloss over obvious signs of stress and tension in a child. Next there is the exploratory and screening function. Once a teacher begins to look at pupils from the counselling viewpoint he begins to see things he had not previously registered and he initiates action. Usually he confirms his feelings by brief investigation before alerting the counsellor. Another aspect of the classroom counselling role is that of linkage between the counsellor and guidance team and the classroom situation. Without this these workers are deprived of essential feedback and the process of counselling becomes more haphazard. The very positive side of this classroom level of counselling is the way in which it is made evident to the pupil that there is real concern for him in the school.

The counsellor may say this, but the real test for a pupil is the attitude in the classroom. No amount of verbal statement by the counsellor will compensate for the lack of obvious signs of concern in the learning situation. The teacher also interprets the role of the counsellor and other workers, and I think we have to see that the form teacher is a credible source of information for the pupil. This means he has to accept this responsibility as part of his role.

## 2. THE INTERMEDIATE LEVEL OF COUNSELLING

Within the school there are a number of teachers whose roles embody pastoral care responsibilities. These are heads of houses, year tutors or heads of guidance departments. The variations are immense, but these teachers occupy a special position in the attempt to incorporate counselling into the school. Their primary responsibility seems to be that of maintaining continuity of concern and of relationships. They will, by nature of their position, have more time for interviews as such and investigation of a more thorough type. Part of their function is the co-ordination of resources and the preservation of essential information which is helpful to those who have to deal with a pupil. When a pupil seems to be especially vulnerable for either physical, social or emotional reasons, then those occupying this intermediate level of counselling will operate the equivalent of an "early warning system". This means that they will undertake systematic periodic checks on the progress and welfare of these pupils, although they make them unobtrusively. Part of the job of counselling at this level centres on the co-ordination of efforts and resources. It is necessary to ensure effective use of scarce resources by avoiding unnecessary duplication of efforts, and also by making sure that interventions are made as early as possible. It is only too easy to allow chronic situations to develop when this intermediate level of counselling is not methodically worked out.

It is clear that this level of counselling involves a great deal of administrative work, including the arrangements for counselling conferences. This heavy weight of administration does not mean sterility, for these workers will also have a great deal of important interviewing to do. They will see both pupils and parents, not only gathering information, but dealing with many vocational and educational guidance problems which do not involve lengthy treatment. They will occupy a key position in the preparation of strategies of group guidance which allow pupils to cope with the discontinuities and choice points they meet within the school. They most certainly will be concerned with the application of the two analytic devices for isolating such situations which I discussed earlier in this chapter.

With the growth of comprehensiveness at the secondary level we have become aware of the importance of adequate communication systems within the school. Not only should those who work at the intermediate level operate an efficient system for the storage and retrieval of information, but they should also function as the focal figures in an internal system of links between pastoral care workers and teachers. This means that we have to develop fairly sophisticated systems of communication which are reliable, linking not only teachers with teachers, but pupils with teachers. Rowe (1970) shows the way in which he achieved this, and Moore (1970) also describes the methods developed in five schools. Without this, it is possible for people to work in isolation or to pull different ways, when a concerted effort is really what is needed. The discussion has been brief, but I would like to make it clear that this level of counselling where resources are co-ordinated is the keystone without which counselling falls to the ground.

### 3. THE SPECIALIST LEVEL OF COUNSELLING

Trained counsellors are very thinly spread over our schools, and to use them when other members of the pastoral care team could work with pupils is a grossly inefficient use of resources. This means that we may have to think hard and isolate the type of pupil where the specialist level of counselling is necessary. The two-phase model of counselling provides a guide line. When the cause of the difficulties primarily reside within the pupil rather than in his environment, then the trained counsellor becomes essential. Such pupils might, for example, have a very negative self-picture, a deep and harsh sense of failure, hostile attitudes towards school and adults and failure in some area of the crucial developmental tasks. This does not mean that we are concerned with the pathological or grossly neurotic conflict, for this is the concern of the child guidance services. Pupils of this type can be helped by groups just as much as by individual methods of counselling. If the pupil has a prediction system which impedes his performance and the acquisition of good interpersonal relationships, then the first phase of counselling is likely to be both important and prolonged. This is the major criterion for using the specialist level of counselling. The need for this extended period of concern with intra-psychic factors is not always evident, but when the form teacher finds that he is not achieving much success, then a closer look is advisable.

Other important factors exist. When it becomes clear that a number of complicating conditions are present, especially where home factors are central, where stress is acute or a chronic situation has been missed by the school, then the trained counsellor has to focus his skills to mount a disciplined attack on the problem. As stated there is a limit to the amount of adaptation that can be made within the form situation, and when considerable adaptation is necessary then we need special skills. Some of these adjustments have to be made carefully, for often there is a danger of reinforcing a delinquent viewpoint or increasing guilt and anxiety. In some pupils manipulative and collusive techniques are well developed, but these pupils have to be helped. This means that someone has really to cope with these behavioural mechanisms and yet not be pushed into rejecting or punishing the pupil. At the same time one should be modifying his behaviour and building up his constructive sides. Only yesterday, I saw a girl who has been in great difficulties. She remarked, "When I'm punished I do it again". She saw punishment as giving her a reason—if not actually a licence—to indulge in stupid activities. The constructive approach was to begin to build up her positive side and provide her with success through the co-operation of the staff.

The skilled level of counselling is needed in the following situations: when underfunctioning and unrealistically high or low levels of aspiration distort the pupil's response to the learning situation; where discrepancy between his development socially and emotionally and the demands of the school are such that most people tend to see him as immature; when there is a pressing need for contact with a competent model, especially in fatherless or motherless families; where the powers of communication are deficient. The specialist level assumes importance when insights are needed by the pupil, when they have difficulty in communicating with adults and are confused about their emotions and reactions, and where irrationality seems to be playing a large part in their problem.

It may not be so clear that the trained counsellor is necessary when group methods of counselling are to be employed. These are very effective, if not essential, when the problem lies in the field of social skills and interpersonal relationships with peers. Group counselling calls for a displined and sensitive approach based on a real knowledge of group dynamics and the mechanisms of groups. Complex interaction such as the processes of role-sending and role-taking have to be perceived, analysed accurately and then modified. This calls for the precise timing of interventions, the capacity to handle tensions by containing them without suppressing feelings and strengthening positive behaviours and feelings. I have stressed this point because sometimes people seem to think that group counselling requires little skill; in fact it is an extension of individual counselling which calls for added knowledge and skills.

The specialist counsellor is also necessary where the outside agencies are involved and where mutual collaboration is necessary. His function will usually be that of initiating contacts, linking up the people who are working with the pupil inside and outside the school in a constructive way. He will also have a great deal to do with the content of counselling conferences, helping to work out viable strategies. Perhaps the most important part of his function is that of diffusing his skills among the rest of the pastoral care team and those interested in developing this side of their teaching role. He must run in-service training groups and pass on his skills and knowledge to his colleagues, rather than try to preserve an isolated position as expert. This is essential in the active model of counselling, where colleagues have to be invited to take up a participant rather than a bystander's role. It is pleasant to record that even students are asked to pass on their skills. One Welsh girls' school has had a student counsellor for the first time, and although there was initial suspicion and doubt, in the second term the student was asked to arrange lunchtime meetings with a group of the staff when they could to discuss the methods of counselling and their role as helpers. This seems to be much healthier and more professional than the situation implied by people who say, "one part of the job of the counsellor is to counsel the staff". I would suspect both separation from the teacher role and a distasteful omnipotence exists in those subscribing to this view. It seems to me to be better to see the need to work together to understand what we are doing to help, and to try to develop better ways of doing it. The counsellor should be intimately involved in in-service training within the school, not confining his activities to passing on what he knows, but working with his fellow teachers to devise new and more creative approaches to counselling.

The argument has been that the viewpoint of the school, counselling and pastoral care is concerned with the processes by which pupils affiliate with or alienate themselves from the school. We have argued that the school is concerned with the developmental process of socialization, simply because it prepares immature personalities for full membership of the adult society. This requires us to detect resources and the situations in which those resources have to be used. To help in this, the idea of a critical incident analysis and the use of a model of socialization was produced, followed by an analysis of the levels of counselling. These are tools to be used, which have no meaning apart from a particular school. Some readers may feel disappointed that no exact prescriptions for action have been offered; to attempt to do this would be charlatanism. The variety of provision for the secondary stage shows this. We have schools for the 11- to 18-year-old, various two-tier and "end-on" systems such as 11 to 16 followed by 16-plus provision, 13 to 16 followed by 16 to 18; 11 to 14 followed by 14 to 18. When this variety is linked with differences in buildings, intake and teaching methods, it is easy to see why one formula for pastoral care and counselling would be meaningless. It has seemed to me that the most useful step is to provide a general guide to which individuals add specific content. The analysis of levels of counselling represents an attempt to spell out what is involved, but in every school a different solution would be found.

Sometimes the trained counsellor would be given a greater loading of the administrative components which have been included in the intermediate level. The object of the exercise is to spell out the different activities which will have to be included in a viable system of pastoral care and counselling. If we wish to make the principle of comprehensiveness a reality, then we have to provide counterbalancing factors to those which mitigate against the realization of potential by pupils, accepting that for equality of opportunity some pupils need more and better education than their less disadvantaged peers. Guidance and counselling can be one form of positive discrimination.

### Pastoral care systems

The discussion on this will be brief, because excellent discussions already exist, e.g. Rowe (1970), Moore (1970), Miles (1968), Benn and Simon (1970). It seems that pastoral care systems need to meet several basic needs. These are that somebody in the school should really know every pupil, and that relationships are built up which have both continuity and depth, thereby expressing care and concern in a way which is evident to the pupil. The other need is the need to prevent the school being fragmented into autonomous units between which there is little connection and hence little co-ordination.

The house system is one solution which splits the school into vertical units. It has been stated that houses often become little more than a basis for competition and a unit for convenient administration. This need not be the case, but there is some danger in the autonomy of the house system. The keener the house head and the more closely knit the house staff, the greater is the likelihood of their separation from the rest of the school, creating a situation in which units have minimal links with each other. The other basic form of organization is horizontal, making age bands. This can be given a strong form in the division of the school into lower, middle and upper schools, each having someone charged with responsibility for them. The weaker form is that of year group or tutor groups. The advantage of the strong form of division is that it becomes possible to make adjustments to the needs and age of the pupils in terms of demands and discipline. The lower school can become a bridge between the primary school and the later stages of discipline, whilst in the upper school appropriate changes in teacher— pupil relationships can take place for the sixth form and leavers. The danger is that these units become autonomous with only superficial contact taking place between them. Such isolation is facilitated by the fact that usually staffrooms are in each section, and so the teachers themselves do not mix. Planning should incorporate conscious decisions about the way each regime prepares the pupil for the next stage. The middle school should move towards the type of relationship between teachers and pupils which prevails in the upper school, whilst the lower school has a graduated system of demands which prepares pupils for those met in the middle stage. The greatest amount of thought may have to go into the middle school stage, for this is crucial for affiliation to the school. In this stage pupils seem to acquire negative attitudes very easily, both towards themselves and towards the school, because of increasing pressure.

The weak form of horizontal organization involves year tutors, but it is possible to combine vertical and horizontal methods of organization. Continuity of relationship is preserved by the year tutors moving up through the school with their group, even though they do not usually continue the relationship into the sixth form. In many ways, this is a pity, because sixth formers are strongly concerned about relationships and still need the assurance that they are valued as persons. Certainly the year tutor who has followed his group up through the school and done his job thoroughly not only has real relationships and valuable knowledge about individuals, but feels frustrated and resents the fact that he is being denied responsibility for pastoral care in the last years at school. If pupils are followed up through the school by the same person, several things have to be taken into account. We have to recognize the need to adjust again to the first year and the difficulties in making a relationship with a new group after having guided the development of a group for at least four years. This needs conscious attention, otherwise pupils will not get the supports they require during the vulnerable period of adjustment to a new school. This type of system also makes the intermediate level of counselling and pastoral care more important. The senior tutor or head of year has to ensure that efforts are co-ordinated and that records which are comparable are being produced. He has to detect the innovations and changes in procedures which can occur and bring these into the open for discussion by the team. Without this, the system becomes fragmented and unrelated.

It seems to me that the system of guidance will be influenced by the size of the school. The larger it is, then the greater is the need to clearly allocate responsibility and the more relevant is the type of analysis presented in this chapter. This analysis should not be seen as a once-for-all process, but as something to be applied periodically in a systematic way. Our guidance and counselling programmes will have to adjust to skewed intakes, especially in the field of ability. Rowe (1970) shows one way of coping with this. The poorer the neighbourhood, the more emphasis we have to give in our guidance systems to contact with parents. Much effort has to be directed towards them, although not necessarily through home visiting. We see the way in which the different aspects of the system interact, for continuity of staff is essential for good counselling and guidance. We do know, however, that satisfaction in work is at least partially dependent upon commitment and involvement, and the creation of a pastoral care team commits teachers to the school, providing them with many important sources of professional satisfaction. This is one of the ways in which a guidance system helps the school reach its objectives.

### The counsellor and social education

The fact that so many pupils disassociate themselves from the school is evidence that we are failing to provide them with what they need. Superficial adaptations are of little use and we need to rethink our whole approach to secondary education. Many schools are doing this, but we can still fail to see ways in which we can provide pupils with independence and autonomy. We are concerned about the growth of violence and aggression, although it is easy to exaggerate this. We learn to examine the meaning of violence for those who engage in it and understand that it serves a real purpose in their lives. If we create social climates in which teachers are seen as persons whose defeat provides an adolescent with the only reward he is likely to get out of the school situation then we can only blame ourselves. It seems to me that it is the exceptional teacher and school who does this, but we have to admit honestly that we have been unsuccessful in providing meaningful experiences for many pupils. Many of our pupils come from backgrounds where they learn that a wide range of situations justify a violent reaction and they tend to see the world in violent terms. It is helpful to see that many of our pupils react to frustration by violence and are especially sensitive to threats to their status and independence. It is even more helpful to realize that those pupils who react aggressively and choose violent solutions to their dilemmas are those who are insecure. What we often fail to understand is that it is the pupil without social skills who is liable to resort to violence as a means of reducing pressures and giving vent to his feelings.

This means that we should build up social competence in pupils, providing them with ways of expressing themselves constructively. There are boys who present a picture of churlishness or aggressiveness, yet who are very far from being either. A set of transactions builds up between them and their teachers which confirms this identity and the whole destructive process, which begins very early on in the secondary school, gains momentum until that boy has an inescapable identity as a hooligan. Social education programmes which provide pupils with constructive strategies in interpersonal relationships and allow them to find ways of expressing themselves without violence are a partial answer to this. With this in mind, I offer you a very limited view of social education as an educational process which specifically focuses on:

1. The techniques by which we send signals about ourselves to others.

2. The way in which we can gain competence in communication.

3. Building the ability to make good relationships and learning to co-operate with others to our mutual advantage.

If we say that social education is concerned with social competences and the constructive presentation of self, then we are also saying that it is dealing with interpersonal perception, the development of the self-concept, the bargaining processes taking place in groups, the systems of communication which we build up with others and group dynamics. The fact is, however, that this formidable list of abstractions can be made meaningful to even those pupils we call less able provided that we put them into a familiar practical context and deal with them through activities rather than relying on traditional methods.

Pupils scan the learning situation for enjoyment and relevance and social education provides them with this if we provide role playing, simulation, games, drama and projects. It is an old idea that effective teaching means a movement from the known to the unknown. If this is combined with positive use of our frequent observation that the adolescent is deeply concerned with his own feelings and reactions, then we can see the need to devise programmes which move outwards from feelings and examination of themselves to the exploration of group interaction.

In social education pupils still need signs of achievement and success. Few of us would be prepared to labour without reward and we should not expect pupils to do what we would not do. They want an end product which is concrete. The suggestions made when the resources centre for counselling and guidance was discussed can be used in social education programmes. The fact that we are dealing with the development of interpersonal skills does not mean that we are confined to intangibles. Before I present some suggestions for the content of such a programme it seems sensible to make several points. Social education is a carefully planned attempt to develop general social skills, whilst group counselling is intended to resolve the specific problems of individuals. Social education is a considered attempt to bring the first three items of the output listed in the socialization model to the highest possible level.

The outline which follows merely suggests the content and this can be given many levels of difficulty to suit the ability of pupils. In my work I find that pupils suggest the concrete situations which form the basis for the activities. To show that the topics hold real intellectual content the psychological and interpersonal implications have been put after each one.

### STAGE ONE. SELF PRESENTATION

1. *How others see me.* This is concerned with the processes of sending and maintaining a picture of oneself. It implies the examination of the signals we send to other people and our evaluation of their reactions.

2. *Keeping face.* We can draw pupils' attention to their reactions when they feel threatened, the way they respond to blame and disapproval, the people they wish to emulate and the way they cope with social blunders.

3. *How I judge other people.* The judgement of others is of great concern to young people. They are concerned with the results of their evaluation of others and are uneasily aware that they are responding to cues of similarity and difference in an intuitive manner. They often wish to modify their reactions to minority groups but find themselves unable to do so until they understand the perceptual processes involved.

4. *Getting my own way.* This is an area of social competence which produces many guilts and anxieties because it produces conflict between the altruistic and egoistic tendencies in the young person. They are partially aware of their strategies of negotiation and bargaining, although they often feel these are not under their control.

5. *Competing with others.* Competition is a source of stress for the adolescent particularly when they wish to avoid exposure and failure. They sometimes experience great difficulty in competing with the opposite sex and resort to very clumsy attempts at dominance.

6. *Being able to change my mind.* A drive towards consistency is present in all of us and is invested with an element of virtue. The pupil who is insecure or uncertain often takes up a rigid position which he is unwilling to modify. He may take refuge in rigid labelling processes, especially of the older generation and the more able amongst his peers. This topic leads into discussion of

the unpleasant aspects of attitude change and the need to be able to justify changes of opinion.

7. *Anger and threat.* These two elements are inextricably mixed in many of us and the adolescent is helped by understanding the defensive function of aggression. It is possible to build in comprehension of the contribution of social anxieties and the way in which anticipation of rejection or failure produce behavioural patterns which lead to those very things.

8. *The kind of person I try to be.* Modelling and identificatory processes can be examined, but the concept of the ideal self and the reference group from which values are drawn can be included.

9. *Trying to understand others.* This topic can lead to an examination of standpoint taking, empathy and the need to suspend judgements long enough to appreciate what the other person is like.

10. *Why they think I am not like them.* Adolescence is the age of conformity despite all the striving after individuality. It helps if they gain some idea of normative sanctions, the type of signal that leads to the idea that they are different from their peers and their vulnerability to pressures from those of their own age.

11. *Changing my behaviour.* So often the teenage pupil wishes to change his behaviour but is thwarted because he does not know how to begin. His attempts at change are liable to produce incredulous reactions from others which make him revert to his original position. We have to prepare him for this by "innoculating" him against adverse comment and ridicule.

### STAGE TWO. WORKING IN A GROUP

This stage helps pupils look at their behaviour in important groups, including the classroom. The aim is to help them understand the dynamics of groups and work constructively within a group.

1. *What do I get out of the group?* This draws their attention to the needs for approval, acceptance and status which are met by the

membership of the group. It helps them voice dissatisfactions in a non-aggressive way.

2. *My role in the group.* This explores the nature of leadership, the allocation of roles such as the scapegoat and the way in which they can change their role in a specific group.

3. *Can I change the group?* This question provides a focus for analysis of coalitions, conflict and innovation within a small group. Persuasive communication and the credibility of oneself as a source of innovation also come into the discussion and activities.

4. *This group and other groups.* Comparison processes, the existence of boundaries and the qualifications for membership would be considered.

5. *The kind of people I like in the group.* The nature of interpersonal attraction and the qualities of those liked by the individual result in a great deal of self-knowledge as well as increased understanding of the group dynamics.

6. *Getting things done within the group.* Co-operation, decision making and goal setting are relevant to this topic.


### STAGE THREE. THE COMMUNITY.

This stage links the programme with other activities in the school. Economy of effort and the limits of time may cause the counsellor to confine himself to the first two stages, although he will find it profitable to help with the final stage.

1. *Our class and its place in the school.* This reveals the evaluation that they place on their own form in relation to others. Once they voice feelings, it is possible to work to improve the status of that class. They should be given some understanding of the school as a social system and the objectives of education.

2. *The neighbourhood.* Before pupils are sent out into the community, they should be provided with the skills for studying it. Simulations and games can be used to provide them with awareness of

crucial questions and the considerations which lie behind community life. A local survey and study can follow, which in turn is succeeded by a re-planning of the neighbourhood. Models, tape recordings, art, booklets, plays and recordings which encourage empathy with other sections of the population such as the aged and unemployed should be encouraged.

3. *Pollution*. The basic issues could be explored. These should include the conflict between important factors such as the need for employment and the provision of amenities.

4. *Employment*. Local patterns, the siting of factories and the reasons for the presence or absence of certain occupations should be explored.

5. *Industrial relationships*. Collective bargaining, negotiation and the changes that will probably occur in the future suggest the kind of topic that produces intense absorption in pupils.

These are merely suggestions about the form that such a social education programme could take. The purpose in setting them out has been to show the way in which the work of the counsellor, which seems to be remote from the classroom at first sight, is very relevant. What appears to be separated, not only can be integrated, but leads into these important areas of the curriculum. The application of the counsellor's skills to such areas of the curriculum provides increased effectiveness. Those of us who have been involved in social education are aware of the danger of "boomerang". This means that we may unintentionally harden constricting views of life in pupils, increase prejudice and the tendency to stereotype others in a rigid way. If we utilize the counsellor's skills in relationships and interpersonal perception in these activities then pupils are more likely to develop the self-awareness and the competences that we desire for them.

### Peer counselling

In planning the system of counselling it is inadequate only to consider staff as resources; we have to include pupils as resources if our planning is to produce results. This may sound surprising, but we should see that the concept of counselling as coming solely from the staff disguises a benevolent paternalism which will become increasingly irrelevant. Our major task in secondary education is that of improving the quality of interpersonal relationships of all those involved. This does not mean a modification of teacher—pupil relationships alone, but also a change in pupil—pupil relationships. Many pupils now reject the prefect role. This is not because they negatively question the concept of authority, although they most certainly question it, but because they see the responsibilities allocated to them as derogatory and infantile. They are not interested in standing in corridors, herding younger pupils into lines, neither will they accept the role of punisher of younger pupils or reporter of misdeeds. Certainly such a concept of prefect role is at best only fit for those who intend to be traffic wardens or police informers. Despite our good intentions, this seems to be how the older pupils perceive out attempts at giving them authority and responsibility. Somehow or other, we have failed to communicate to them what we want from them or to provide them with the opportunity to serve the school and fellow pupils in a way which enhances their own self-respect and identity. Peer counselling gives us the chance to provide this experience.

Peer counselling may sound risky and perhaps an almost outrageous abdication of responsibility by the counsellor. A second thought however may hint that it represents an attempt to formalize and use a situation which already exists. For the adolescent the opinions of his friends and those slightly older than himself are more important than the comments and ideas of the middle-aged. This does depend upon the attitudes and approach of the middle-aged, but the meaningful rewards tend to come from peers rather than from those of an older age group. There are a number of situations in which pupils not only respond better to peers, but where peers or near-peers can appreciate the situation more sensitively and provide more relevant help. In peer counselling, the counsellor is not seen as being contaminated by authority or separated by age and social position, therefore the barriers which impede counselling with *some* pupils do not exist. There are intelligent adolescents who are deeply suspicious of our motives, and this prevents them using our services. Their attitudes to adults and their powers of communication may be so deficient that they feel threatened and unable to cope with the adult-adolescent counselling situation. In these cases, peer counselling provides a source of support which may eventually lead to the development of trust and interaction with an adult counsellor.

We have, in fact, already talked about peer counselling at several points in this book. The suggestion of using a friend as a source of information about behaviour is one example, whilst setting two or three pupils to work together to give mutual help and support as part of group counselling is another. It is now time to look at peer counselling in a wider way, noting that the remarks above are not only obvious, but almost negative in their lack of drive. There is a much more positive side to it, which is related to our basic theme of trying to help pupils affiliate with the school and use the resources for their own benefit. It is a tool by which pupils can serve their fellows and the school, gaining a sense of worth as they do it and accelerating their own rate of personal development. The very fact of helping creates a sense of autonomy and worthwhileness, which in turn is spread amongst other pupils, for those who are helped usually develop the desire to help. The creation of a system of peer counselling produces a new climate into the school and introduces a new element of positive co-operation into relationships between staff and pupils. The division into those who do things and those who have things done to them disappears, for this is implicit in many formal teaching and school situations. In recent years we have often questioned the passivity of pupils during school assemblies and we have tried to find ways of involving them. This attitude is at least as important in the field of counselling and pastoral care.

How do we introduce and develop peer counselling? The critical incident analysis provides one hint, whilst the socialization model provides another. The first suggests that we isolate the critical periods and incidents, proceeding to use as peer counsellors those who have passed through them. The basic principle here is that the peer counsellor is one who is fairly near in age and who has just passed through the situation on which the counselling is focused. This means that they have not forgotten the impact of the experience. We have to be realistic about the short time span and the rapid loss of memories due to the intensity of life for the adolescent. I am now reminded of the sixteen-year-old who said to me gravely, "When I was very young I wanted to be a rebel and joined the Young Socialists". Very young meant fourteen years of age. The peer counsellors are not restricted to those who have been extremely successful, for those who had difficulties and are still struggling with them make good counsellors, and by helping others also help themselves. The socialization model reveals another strategy. We use peer counsellors at those periods when the influence of peers is strongest and that of teachers and school weakest. Such periods will come in the second and third forms where the pulls toward effort and affiliation are not very strong because examinations are still distant and where the pupil has begun to opt out of school because he is leaving. Many pupils need peer supports during the last year when they are not taking examinations. Another point made clear by the socialization model is related to the choice of the counsellor. He must not be too different either in terms of age or social class. To send peer counsellors who are obviously different in level of aspiration and social class is to risk creating the situation in which they are rejected as "snobs" or "posh kids". We must work out the degree of difference which is sufficient to promote change, but not so great that it renders the peer counsellor ineffective. Perhaps the forms in the middle of the bands or streaming system are those which may benefit most from peer counselling, although much can be done to help the lower ability pupils through the technique. Indeed, it may be highly constructive for those pupils who have experienced signals of failure in a concentrated way to be helped to see that they can help themselves. The whole approach opens the way for creative experiments in school counselling which are linked with innovation in educational method, especially the development of team teaching and individual programmes of learning.

Where do the pastoral care team and the trained counsellor come into the peer counselling scheme? It is important that the peer counsellors are given support and that they have a chance to voice their difficulties and anxieties. The counsellor functions as a resource person, not only helping them to gain insights and develop techniques for dealing with difficult situations, but sharing in the development as an equal partner.

I have been privileged to talk to sixth formers starting this work and found that it was a process of sharing in which I learnt at least as much from them as I shared with them. The ability to learn and adapt is very important in the members of staff who are going to be concerned with the support groups which back peer counselling. We have no right to initiate this work without providing help and a platform of support for the boys and girls who undertake it. Peer counsellors work in groups sharing their insights and the trained counsellor leads these groups in a way which reflects the ethos of counselling. The success gained by such pupils is amazing, although even this brings its difficulties. Some sixth formers who were successful in affiliating previously alienated pupils with the school and created enthusiasm in them for school activities found themselves the object of attack by the gang leaders who saw their power dissolving. This kind of situation is inevitable; we have to face the challenges they postulate without retreating from the difficulties. If we run away from the complications, then little is likely to happen, and we lose a valuable opportunity.

Peer counselling is very much concerned with reactions to authority, adults, feelings about achievement and success and the problems of peer relationships. We can help by including these problems in our social education programme, opening up ideas and new horizons, but we must see that our own attitudes of trust and the expectations we generate are the crucial factors. If we take the viewpoint that we have to tell them what to do or they will make mistakes, then we kill the whole thing. Indeed we delude ourselves, for we are trying to pretend that we never make mistakes. Our own actions are often blind and based on intuition: they often represent an act of faith. Can we therefore deny young people this very basic experience?

Peer counselling requires careful planning and slow developments. Peer counselling is not a venture into which we rush lightly, for it needs to be based upon a well-developed system of counselling. It represents the final step in making counselling part of the everyday life of the school. A carefully phased way of introducing it should be developed, although we need not automatically begin with the sixth form. It does seem, however, that peer counselling within the sixth form will be particularly valuable when we consider the changes in the composition of the sixth. The step by step approach has the merit of allowing consultation with pupils, developing it according to their needs. Those of us who work in secondary schools know that pupils have very original, yet realistic, ideas about the ways in which their needs can be met. They often make suggestions which can be developed into very effective procedures. This cannot be hurried and it does not happen at once; two to three years is a reasonable time to allow for the evolution of a reasonable system of peer counselling. In this area of counselling even more than in the other approaches we must keep our approach flexible and modify the system as the needs of pupils change. Once our system of counselling reaches this stage, then our objectives of building controls from within the young person, stimulating autonomy, responsibility and decision making are well within reach.

## A concluding note

This book has presented no recipes, although it gives an honest view of counselling as seen by the writer. It is based on a belief in the creative nature of education and the professional status of teachers. This final chapter has offered two possible tools for analysis of the needs of the school, but many other such tools exist. If we have faith in what we do as teachers, then we really need to study the processes by which pupils disassociate themselves from the school or the ways in which they can use the experiences we provide for their personal development. No prescriptions are possible because each school has to work out a plan which suits all those involved in the educative process. This book has been written in the hope that it will stimulate teachers to work out in groups the way in which they implement their professional responsibilities for counselling. The levels of counselling I have described are all equally important, but the way in which they are finally blended into counselling roles is the responsibility of the staff of the school. My final remark is to stress that counselling is only fully meaningful when we use the pupils themselves as agents in the process of development. Without peer counselling, not only is the system of counselling incomplete, but we have deprived ourselves of the most potent agency for achieving our aims. When we use pupils, then, strangely enough, the role of the counsellor does become the perfection of the role of the teacher.

---

## REFERENCES

Bandura, A. and Walters, R. (1963) *Social Learning and Personality Development,* New York: Holt, Rinehart & Winston.

Benn, C. and Simon, B. (1970) *Halfway There,* Maidenhead: McGraw-Hill.

Hargreaves, D.H. (1967) *Social Relations in a Secondary School,* London: Routledge & Kegan Paul.

Hayes, J. and Hopson, B. (1971) *Careers Guidance,* London: Heinemann.

Miles, M. (1968) *Comprehensive Schooling,* London: Longman.

Monks, T.G. (1968) *Comprehensive Education in England and Wales,* Slough: N.F.E.R.

Moore, B. (1970) *Guidance in Comprehensive Schools,* Slough: N.F.E.R.

Rowe, A. (1970) *The School as a Guidance Community,* London: Pearson.

Whitehead, A.N. (1959) *The Aims of Education,* New York: Macmillan.

# A BIBLIOGRAPHY
# FOR BACKGROUND READING

Adkins R.W. (1970). "Life Skills Structured Counseling For the Disadvantaged." *J. Personnel Guid.* 49. No. 2.

Allport G.W. (1955). *Becoming.* Yale University Press.

Armstrong A.J. (1970). *An Investigation Into the Work Performed by some Trained Counsellors in English Secondary Schools.* Unpublished Research Report. University of Keele.

Ashley B., Cohens S. and Slater R. (1969). *Introduction to the Sociology of Education.* London. Macmillan.

Bales R. (1970). *Personality and Interpersonal Behaviour.* New York. Holt, Rinehart and Winston.

Banaka W.H. (1971). *Training in Depth Interviewing.* New York. Harper and Row.

Bandura A. and Walters R. (1963). *Social Learning and Personality Development.* New York. Holt, Rinehart and Winston.

Bandura A. (1969). *Principles of Behaviour Modification.* New York. Holt, Rinehart and Winston.

Beers C.D. (1939). *The Mind Which Found Itself.* New York. Doubleday Page.

Benn C. and Simon B. (1970). *Halfway There.* Maidenhead. McGraw-Hill.

Bernstein B. (1971). *Class, Codes and Social Control.* London. Routledge and Kegan Paul.

Bentley J.C. (1968). *The Counselor's Role*. New York. Houghton Mifflin.

Blocher D.H. (1966). *Developmental Counseling*. New York. Ronald Press.

Bloom L. (1971). *The Social Psychology of Race Relations*. London. Allen and Unwin.

Bloomquist E.R. (1968). *Marijuana*. Beverley Hills. Glencoe Press.

Boocock S. (1972). *An Introduction to the Sociology of Learning*. Boston. Houghton Mifflin.

Bradford L., Gibb J. and Benne K. (1964). *T-Group Theory and Laboratory Method*. New York. Wiley.

Butcher H.J. (1968). *Human Intelligence*. London. Methuen.

Carkhuff R.B. (1969). *Helping and Human Relations,* Vols. 1 and 2. New York. Holt, Rinehart and Winston.

Carson R.G. (1970). *Interaction Concepts of Personality*. London. Allen and Unwin.

Cave R. (1971). *An Introduction to Curriculum Development*. London. Ward Lock.

Christenson H. (Ed.) (1964). *Handbook of Marriage and the Family*. New York. Rand McNally.

Christie R. and Geis F. (1970). *Studies in Machiavellianism*. New York. Academic Press.

Coleman J. (1961). *The Adolescent Society*. Glencoe. Illinois. Free Press.

Coopersmith S. (1967). *The Antecedents of Self Esteem*. San Francisco. Freeman.

Crites J. (1969). *Vocational Psychology*. New York. McGraw-Hill.

Crown D. and Marlowe P. (1964). *The Approval Motive*. New York. Wiley.

Dager E.Z. (1971). *Socialization*. Chicago. Marham.

Dennison G. (1972). *The Lives of Children*. London. Penguin.

Dolliner R.H. (1965). " 'Expressive' and 'Instrumental' as Conceptualizations of Counseling." *J. Couns. Psychol.* 12. 414–417.

Eliot K. (Ed.) (1970). *The Family and Its Future*. London. Churchill.

Elkind D. (1970). *Children and Adolescents*. New York. Oxford University Press.

Erikson E.H. (1965). *Childhood and Society*. London. Penguin.

Erikson E.H. (1968). *Identity*. London. Faber and Faber.

Evans K.M. (1965). *Attitudes and Interests in Education*. London. Routledge and Kegan Paul.

Fagan J. and Shepherd I. (Eds.) (1972). *Gestalt Therapy Now*. London. Penguin.

Ferri E. (1971) *Streaming: Two Years Later*. N.F.E.R. Slough.

Feshbach S. and Singer R. (1971). *Television and Aggression*. Jossey Bass. San Francisco.

Festinger L. (1964). "Behavioural Support for Opinion Change." *Public Opin. Quar*. 28. 404–417.

Fisher R. and Smith W. (1972). *Schools in an Age of Crisis*. New York. Van Nostrad.

Ford J. (1969). *Social Class and the Comprehensive School*. London. Routledge and Kegan Paul.

Foren R. and Bailey R. (1968). *Authority in Social Casework*. Oxford. Pergamon.

Foster J. (1971). *Creativity and the Teacher*. London. Macmillan.

Friedemann F. (1971). *Youth and Society*. London. Macmillan.

Friedenberg (1967). *The Image of the Adolescent Minority*. California Monthly June/July. 37–42.

Glasser W. (1965). *Reality Therapy*. New York. Harper and Row.

Glasser W. (1969). *Schools Without Failure*. New York. Harper and Row.

Goffman E. (1959). *The Presentation of Self in Everyday Life*. New York. Doubleday.

Goffman E. (1967). *Interaction Ritual*. London. Allen Lane.

Goodman P. (1971). *Compulsory Miseducation*. London. Penguin.

Gribbons and Lohnes (1965). "Shifts in Adolescents' Vocational Values." *Personnel Guid. Jn*. 44. 248–252.

Grossack M. and Gardner H. (1970). *Man and Men*. Scranton, Pennsylvania. International Textbook Co.

Guerney B.G. (Ed.) (1969). *Psychotherapeutic Agents*. New York. Holt, Rinehart and Winston.

Hamachek D.E. (1965). *The Self in Growth, Teaching and Learning*. Englewood New Jersey. Hall.

Hannam C. *et al*. (1971). *Young Teachers and Reluctant Learners*. London. Penguin.

Hansen (Ed.) (1969). *Explorations in Sociology and Counseling*. Boston. Houghton Mifflin.

Hargreaves D.H. (1967). *Social Relations in a Secondary School*. London. Routledge and Kegan Paul.

Hargreaves D.H. (1972). *Interpersonal Relations and Education*. London. Routledge and Kegan Paul.

Hartford M. (1972). *Groups in Social Work*. Columbia University Press.

Hayes J. and Hough P. (1971). *Occupational Perceptions and Occupational Information*. Institute of Careers Officers. Bromsgrove.

Hollander E. (1967). *Principles and Methods of Social Psychology*. New York. Oxford University Press.

Hollis F. (1964). *Casework*. New York. Random House.

Hollins T. (Ed.) (1964). *Aims in Education*. Manchester University Press.

Holman R., Lafitte F., Spencer K., and Wilson H. (1970). *Socially Deprived Families in Britain*. London. Bedford Square Press.

Hooper R. (Ed.) (1971). *The Curriculum: Context, Design and Development*. Edinburgh. Oliver and Boyd.

Hordern A. (1971). *Legal Abortion*. Oxford. Pergamon.

Hoose W. and Pietrofesa J. (1970). *Counseling and Guidance in the Twentieth Century*. Boston. Houghton Mifflin.

Holt R. (1971). *Assessing Personality*. New York. Harcourt, Brace Jovanovich.

Hourd M. (1972). *Relationships in Learning*. London. Heinemann.

Hughes M.G. (1970). *Secondary School Administration*. Oxford. Pergamon.

Hughes P. (1971). *Guidance and Counselling in Schools*. Oxford. Pergamon.

Hudson L. (1968). *Contrary Imaginations*. London. Penguin.

Hudson L. (1968). *Frames of Mind*. London. Methuen.

Inhelder B. and Piaget J. (1958). *The Growth of Logical Thinking*. New York. Basic Books.

Jackson B. and Marsden M. (1962). *Education and the Working Class*. London. Penguin.

Jackson P. (1968). *Life in Classrooms*. New York. Holt, Rinehart and Winston.

Jackson R. and Juniper D. (1971). *A Manual of Educational Guidance*. London. Holt, Rinehart and Winston.

Janis I. (1971). *Stress and Frustration.* New York. Harcourt, Brace Jovanovich.

Jensen A.R. (1972). *Genetics and Education.* London. Methuen.

Jersild A.T. (1963). *The Psychology of Adolescence.* New York. Macmillan.

Jones A. (1970). *School Counselling in Practice* London. Ward Lock. Educational.

Jones R. (1972). *Fantasy and Feeling in Education.* London. Penguin.

Jordan W. (1970). *Client-Worker Transactions.* London. Routledge and Kegan Paul.

Kahn J. (1971). 2nd Edition. *Human Growth and the Development of Personality.* Oxford. Pergamon.

Kandel D. and Lesser G. (1972). *Youth in Two Worlds.* San Francisco. Jossey-Bass.

Katz D. and Kahn R. (1966). *The Social Psychology of Organisations.* New York. Wiley.

Katz R.L. (1963). *Empathy.* Glencoe. Illinois. Free Press.

Kell, B. and Burow J. (1970). *Developmental Counseling and Therapy.* Boston. Houghton Mifflin.

Kellmer Pringle M. (1970). *Able Misfits.* London. Longmans.

Kelly G. (1955). *The Psychology of Personal Constructs.* Vols. 1 and 2. New York. Norton.

Kemp C.G. (1970). *Foundations of Group Counseling.* New York. McGraw Hill.

Kretch D., Crutchfield R. and Ballachey E. (1962). *Individual In Society.* New York. McGraw-Hill.

Krumboltz J.D. (Ed.) (1966). *Revolution in Counseling.* Boston. Houghton Mifflin.

Krumboltz J. and Thorensen C. (1969). *Behavioural Counseling.* New York. Holt, Rinehart and Winston.

Laing R. (1965). *The Divided Self.* London. Penguin.

Landfield A.W. (1971). *Personal Construct Systems in Psychotherapy.* Chicago. Rand McNally.

Laurie P. (1967). *Drugs.* London. Penguin.

Lawson R. (1965). *Frustration.* London. Macmillan.

Lawton D. (1968). *Social Class, Language and Education*. London. Routledge and Kegan Paul.

Laycock A. (1970). *Adolescence and Social Work*. London. Routledge and Kegan Paul.

Lazarus R.S. (1966). *Psychological Stress and the Coping Process*. New York. McGraw Hill.

Levitt E.E. (1968). *The Psychology of Anxiety*. London. Staples.

Lewis E.C. (1970). *The Psychology of Counseling*. New York. Holt, Rinehart and Winston.

Lytton H. and Craft M. (1971). *Guidance and Counselling in British Schools*. London. Arnold.

Mahl G. (1971). *Psychological Conflict and Defense*. New York. Harcourt, Brace, Jovanovich.

Maslow A. (1954). *Motivation and Personality*. New York. Harper and Row.

Marsden D. (1969). *Mothers Alone*. London. Allen Lane.

McCulloch J. and Phillip A. (1972). *Suicidal Behaviour*. Oxford. Pergamon.

McGinnies E. (1971). *Social Behaviour. A Functional Analysis*. Boston. Houghton Mifflin.

Megargee E. and Hokanson J. (1970) *The Dynamics of Aggression*. New York. Harper and Row.

Miller D. (1964). *Growth to Freedom*. London. Tavistock.

Miller D. (1969). *The Age Between*. London. Hutchison.

Monks T.G. (1970). *Comprehensive Education in Action*. N.F.E.R. Slough.

Moore B.M. (1970). *Guidance in Comprehensive Schools*. N.F.E.R. Slough.

Morrison A. and McIntyre D. (1969). *Teachers and Teaching*. London. Penguin.

Morrison A. and McIntyre D. (1971). *Schools and Socialisation*. London. Penguin.

Musgrove F. and Taylor P. (1969). *Society and the Teacher's Role*. London. Routledge and Kegan Paul.

Morton R.S. (1972). *Venereal Diseases*. London. Penguin.

Mussen P. and Jones M. (1957). "Self-conceptions, Motivations and Interpersonal Attitudes of Late and Early Maturing Boys." *Ch. Dev*. 28. 243–256.

Natale S. (1972). *An Experiment In Empathy*. Slough. N.F.E.R.

Nelson D.M. (1968). "Predictive Value of the Rothwell-Miller Interest Blank." *Occup. Psychol.* 52. 123–131.

Nettleton J. and Stacey E. (1969). "Counselling in Schools: Courses for Teachers." *Voc. Aspect of Educ.* 22. 143–145.

Norther H. (1969). *Social Work with Groups*. Columbia. University Press.

Nuttall D. and Willmott A. (1972). *British Examinations: Techniques of Analysis*. N.F.E.R. Slough.

Oeser O. (Ed.) (1970). *Pupil, Teacher and Task*. London. Tavistock.

O'Hara R. and Tiedeman D. (1959). "The Vocational Self Concept in Adolescence." *J. Couns. Psychol.* 6. 292–301.

Parker C.A. (Ed.) (1968). *Counseling Theories and Counselor Education*. Boston. Houghton Mifflin.

Parkes C.M. (1972). *Bereavement*. London. Tavistock.

Parsons F. (1906). *Choosing A Vocation*. Boston. Houghton Mifflin.

Parsons T. and Bales R. *et al.* (1955). *Family, Socialization and Interaction Process*. Illinois. Free Press.

Pidgeon D.A. (1970). *Expectations and Pupil Performance*. Slough. N.F.E.R.

Piaget J. (1952). *The Origins of Intelligence in Children*. New York. Norton.

Reddin W. (1970). *Managerial Effectiveness*. New York. McGraw-Hill.

Rice A. (1965). *Learning for Leadership*. London. Tavistock.

Richardson S., Dohrenwend B. and Klein D. (1965). *Interviewing—Its Forms and Functions*. New York. Basic Books.

Richmond K. (1967). *The Teaching Revolution*. London. Methuen.

Roberts K. (1971). *From School to Work*. Newton Abbot. David and Charles.

Rogers C. (1942). *Counseling and Psychotherapy*. Boston. Houghton Mifflin.

Rogers C. (1951) *Client Centred Therapy*. Boston. Houghton Mifflin.

Rogers C. (1971). *Encounter Groups*. London. Allen Lane.

Rosenshine B. (1971). *Teaching Behaviours and Student Achievement*. Slough. N.F.E.R.

Rosenthal R. and Jacobson L. (1968). *Pygmalion In the Classroom*. New York. Holt, Rinehart and Winston.

Rowe A. (1971). *The School as Guidance Community.* London. Pearson.

Rubin L.J. (1970). *Frontiers In School Leadership.* Chicago. Rand McNally.

Rutter M. (1972). *Maternal Deprivation Reassessed.* London. Penguin.

Sactuary G. and Whitehead C. (1972). *Divorce and After.* London. Penguin.

Sandström C. (1968). *The Psychology of Childhood and Adolescence.* London. Penguin.

Schact R. (1971). *Alienation.* London. Allen and Unwin.

Schofield M. (1968). *The Sexual Behaviour of Young People.* London. Pelican.

Schools Council (1968). *Young School Leavers—Enquiry 1.* London. H.M.S.O.

Schools Council (1972). *Careers Education in the 1970's.* Working Paper 40. London. Evans/Methuen.

Sherif M. and Cantril H. (1947). *The Psychology of Ego. Involvements, Social Attitudes and Identifications.* New York. Wiley.

Shouksmith G. (1970). *Intelligence, Creativity and Cognitive Style.* London. Batsford.

Silverman D. (1970). *The Theory of Organisations.* London. Heinemann.

Smith C. (1968). *Adolescence.* London. Longmans.

Starishevsky R. and Matlin N. (1968). In Hopson B. and Hayes J. *The Theory and Practice of Vocational Guidance.* Oxford. Pergamon.

Stott D.H. (1966). *Studies of Troublesome Children.* London. Tavistock.

Sumner R. and Warburton F. (1972). *Achievement in Secondary School.* Slough. N.F.E.R.

Super D. (1957). *The Psychology of Careers.* New York. Harper and Row.

Super D. and Overstreet P. (1960). *The Vocational Maturity of Ninth Grade Boys.* New York. Teachers College Bureau of Publications.

Super D. and Crites J. (1962). *Appraising Vocational Fitness* (Rev. Ed.). New York. Harper and Row.

Super D. et al. (1953). *Career Development. Self Concept Theory.* New York. College Entrance Examination Board.

Super D. and Jordaan P. (1973). Career Development Theory. *Br. J. Guid. and Couns.* 1. 1.

Tansey P. and Unwin D. (1969). *Simulation and Gaming in Education.* London. Methuen.

Tansey P. (Ed.) (1971). *Educational Aspects of Simulation.* London. McGraw Hill.

Taylor H.J. (1971). *School Counselling.* London. Macmillan.

Taylor L. (1971). *Resources for Learning.* London. Penguin.

Truax C. and Carkhuff R. (1967). *Toward Effective Counseling and Psychotherapy.* Chicago. Aldine.

Turner R.H. (1970). *Family Interaction.* New York. Wiley.

Tyler L. (1960). "Minimum Change Therapy." *Personnel Guid. J.* 38. 475–479.

Tyler L. (1964). *Antecedents of Two Varieties of Vocational Interests.* Genetic Psychol. Monographs. 70. 177–227.

Tyler L. (1969). *The Work of the Counselor.* 3rd Edn. New York. Appleton-Century-Crofts.

Vaughan T.D. (1970). *Education and Vocational Guidance Today.* London. Routledge and Kegan Paul.

Venables E. (1971). *Counselling.* London. National Marriage Guidance Council.

Vernon P.E. (1972). *Intelligence and Cultural Environment.* London. Methuen.

Young T.R. (1972). *New Sources of Self.* Oxford. Pergamon.

Wall W.D. (1948). *The Adolescent Child.* London. Methuen.

Wall W.D. (1968). *Adolescence in School and Society.* Slough. N.F.E.R.

Wenar C. (1971). *Personality Development.* Boston. Houghton Mifflin.

Wiener R.S. (1970). *Drugs and Schoolchildren.* London. Longman.

Williams F. (Ed.) (1970). *Language and Poverty.* Chicago. Markham.

Williams G. (1967). *Counselling for Special Groups.* Paris O.E.C.D.

Williams N. and Williams S. (1970). *The Moral Development of Children.* London. Macmillan.

Wolpe J. (1969). *The Practice of Behaviour Therapy.* Oxford. Pergamon.

Wrenn G. (1957). "Status and Role of the School Counselor." *Personnel Guid. J.* 36. 175–183.

Wylie R. (1961). *The Self Concept.* The University of Nebraska Press.

Zander A. (1971). *Motives and Goals in Groups.* New York. Academic Press.

# GLOSSARY

*Abstractive verbal skills:* The ability to separate one aspect of behaviour or an object from the whole to which it belongs. To deal with ideas rather than the concrete.

*Affiliation:* The desire to be connected with or attached to some group or person. The act of so connecting or attaching oneself.

*Alienation:* A separation between a part of the personality or the total personality and important areas of the world of experience, e.g. alienation from work.

*Ambivalent:* The simultaneous possession of positive and negative feelings about an object or person.

*Boundary exchanges:* Related to a social system. This is seen as having boundaries, e.g. the counselling situation or the classroom situation. Across the boundaries go actions which affect the larger system which itself sends input into the smaller system. Both have an influence on the other.

*Coding:* The relating of information to a system of meanings or signals. An act of translation into a particular system of signals.

*Circular speech:* A way of describing patterns of speech focused on one idea, or having limited content, which is repeated in various ways, but little planning is present and little new content emerges.

*Collusion:* The situation in which the social worker or counsellor goes beyond seeing the pupil's view, and supports him in ideas and actions which are not based upon the reality of the situation.

*Conceptual framework:* A structure of ideas used by a person as a basis for interpreting events and information.

*Conditioning:* The process by which a response comes to be elicited by an event, object or situation other than the original or usual one. A process in which things are associated together.

*Conformity:* Adaptation to rules, social customs and expectations.

*Congruent:* In accordance with; mutual correspondence between.

*Coping strategies:* The behaviour typically used by an individual to deal with stresses, tensions and other problematical situations met during the course of everyday life.

*Construct:* Ideas and groups of ideas through which the world is viewed. These constructs allow one to chart a course of action and make predictions about the consequences (Kelly, G., 1955).

*Feedback:* A term derived from work on systems and social groups amongst other sources. Information or energy coming back to a person or social system. Positive feedback facilitates the occurrence of the behaviour or the action to which it refers, whilst negative feedback would inhibit it.

*Halo effect:* The tendency in assessments and judgements of people to assume that certain characteristics and behaviour are always associated, e.g. in rating scales to assume that a pupil who is good or bad on one quality is the same on others.

*Identification:* An emotionally based merging with a model in which the child takes over the standards of the model.

*Idiosyncratic:* Peculiar to an individual.

*Impaired vocational choice:* The situation where a person cannot make a realistic vocational choice due to heavy external pressures, emotional disturbance etc. A choice where rational considerations are minimal.

*Impermeable structures of thought:* Ideas and groups of ideas which cannot be modified easily because it is very difficult to attach new ideas and associations to them (From Kelly, G., 1955).

*Construct theory:* The theory of Kelly, G. which is based on the fact that men make representations of their world, thereby being able to predict consequences and devise courses of suitable action.

*Counter transference:* Positive or negative feelings coming from the person taking the helping role and directed towards the person who is being helped. Often of an irrational nature.

*Developmental counselling:* Counselling which is concerned with the normal processes of growth and maturation, and which emphasizes the future rather than the past.

*Discriminative verbal skills:* The ability to categorize accurately and distinguish differences within events, ideas and perceptions. The ability to isolate slight differences and express these verbally.

*Empathy:* The capacity to feel into a person and understand his unique reactions and feelings.

*Empirical:* Based upon facts rather than opinion. Derived from systematic observation and experiment.

*Family regime:* The type of relatively permanent interaction which develops between the members of a family, e.g. democratic, authoritarian.

*Inoculatory device:* The technique used in persuasive communication and attitude change which aims to reduce the impact of contrary information and arguments which the individual is likely to meet. This is achieved by providing preparatory exposure to weakened forms of the arguments and giving counter arguments before they are met in real life.

*Interaction:* A process of mutual adjustment and reaction between a person and others, or between a person and an aspect of his environment.

*Interpersonal perception:* The way in which one person sees another, and the process of attributing intentions and purpose to that other.

*Life field:* A method of seeing a pupil's actions as being set in fields composed of goals, obstacles and other positive and negative forces.

*Level of aspiration:* The standard of achievement to which someone aspires. This standard provides him with the basis for feelings of success or failure.

*Looking glass self:* The picture of oneself that is reflected back by the behaviour and statements of others.

*Machiavellian:* A name given to the type of person who is greatly concerned with power in social relationships and who is highly manipulative.

*Maladaptive responses:* Behaviour which is a response to some situation or event which is harmful to the individual performing it and to others at times. Behaviour which is inefficient because it is not fitted to the situation.

*Manipulative:* To use other people for one's own ends, treating them as objects rather than as persons.

*Mobilizer of resources:* That part of the role of the counsellor-teacher concerned with initiating action which makes previously unused resources within the school available to a pupil.

*Occupational field:* A broad area within the occupational structure determined by some central characteristic, e.g. outdoor, mechanical, social work. Within the field many jobs of widely varying character are found.

*Occupational stereotype:* The view that people hold of the characteristic common to workers within a specific occupation.

*Perception:* The process of becoming aware of something and identifying it. Used in the discussion to cover all the ways people have of getting to know their physical and social environments.

*Phantasy:* Images and fancies deriving from a person's needs and wishes.

*Primary appraisal:* The first part of the process by which a person copes with threat and danger. In this he estimates the nature and degree of threat (Lazarus, 1966).

*Projection:* The attribution of feelings and motives to other people which actually belong to the person attributing them. The aim being the avoidance of recognizing these things in oneself.

*Psycho-logic:* One's concept of what is associated together and of the nature of the relationships between them in mental, personal and social behaviour.

*Psychotherapy:* The treatment of abnormalities by psychological methods.

*Reaction formation:* A term from psychoanalytic theory. The unknowing development and use of behaviour which is the opposite of that which is possessed but is unacceptable to the person, e.g. the development of a strong puritanical outlook in a person actually possessed of strong sexual drives.

*Reactive being:* The concept of a person as controlled by pushes and pulls coming from his environment.

*Reference group:* The group from which a person draws his standards and values and to which he compares himself.

*Reinforcement:* The rewards and responses which increase the likelihood of a response being repeated.

*Retarded vocational choice:* An occupational choice based on the factors and considerations used by much younger pupils in talking about choices, e.g. reliance upon interest and liking alone in a sixteen-year-old.

*Role-playing:* A technique intended to aid understanding of a particular role by acting the part.

*Role-sending:* A process between individuals in which one provides the other with clear indications of the type of role he is expected to occupy.

*Secondary appraisal:* The second stage of dealing with threat or danger. It involves devising ways and means of coping with threat and danger coupled with estimation of the costs of the coping strategies (Lazarus, R., 1966).

*Self-concept:* The image a person has of himself. Partially derived from the reactions of others to him.

*Self-esteem:* The degree of positive regard and feelings of worth a person holds about himself.

*Self-fulfilling prophecy:* The making of a prediction which then leads to actions and attitudes on the part of those involved causing the prediction to be met.

*Self-image:* The picture held by a person of himself.

*Self-perceptions:* The way in which a person sees himself.

*Simulation:* A method of learning based upon an attempt to replicate the salient parts of a learning or social situation, e.g. simulation of occupational tasks or situations.

*Social comparison process:* The tendency not only to evaluate, but to define oneself by reference to a group or an individual.

*Social desirability:* The tendency to make responses, verbal and behavioural, based on the individual's ideas of what relevant groups tend to approve or disapprove.

*Standpoint taking:* The capacity to reconstruct in imagination the role of the other person.

*Status equal interaction:* Interaction between people which is on the level of equals, rather than between superior and subordinate.

*Stimulus question:* A question devised to get more information from the pupil. Framed (i) to initiate a particular train of thought, or (ii) so that it can be answered in many ways.

*Subjective meaning:* The meaning an event or situation has for a specific person. Meaning which arises from the individual's interpretation of the situation, rather than the situation as such.

*Superordinate construct:* Those constructs which include a number of other constructs, thereby being very important in the mental life of an individual, The superordinate construct controls those subordinate to it (Kelly, G., 1955).

*Therapeutic:* Methods of treatment concerned with the cure of disease, either mental or physical.

*Transference:* The development of an emotional attitude, usually unrealistic towards the person taking the helping role by the person who is being helped It i s a form of projection shaped by past experiences. Psychoanalytic term.

# INDEX

## SUBJECT INDEX